☐ MASTERING C

☐ MASTERING C

CRAIG BOLON

San Francisco • Paris • Düsseldorf • London

Cover art by Jean-Francois Penichoux
Book design by Jeffrey James Giese

Unix is a trademark of AT&T Bell Laboratories.
VAX is a trademark of Digital Equipment Corporation.

SYBEX is a registered trademark of SYBEX, Inc.

SYBEX is not affiliated with any manufacturer.

Library of Congress Card Number: 85-63325
ISBN 0-89588-326-0
Manufactured in the United States of America
10 9 8 7 6 5 4 3

For Judy, David, and Daniel

☐ Acknowledgments

The author acknowledges with thanks the assistance of reviewers, including Michael McCallig, John Tortora, Kathryn Jennings, Craig Goss, Sarah Freeman, Alex Gold-Pitegoff, Farrell Golden, Allen Andersson, and Jeffrey Tecosky, and the efforts of SYBEX editors and staff, including Carole Alden, Karl Ray, James Compton, Daniel Tauber, Joel Kroman, Dawn Amsberry, Elizabeth Wilcox, Laura Hurd, Jeff Giese, Donna Scanlon, Olivia Shinomoto, and Dave Clark.

CONTENTS

PART IV: PROGRAMMING ENVIRONMENTS

PART 1

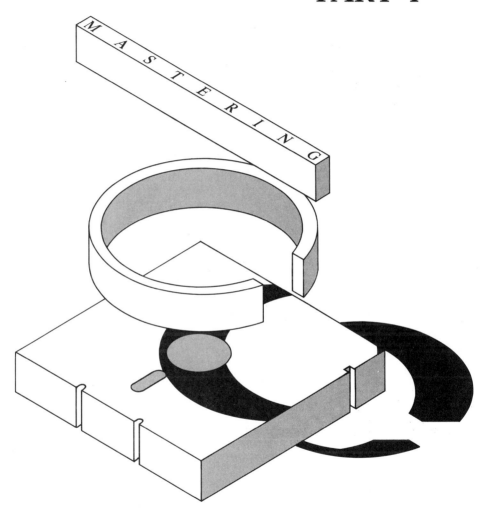

MASTERING

INTRODUCTION

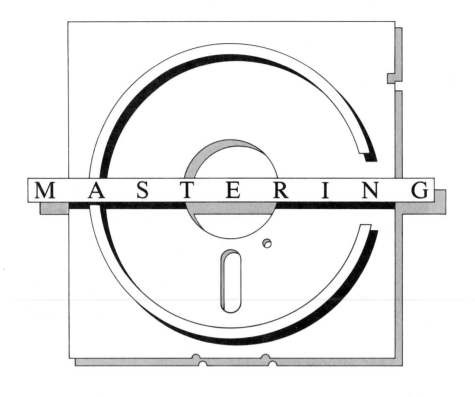

CHAPTER 1

CHARACTERISTICS OF C

This chapter discusses the background and characteristics of the C language, including these topics:

- the origin of the C language
- the features of C
- structured programming
- advantages of C
- limitations of C
- implementations of C
- systems that support C

□ THE ORIGIN OF THE C LANGUAGE

The C language was invented by Dennis Ritchie at Bell Telephone Laboratories (now an AT&T division) in the early 1970s. Ritchie wanted a high-level language suitable for writing an operating system, which manages the input and output devices of a computer, allocates its storage, and schedules the running of other programs. Operating systems had usually been written in the machine instructions of a particular computer, using an *assembler* language. By writing in a high-level language, Ritchie hoped to speed the work of programming and to transport the operating system easily from one type of computer to another.

The outcome of Ritchie's project was a new version of the Unix system, which was being developed at Bell Labs by Kenneth Thompson. The project was generally regarded as a success. In a relatively short time, versions of Unix were brought up on a variety of computers. By the mid-1980s, Unix was available on more than a hundred different computers. About 80 to 90 percent of a typical Unix operating system is written in C.

□ THE FEATURES OF C

C is a high-level, procedural language. In part, it resembles other procedural languages, such as Pascal, FORTRAN, BASIC, Algol, PL/1, and Ada. When using a procedural language, a programmer writes explicit directions for a computer about the steps it is to perform. The programmer must understand the meaning of the data, the steps being

2 □ MASTERING C

performed, and the results. A high-level language frees the programmer from having to work with machine instructions and from having to determine the locations of data in main storage. These details are provided by a *compiler,* which translates a program from *source code,* in the high-level language, to machine instructions.

The C language has a distinctive appearance. For some types of work, it has substantial advantages over other languages. The features of C include:

- *System independence.* The C language was designed to require no operating system services, since Ritchie intended that programs written in C were going to supply them.

- *Limited data types.* Originally, C provided only characters and integers. Later, "long" and "short" integers were added, as well as floating-point data.

- *Detailed data manipulations.* The C language provides flexible data structures and a wealth of detailed data manipulations. However, it does not provide automatic operations for most data aggregates, such as matrices and strings.

- *High efficiency.* C compilers are generally able to translate source code into efficient machine instructions. C language data and control mechanisms are well matched to most small computers and microcomputers.

□ STRUCTURED PROGRAMMING

In the 1960s and early 1970s, theorists interested in algorithms developed techniques called *structured programming.* Because structured programs are easier to understand and test, they are usually more reliable than unstructured programs. The C language is designed to support structured programming techniques.

Structured programming is an orderly arrangement of what a program tells a computer to do. Older computer languages used an arrangement of instructions like this:

1: Do the first thing.

2: If a condition is satisfied, go to instruction number 5.

3: Do a second thing.

4: Do a third thing.

5: Do the last thing.

This program will do only the first and last things, in that order, if the condition is satisfied. Otherwise, it will do all four things.

An equivalent structured program will use an arrangement like the following:

Do the first thing.
If a condition is not satisfied, then:
    Do a second thing.
    Do a third thing.
Do the last thing.

In a structured program, the instructions are not numbered or labeled. There is no provision for "going to" a particular instruction.

In a structured program, instructions are executed in the order written, but they may be grouped into blocks, controlled by an instruction just before or after a block. As you can see from the example above, a structured program tends to resemble an outline. Structured languages have different ways of denoting blocks of instructions; the C language puts braces around them.

□ ADVANTAGES OF C

Because the C language is relatively simple and orderly, C compilers can be made to run on small computers. The language is also designed so that compilers can translate it into efficient machine instructions. The C language provides more flexibility in detailed data manipulations than other high-level languages. These characteristics have made C attractive for microcomputers and for applications such as user interfaces, communications, control systems, automatic test equipment, operating systems, database managers, computer-aided design, spreadsheets, and text processors.

In the microcomputer's first decade, C met a need for a general-purpose language simple enough to use with microcomputers but powerful enough to write substantial programs. Because it supports structured programming, most users find it easier to write reliable programs in C than in "ghetto" languages, such as BASIC or Forth. The Pascal language shares a similar approach and has provided many of the same benefits. Comparing C to Pascal, experienced programmers value the flexibility of C's data manipulations, the compactness of its statements, the generality of its data structures, and the portability of its source code.

□ LIMITATIONS OF C

The flexibility of C can be a problem for an inexperienced programmer, because a mistake in a program will often result in some valid, although unwanted interpretation. Programmers occasionally overuse compact forms of statements and create programs that are hard to read, understand, and test. To be used effectively, C requires a more developed sense of software organization than other languages.

C does not provide a machine-independent way to specify the precision of data. There are some generally observed practical standards, explained in this book, that meet most needs. For numerical analysis, however, this deficiency can become a major problem. Other languages, particularly FORTRAN, are generally preferred over C.

C has no input or output facilities. Under Unix, these services are provided through functions available to any C program that is not a part of the operating system. The Unix services have become a practical standard. A Unix format function library is supplied with most C compilers. Unix services are oriented toward unstructured, printable characters in files. Additional services are needed by programs that respond rapidly to interrupts, process binary data, produce displays, handle high-speed communications, and use large or numerous files of interrelated data.

For many applications, additional services are provided by writing parts of a program in an assembler language or by linking C code to code written in another high-level language. For some applications, including financial accounting, engineering data analysis, and high-reliability control systems, different languages—COBOL, APL, or Ada—may provide more appropriate capabilities.

□ IMPLEMENTATIONS OF C

C compilers are now available for most popular microcomputers, minicomputers, and small mainframe computers. These compilers implement the language in a remarkably consistent way. In contrast to the situation with Pascal, most writers of C compilers have refrained from adding features or changing the interpretation of statements. Because of this, programs written in C are usually easier to transport from one type of computer to another than programs written in Pascal and other procedural languages.

Through the mid-1980s, there was no standard for the C language comparable to the FORTRAN defined by the American National Standards Institute or the Pascal defined by the International Standards Organization. A book by Brian Kernighan and Dennis Ritchie[1] served as a reference from the late 1970s. In 1983, the American National Standards Institute authorized a committee to prepare a standard. A language standard for C was scheduled for release in 1986.

Despite the lack of an official standard, there was never much interest in "dialects" of the C language. This is a striking indication that the C language, as originally designed to solve some practical problems, does in fact meet a wide range of needs.

□ SYSTEMS THAT SUPPORT C

Nearly all elements of the C language described in this book are implemented as shown by systems that claim to support the "full" C language, with two exceptions. The first is support for floating-point numbers, described in Part IV of this book; many small computers provide instructions only for integer numbers.

The other exception is the so-called "standard" library services. These provide frequently used procedures, such as reading data from a file, allocating portions of the computer's main storage to a program, or printing messages on a terminal. The library services described in this book are sometimes called the "portable" Unix subset. There are many variations of these functions, described in Chapters 18 and 19.

Major exceptions to Unix format functions are certain compilers and function libraries produced by Whitesmiths, Ltd., which have completely different function names and slightly different procedures. Readers who will be using such a compiler or library should consult their Whitesmiths manuals for information on using these functions.

□ THE APPROACH OF THIS BOOK

For the first decade of its existence, the C language was used mainly by professional programmers. Few schools offered courses using it.

---

[1] Brian W. Kernighan and Dennis M. Ritchie, *The C Programming Language,* (Englewood Cliffs, N.J.: Prentice-Hall, 1978).

This gave the language a kind of mystique and an undeserved reputation for being obscure or difficult. Actually, the C language is no harder to learn or use than other high-level, procedural languages.

This book has three objectives: the first is to show readers how to do simple things immediately; the second is to encourage software planning, using C as a structured language; and the third is to teach the full powers of the language. At the end of many chapters are exercises, exploring the topics of the chapter. They assume familiarity with the preceding chapters. The reader is urged to work out solutions for these exercises or to invent his own. Learning a computer language is learning a skill, and as with all skills, mastery comes only with practice.

This book aims to teach a generic, highly portable C language. Those features of the language that make programs dependent on the details of a particular computer or operating system are postponed to the last part of the book. As much as possible, this book avoids the jargon and programmer's slang that have crept into common, but inconsistent, use. Portability is a major reason for the rapidly growing use of C in commercial software. Moving a C program from one computer to another usually requires far less work than writing the original program.

Occasionally, writing a program for portability means giving up efficiency. Some programmers write machine-dependent C programs instead of writing parts of a program in the actual instructions of a particular computer. This is not always a satisfactory compromise; it can become confusing and nonportable yet remain much less efficient than good machine code. There are often better ways to achieve efficiency than machine-dependent C programs. This book encourages such alternatives.

□ HOW TO USE THE BOOK

This book has been designed for readers who are already familiar with computers and who know how to use some type of computer language. Its emphasis is on developing a thorough understanding of the C language, including skill at developing programs of practical sizes and complexity. The book's organization is based on functional aspects of the language, rather than on a strictly tutorial approach.

The book is divided into four parts, with a total of 20 chapters. Each part of the book is designed to teach a major area of the language or its use. Each chapter is designed to teach an individual topic, suitable for a few hours of attention in one day. A semester- or quarter-long course can usually cover one chapter per class period. A short course for advanced programmers might cover only Parts II and III, in as little as five or six sessions.

Part I of this book is an introduction to the C language and to the types of software organization helpful in using the language. The major topics are:

- how to write simple programs

- how to use the C function library

- how to plan and test programs

Parts II and III present the major capabilities of the C language in a traditional format. Data elements are explained in Part II, including arrays, structures, and pointers. The flexibility of C data definitions is essential to sophisticated programs. This part of the book explores all aspects of the subject, including most features of recent compilers. The use of structures and arrays for connective data organizations is presented in detail.

Part III is devoted to program control, including the rich repertoire of C operators. The focus of this section is on features of the language that support structured programming. Chapter 12 demonstrates effective uses of recursive functions. Chapter 13 includes a detailed chart of all C operators and their uses.

Part IV discusses machine- and system-dependent features of the language, including sizes of data elements, floating-point data, preprocessor capabilities, and the major system services provided by Unix format libraries. The discussion is intended to help you use the C language for developing substantial program packages in realistic programming environments. This part of the book also covers methods of testing and maintaining C programs.

□ TYPOGRAPHICAL CONVENTIONS

In this book, programs and parts of programs are distinguished from other text by a distinctive font or typeface, as in the following example:

```
if ( vertical % 5 == 0 )
    printf( "X" ) ;
else if ( horizontal % 10 == 0 )
    printf( "X" ) ;
```

```
else
    printf( " " ) ;
```

Like many other languages, C reserves a number of keywords for special uses. In this book, you will see keywords in a **boldface** form of the program font, as above. When you write a program, no special emphasis for keywords is necessary, but you must avoid using the keywords for anything other than their reserved purposes.

Prototypes of program components appear in a boldface form of the text font:

pointer + value

When input or output is shown, it appears in the program font, in a "screen":

```
To market,
To market,
```

CHAPTER 2

WRITING SIMPLE C
PROGRAMS

This chapter explains what is needed to create and run simple C programs. It does not give detailed instructions about operating-system commands, because they vary greatly among systems. Instead, it describes the major elements of C programs, comparing them to other languages, and covers the basic necessities for writing and running your programs, including these topics:

- using a computer system for C
- a short test program
- comparison of C with other languages
- a program example using a loop
- spacing, case, and keywords
- character and integer data
- arrays and strings
- quantities that are TRUE or FALSE
- a pattern-making program example
- conditional cascades

☐ USING A COMPUTER SYSTEM FOR C

Most available versions of C are supported by compilers. To write and run programs involves the following basic sequence of steps:

1. Write source code, using a text editor.
2. Compile the program.
3. Link the compiler output with functions from a C library, supplied with the compiler.
4. Run the linked program.

Most C programming is done interactively. The programmer uses a terminal with a keyboard and either a printer or a screen display. When you begin to type in your commands to such a computer, you are communicating with its operating system. The operating system will load and run a variety of programs for you, including those you write.

In order to develop C programs, you need to know how to use some of the operating-system services. The essential ones are these:

- logging on and off
- running a text editor
- running a C compiler
- running a program linker
- getting access to the C library
- running file-management utilities
- running a program you've written

The instructions for these things differ greatly from one computer to another. If you are working with an unfamiliar system, get the information from a reliable source, such as a course instructor, the computer staff, manuals, or your computer dealer.

Some C compilers produce assembler language output; this output must be processed by an assembler to produce a linkable program. If your compiler works this way, you need to know how to run the assembler. A few C compilers do not recognize all conventional C statements. Find out whether your compiler has any language restrictions. If so, get a list of the capabilities it omits.

Some computer systems provide combined compile and link procedures, including the "cc" command of Unix. Others make a linker "invisible," by performing the link procedure automatically when you run a simple program. If your computer works this way, you may not need to use a linker directly.

Since the operations described in this section are frequent and repetitive, many computers provide a "command procedure" that will perform them automatically. Such a procedure might need as little as the name of a source file to carry out the remainder of the steps. If such a procedure is available for compiling or linking C programs, you should find out how to use it. If a such a procedure is not available on your computer but could be created, you may want to make one.

Besides entering, compiling, and running your programs, on most computers you will also need to know how to locate and manipulate program and data files. Most operating systems provide utility services, controlled by commands. You should know how to do these things:

- list the files you have made

- copy a specified file

- delete a specified file

□ A SHORT TEST PROGRAM

To check out the operating-system services you will be using, try entering the following short test program:

```
#include <stdio.h>
main( )
{
    printf( "It works!\n" ) ;
}
```

When this program has been correctly typed into a source file and then compiled, linked, and run, the computer should print or display:

It works!

In C, a program is normally written in several independent sections, called *functions*. Each such function does its work when it is invoked by another function. A function named main has special significance; it is the function that first gets control when an ordinary program starts to run. The line #include <stdio.h> is needed at the start of most programs that perform input or output.

The short program that prints

It works!

has only one function, named main. The braces after the function name tell the C compiler that you are about to start writing the body of a function, which consists of C statements. The statements that make up a function are contained between paired braces. The main function in the test program has only one statement:

```
printf( "It works.\n" ) ;
```

This is a "simple" C statement, and it ends in a semicolon.

The C language uses punctuation, including parentheses, braces, and semicolons, to indicate where one element of a program ends and another begins. Because of this, a C statement need not be contained in a single line of a source file. You can put many statements on one line or one statement on many lines. The little program just shown would work in exactly the same way if it were written as:

```
#include <stdio.h>
main(){printf("It works.\n");}
```

Because clear style is particularly useful in C, this book will continue to use the program arrangement originally shown, placing each statement on a separate line and indenting certain statements. Choices in style are discussed in a later chapter.

The single statement in **main** invokes another function, named **printf**. This is normally available from a Unix format C library. It prints or displays character information on some standard device, ordinarily the user's terminal. You give **printf** instructions about what to print. These appear between the parentheses.

The **printf** function was called with a single *argument*. When a function is called with more than one argument, the arguments will be separated by commas. In this instance, the argument was a *character string* enclosed in quotation marks. The quotation marks serve only to mark the beginning and end of a string; the string consists of the characters they enclose. The last character in this string was represented by \n and is called a *newline* character. When printed, this character causes the line on which it occurs to end; any subsequent printing will take up at the left margin of the next line.

□ COMPARISON OF C WITH OTHER LANGUAGES

The C language has similarities to other high-level, procedural languages. This section will compare some features of C with their equivalents in Pascal, FORTRAN, and BASIC. All of these languages share the following characteristics:

- Programs are composed of statements, executed in order, which describe a precise sequence of operations for a computer to carry out.

- There are several types of data elements; each has a specific range of allowed values.

- Data elements are referred to by name. The language compiler and linker allocate the required storage automatically.

- Each data element has a current value. When the current value changes, the previous value is lost.

- Program statements can cause expressions that depend on values of data elements and the meanings of operators to be evaluated.

- Program statements can assign the results of expressions as new current values of data elements.

- Program statements can test the values of expressions to control whether other statements are executed, either once or repeatedly.

High-level languages differ in their repertoire of data elements and operators. Pascal, FORTRAN, BASIC and C all provide some form of numeric data. They all include operators for addition, subtraction, multiplication, and division of numbers. They all allow the names of numeric data elements to be composed of letters and digits, with the first character a letter. They all recognize a priority of operators, with multiplication and division performed before addition and subtraction.

The following shows equivalent statements using numeric data in the Pascal, FORTRAN, BASIC, and C languages:

Pascal:

```
Amount := Initial + Rate * Time ;
```

FORTRAN:

```
AMOUNT = INITIAL + RATE * TIME
```

BASIC:

```
20 LET AMOUNT = INITIAL + RATE * TIME
```

C:

```
amount = initial + rate * time ;
```

Notice that Pascal and C often use lowercase letters. Unlike Pascal, however, C is case-sensitive. Statements in Pascal and C end in semicolons. Pascal sometimes omits the semicolon, while C always requires it. FORTRAN and BASIC generally use uppercase letters only and do not require semicolons to end statements.

High-level languages differ in their capabilities for recognizing data names. FORTRAN and BASIC recognize names of data elements automatically and assign default data types. Pascal and C lack automatic data types; a program must declare the type of each data element. FORTRAN allows explicit data declarations, but BASIC does not. The following are equivalent declarations of integer variables:

Pascal:

VAR Initial, Rate, Time : **INTEGER** ;

FORTRAN:

INTEGER INITIAL, RATE, TIME

BASIC: (no equivalent)

C:

int initial, rate, time ;

All high-level, procedural languages have some form of statement to test the value of an expression and control whether one or more other statements will be executed. If the controlled statements can be executed repeatedly, the form of control is known as a *repetition* or *loop*. If the controlled statements will be executed either once or not at all, it is called a *conditional*. Languages differ substantially in the forms of control they provide.

Pascal, C, and FORTRAN (in the 1977 ANSI standard) all support structured programming. They permit repetitions and conditionals to control blocks of statements. In Pascal, a block of statements starts with **BEGIN** and stops with **END**. In C, a block starts at an opening brace and stops at a closing brace. In FORTRAN 77, blocks start and stop at different keywords, depending on the type of control. Conventional versions of BASIC support structured programming for some loops (in a manner similar to FORTRAN) but not for conditionals. However, structured programs can be written in BASIC by properly controlled use of **GOTO**.

Here is a series of equivalent conditional statements that control another pair of statements, in the Pascal, FORTRAN, BASIC, and C languages:

Pascal:

```
IF Amount > Limit THEN
BEGIN
    Initial := 0 ;
    Rate := Rate − Delta
END ;
```

FORTRAN 77:

```
IF (AMOUNT .GT. LIMIT) THEN
    INITIAL = 0
    RATE = RATE – DELTA
END IF
```

BASIC:

```
40 IF AMOUNT < = LIMIT GOTO 70
50    LET INITIAL = 0
60    LET RATE = RATE – DELTA
70
```

C:

```
if (amount > limit)
{
    initial = 0 ;
    rate = rate + delta ;
}
```

The following are equivalent repetition statements that control another statement, in the Pascal, FORTRAN, BASIC, and C languages:

Pascal:

```
FOR N : = 1 TO Max DO
    Total : = Total * (1.0 + Rate) ;
```

FORTRAN 77:

```
DO N = 1, MAX
    TOTAL = TOTAL * (1.0 + RATE)
END DO
```

BASIC:

```
70 FOR N = 1 TO MAX
80    TOTAL = TOTAL * (1.0 + RATE)
90 NEXT N
```

C:

```
for ( n = 0 ; n < max ; n = n + 1 )
    total = total * (1.0 + rate) ;
```

Most high-level languages make it possible to divide a program into independent sections, any one of which can invoke another and supply it with data to process. Pascal has procedures and functions; FORTRAN has subroutines and functions; and BASIC has functions, although conventional versions of BASIC recognize only certain predefined functions. Functions return to the caller a single data value. Procedures and subroutines do not return a value.

The C language has only functions. As in the other languages, data values are transmitted through arguments when a function is invoked. A C function may or may not return a result; the caller is free to ignore any result returned. Functions are invoked by writing the name of the function followed by a pair of parentheses. Between the parentheses are the arguments, expressions separated by commas. Like FORTRAN and BASIC, but unlike Pascal, C always requires the parentheses.

□ A PROGRAM EXAMPLE USING A LOOP

Figure 2.1 is a short program written in C. It is not intended to do anything particularly useful, but simply to show how some of the elements of C are used, including conditional control and the most common type of loop, controlled by **while**.

When this program has been correctly typed in and then compiled,

```
#include <stdio.h>
main( )
{
    int count ;
     count = 3 ;
    while ( count )
      {
          printf( "To " ) ;
          if ( count > 1 )
              printf( "market,\n" ) ;
          else
              printf( "buy a fat pig.\n" ) ;
          count = count - 1 ;
      }
}
```

Figure 2.1: *A program using a loop.*

linked, and run, the computer should print or display:

```
To market,
To market,
To buy a fat pig.
```

The first statement inside the **main** function of the program is a *declaration* statement, declaring that the program uses a particular *variable:*

```
int count ;
```

This program has a variable named **count**. The **count** variable is of type **int**, the standard way in C to specify a variable that can take on integer values, both positive and negative. Both the name and the type of this variable are stated, and these specifications are made at the start of the function. This is required practice in C. For this program, you must tell the C compiler to reserve space for a quantity, **count**, that will be given integer values.

The next statement is the first *executable* statement. This statement assigns to **count** a value of 3:

```
count = 3 ;
```

In C, when the name of a variable appears in a statement, this ordinarily means, "Use the current value of the variable in calculating an expression." However, when the name of a variable appears to the left of an equal sign, it means, "Calculate whatever appears to the right of the equal sign, and assign that value to the variable." Such a value will be retained by a variable until it is changed by another assignment.

The next part of the program uses one of the two main types of control in a structured language—a repetition, often called a "loop":

```
while ( count )
{
  . . .
  count = count - 1 ;
}
```

The omitted statements, shown as ellipsis dots (. . .), do printing. The particular form of control used here is the **while** repetition. In C, this consists of the keyword **while** followed by an expression in parentheses, then followed by a C statement or block of statements. The rule for **while** is that the statement or block it controls will be repeatedly executed as long as the expression in parentheses has a nonzero value.

In Figure 2.1, the expression in parentheses for the **while** statement is simply the value of the variable count. This particular **while** will repeat as long as the value of count is not zero. What is repeated here is a whole group of statements; this is called a *compound* statement, or *block*.

In C, *simple* statements specify information to the compiler or cause an action to be performed; they end in a semicolon. A compound statement or block consists of one or more simple statements enclosed between braces. A block can be used wherever a simple statement is permitted. There is no semicolon after the closing brace of a block, but there is a semicolon after the last statement inside a block.

In the looping program, what will be repeated under the control of **while** is the whole block of statements found between the braces after **while**:

```
{
    printf( "To " ) ;
    if ( count > 1 )
        printf( "market,\n" ) ;
    else
        printf( "buy a fat pig.\n" ) ;
    count = count − 1 ;
}
```

This block will be executed as long as the value of the variable count is not zero. The format shown in this program, with the braces standing out by themselves and the block of simple statements indented, was chosen to emphasize the part of the program controlled by **while**. This format is not required by the C language. It is a matter of style, intended to emphasize the scope of **while** control.

Just how does **while** provide three repetitions of the block of statements? The last statement in the **while** block calculates the value of an expression:

```
count = count − 1 ;
```

The current value of the variable count, minus 1, is calculated. It is then assigned as a new value of count. Thus the value of count is reduced by one each time this statement is executed. Before the **while** statement, count was set to 3. Each time the **while** block is executed, count is reduced by one. During executions of the **while** block, count therefore has successive values 3, 2, and 1.

A **while** control expression is evaluated and tested just before each repetition. If the expression has a nonzero value, the statement or block controlled by **while** is executed. Otherwise, the repetition stops and the next statement after the controlled statement or block is executed. In the looping program, after the **while** block has been executed with **count** at one, the last statement of the **while** block will change **count** to zero. The **while** test will detect this value, and the repetition will stop. The **while** block will not be repeated with **count** at zero.

Inside the **while** block of statements is an example of the second main type of control in a structured language, a conditional:

```
if ( count > 1 )
    printf( "market,\n" ) ;
else
    printf( "buy a fat pig.\n" ) ;
```

The forms used here are the **if** and **else** conditionals. In C, the **if** conditional consists of the keyword **if** followed by an expression in parentheses, then followed by a C statement or block of statements. The rule for **if** is that the statement or block it controls will be executed if the expression in parentheses has a nonzero value. Unlike **while**, **if** gets only one pass. Whether its scope is executed or not, a program won't back up and try again.

Immediately after a statement controlled by **if** may appear another statement, controlled by **else**. The **else** conditional consists of the keyword **else** followed by a C statement or block. The rule for **else** is that when the scope of **if** was not executed, the scope of **else** will be executed instead. As with **while**, statements controlled by **if** and **else** are shown indented underneath them. This, again, is not required by the language but is done as a matter of style, intended to enhance readability.

Now, having gone over the individual statements in the looping program, look at how the whole program works. You now know that the **while** block will be executed three times, with **count** at successive values of 3, 2, and 1.

Each time the **while** block of statements is executed, the printf function is invoked; it prints

```
To
```

with a trailing blank. No end of line occurs, because in C a print line does not end until a newline character has been printed. Next come the **if** and the **else** statements. When **count** is 2 or 3, they print

```
market,
```

with a comma followed by an end of line. When count is one, they print

buy a fat pig.

After this, the value of count becomes zero, and the **while** repetition ends. There are no more statements to execute, so that is the end of the program. When it is finished, the program has printed

To market,
To market,
To buy a fat pig.

□ SPACING, CASE, AND KEYWORDS

Much of the time, C symbols and punctuation are enough to separate one element of a program from another. Blanks may be freely added or omitted when punctuation marks or symbols are present. However, blanks are significant when there is no other separation between elements. Sometimes a blank is necessary. For example, the program in Figure 2.1 had the following statement:

int count ;

Without the blank between **int** and count, a C compiler could not make sense of this statement.

In C programs, unless spacing characters occur inside character strings, these characters—blanks, tabs, ends of lines, and form feeds— all have the effect of blanks and can be used to improve readability. These are sometimes called "whitespace characters" or, more simply, *spacing*. Spacing may not appear within variable names, function names, symbols that have more than one character, or (as discussed shortly) keywords.

C compilers distinguish between the cases of characters that appear in the source text of programs. Variable names may use uppercase, lowercase, or both. Changing the case of even one character will make a different name. For example, these names will all be recognized as different:

acmerug   ACMERUG   AcmeRug   ACMErug

Because of the potential for accidental confusion, most C programmers put variable names completely in lowercase. However, this usage is a matter of style, as discussed in a later chapter.

Some potential ambiguities remain to be resolved. For example, the program in Figure 2.1 invoked printf with this statement:

    printf("To ") ;

Immediately after this, there appeared the following:

    if (count > 1)

When interpreting this, a C compiler might have invoked a function called if evaluating count > 1 and using the value as an argument. However, a C compiler will reliably recognize an **if** conditional, not the invocation of an if function.

C has a small number of reserved words, called *keywords*. The word **if** is one of these. You can use **if** only to introduce a conditional statement, not as the name of a variable, a function, or anything else. The following keywords have already been introduced:

if   **int**   **else**   **while**

Keywords must be spelled correctly, must always appear in lowercase, and may not contain any spacing. In this book, keywords appear in boldface type, to emphasize their use as symbols in C.

□ CHARACTER AND INTEGER DATA

The most useful data types in C are characters and integers. Many programs need only these data types. You declare variables of these types by statements such as

    char asterisk ;
    int count ;

Integer data is the preferred data type of C. There are certain ways, as explained in later chapters, to declare variables without specifying a data type. In all such cases, C assumes a data type of **int**.

A character constant is written as a character enclosed in single quotes. For example, the following assigns a character value that will be printed as an asterisk to the **char** variable named asterisk:

    asterisk = '*' ;

An integer constant is written as an ordinary decimal number. A negative integer is preceded by a minus sign; a positive integer has no sign. You can also make an unsigned octal constant, consisting of octal digits preceded by a zero, and an unsigned hexadecimal constant, consisting of hexadecimal digits preceded by 0x or 0X. Letters representing hexadecimal digits can be in either upper- or lowercase. The following are all valid integer constants:

23 − 59 017 0x4A

Each implementation of C has its own standards for the sizes of integers and characters and the values of character codes. The size of a standard integer is whatever works most efficiently on a particular computer. Mainframe computers and large minicomputers such as the VAX-11 provide an integer of 32 bits or more. Most smaller machines provide at least 16 bits. Character codes are integer values. They are most commonly ASCII codes stored as 8 bits. C does not specify whether character variables are signed or unsigned, but the codes for printable characters always have positive values.

You can assign a character value to an integer variable and an integer value to a character variable. In the latter case, high-order bits of the integer value will be truncated if the value is too large for a character. You can also write expressions that contain both characters and integers. In such expressions, character values are always "widened" to the size of an integer by adding high-order bits.

In C, data elements do not ordinarily have predictable values until a program has assigned them. This means that you must be careful not to use a variable in an expression until some previous statement has assigned a value to it. In particular, *do not* assume that values are automatically zero until changed. While some C implementations may provide this feature, it is not guaranteed by the language, and most implementations do not provide it.

Expressions in C always use the following symbols for the operations of arithmetic:

+ add   * multiply
− subtract / divide

There is no symbol for integer division as there is, for example, in Pascal. The minus sign can be placed alone before a variable or a constant to designate the negative of its value. The following symbols are always used when comparing numerical values:

<	is less than
<=	is less than or equal to
>	is greater than
>=	is greater than or equal to
==	is equal to
!=	is not equal to

Be especially careful with the double equal signs for "is equal to." The single equal sign, used to assign values, has an interpretation that will often allow a mistake to be accepted by a compiler but produce strange results when run.

□ ARRAYS AND STRINGS

The C language provides one-dimensional arrays of all data types. You declare the type and the length of an array by statements such as the following:

```
char line[ 80 ] ;
int day[ 7 ] ;
```

Here, the array line has 80 character elements and day has 7 integer elements. An individual element is used in a statement by placing an *index* value between brackets after the array name, for example:

```
count = day[ 1 ] + day[ 3 ] ;
```

An index can be any expression with an integer value. In C, index values always begin at zero. The line array declared above, for example, has 80 elements, with index values 0 through 79. Array data in C statements can only be manipulated through individual elements. The language does not provide operations on whole arrays or sections of arrays.

The most commonly used array in C programs is an array of characters, also known as a "character string" or simply a *string*. C programs commonly use strings of variable length and mark the end of data in a string with a character that has the code value of zero, sometimes called a "null character" or a *null*. A convention of C guarantees that no printable character will use this code value. For example, a program might store the word "cat" in the line array defined above by the following statements:

```
line[ 0 ] = 'c' ;
line[ 1 ] = 'a' ;
line[ 2 ] = 't' ;
line[ 3 ] = 0 ;
```

C provides a special type of constant for character strings, consisting of characters enclosed in double quotes. These can be used only as initial values for character arrays and as function arguments. Their use with functions will be discussed in later chapters. To create an initial value for a character array, you follow the array name and length in a declaration statement with an equal sign and a string constant. For example, the following will store the word "cat" as the initial contents of the line array:

```
char line[ 80 ] = "cat" ;
```

The C language automatically appends a character with a code value of zero (a null character) to a string constant, so that line, as initialized, will have the same contents that were assigned in the preceding example. However, neither example assigned values to line[4] through line[79]. Until values are assigned to these elements, they are not predictable.

□ QUANTITIES THAT ARE TRUE OR FALSE

An unusual feature of C concerns *logical* quantities, that is, those which must be considered either TRUE or FALSE. These appear most often in the control expressions of repetitions and conditionals. The looping program example, in Figure 2.1, had two such expressions. The repetition of a block of statements in this program was controlled by the following:

```
while ( count )
{
   . . .
}
```

The omitted statements between the braces were executed as long as the expression in parentheses was not zero, that is, as long as the value of count was not zero. One of the statements inside this block was governed by the following:

```
if ( count > 1 )
   . . .
```

The omitted statement was executed when the condition in parentheses was TRUE, that is, when the value of count was greater than one.

In C, numbers are used to express TRUE and FALSE. Numbers are considered TRUE when nonzero and FALSE when zero. When C must evaluate a relation, such as count > 1, it assigns a number as the result. This will be the integer 1 if the relation is true and the integer 0 if it is false. When such a relation appears in a control expression, the statements controlled will be executed when the relation is true, that is, when the result is 1.

The C characteristic of producing an integer result of 1 or 0 when evaluating relations between numbers gives meaning to statements such as this:

```
count = count + ( count > 1 ) ;
```

This statement will add one to the value of count if it was already greater than one; otherwise, will add zero and hence leave the value unchanged. Parentheses ensure that the relation is evaluated before the addition is performed.

There is a logical NOT operation, symbolized by an exclamation point (!), that converts a nonzero value to zero and a zero value to one. This makes it easy to reverse the sense of control for a conditional or repetition. Whenever **if (value)** would execute a statement, **if (!value)** will cause the statement to be skipped. If you apply the logical NOT to a relation, use parentheses

```
if ( !( count > limit ) )
```

□ A PATTERN-MAKING PROGRAM EXAMPLE

The program listed in Figure 2.2 performs a common type of task: it makes a repeating pattern. This program prints out a pattern of rectangular boxes, using the uppercase letter X. It makes a horizontal row of X's every fifth line and a vertical column of X's every tenth print position on a line. In all, there will be five by five boxes printed.

This program has two integer variables, horizontal and vertical, which keeps track of the current printing position. As the position moves from left to right, horizontal increases, starting at zero on the leftmost position of each line. As it moves down the page, vertical increases, starting at zero on the first line. These actions are controlled by two repetitions, one inside the other:

```
vertical = 0 ;
while ( vertical <= 25 )
{
  horizontal = 0 ;
  while ( horizontal <= 50 )
  {
```

```
      . . .
      horizontal = horizontal + 1 ;
  }
      . . .
      vertical = vertical + 1 ;
  }
```

The omitted statements perform the printing.

The repetitions in this program count from 0 to 50, inclusive, for the print positions on eacn line and from 0 to 25 as line numbers. Vertical bars are made by printing X whenever **horizontal** is a multiple of 10. Horizontal bars are made by printing X whenever **vertical** is a multiple of 5. Otherwise a blank is printed, to move the print position along a line:

```
if ( vertical % 5 == 0 )
    printf( "X" ) ;
else if ( horizontal % 10 == 0 )
    printf( "X" ) ;
else
    printf( " " ) ;
```

The symbol % is used in the above expressions. In C, this symbol is related to the symbol / for division. The difference is that % obtains

```
#include <stdio.h>
main( )
{
    int vertical, horizontal ;
    vertical = 0 ;
    while ( vertical <= 25 )
    {
        horizontal = 0 ;
        while ( horizontal <= 50 )
        {
            if ( vertical % 5 == 0 )
                printf( "X" ) ;
            else if ( horizontal % 10 == 0 )
                printf( "X" ) ;
            else
                printf( " " ) ;
            horizontal = horizontal + 1 ;
        }
        printf( "\n" ) ;
        vertical = vertical + 1 ;
    }
}
```

Figure 2.2: *A pattern-making program.*

the *remainder* of a division, rather than the quotient. The remainder is often used to make a repeating pattern. In this example, as vertical assumes the following sequence of values:

0, 1, 2, 3, 4,   5, 6, 7, 8, 9,   10, 11, . . .

the expression vertical % 5 has corresponding values:

0, 1, 2, 3, 4,   0, 1, 2, 3, 4,   0, 1, . . .

By testing whether vertical % 5 == 0, the program can pick out every fifth line printed. In the same way, testing whether horizontal % 10 == 0 picks out every tenth print position on a line. Since vertical goes from 0 to 25 and horizontal goes from 0 to 50, the top line, the bottom line, the leftmost print position, and the rightmost print position will all be occupied by bars of X's.

□ CONDITIONAL CASCADES

The box-pattern program illustrates a type of statement sequence frequently found in C programs—a cascade of conditional statements, with **if** followed by **else if** followed by **else**. Such cascades are needed fairly often in C programs, and so it is important to understand how they work. A conditional cascade has the following general form:

```
if ( condition-1 )
    statement-1 ;
else if ( condition-2 )
    statement-2 ;
. . .
else if ( condition-k )
    statement-k ;
else
    statement-d ;
```

When such a sequence of statements appears, first **condition-1** is checked. When this succeeds, **statement-1** will be executed; none of the remaining conditions will be tested, and none of the statements they control will be executed. When **condition-1** fails, **condition-2** will be checked. If it succeeds, **statement-2** will be executed, and the remainder of the conditions and statements will be bypassed. In this manner, one condition after another is checked, until one of them succeeds. If all of them fail, **statement-d,** controlled by **else,** will be executed.

□ EXERCISES

2.1: Modify the box-pattern program from Figure 2.2. Instead of start-ing horizontal at a value of zero for each line, start at a value equal to vertical. Which way do the bars slant? Why?

Now make the value of horizontal increase by 2 instead of 1 on each repetition. What happens to the slant? Why?

Add another **else if.** Test whether the value of the expression (100 − horizontal) % 10 is zero. Print an X if it is. Now what happens to the pattern? Why?

2.2: Start with the original box-pattern program. This time, make it print a pattern of nine by nine boxes. You will probably have to make each box narrower to fit the pattern within the width available.

Next, print corners of the boxes with the plus sign (+) instead of X. To do this, you will need an **if** that controls a block rather than a single statement. For example:

```
if ( vertical % 5 == 0 )
{
    if ( horizontal % 10 == 0 )
        printf( "+" ) ;
    else
        printf( "X" ) ;
}
```

Now make the horizontal parts print with minus signs (−) and the vertical parts print with with bars (|) to produce "window boxes."

2.3: Reserve two character positions inside each window box to print a special character rather than a blank. To do this, you will need to check the remainders from horizontal and vertical for a nonzero value. Print asterisks in these two positions, so that each box looks something like this:

Next, find a way to number the boxes, using rows 1 through 9, from top to bottom, and columns 1 through 9, from right to left. You will need two new variables, called, say, row and column. Invent statements to calculate their values, based on the values of horizontal and vertical. Now, in place of the asterisks, print the row number and column number. If column represents the column number, one way to print it is with a series of if statements, such as this:

```
if ( column == 0 )
    printf( "0" ) ;
else if ( column == 1 )
    printf( "1" ) ;
. . .
else if ( column == 9 )
    printf( "9" ) ;
```

Finally, multiply the row and column number for each box, using a statement such as

```
times = row * column ;
```

Print the products in the boxes. If the product is a variable called times, you can get the first digit of it with the expression times / 10 and the second digit by using times % 10. With this piece of handiwork, your computer should now be able to produce a neatly formatted multiplication table.

MASTERING

CHAPTER 3

USING THE C LIBRARY

The previous chapter described the basic components of a C program. This chapter is devoted to the use of C functions. It introduces the most commonly needed functions in the C library. The topics include:

- a program example using functions
- program names and comments
- function arguments and return values
- local variables in functions
- the operation of a function
- indefinite repetition
- using functions to read and print
- contents of the C library
- input and output functions
- input and output using data files
- character string functions

□ A PROGRAM EXAMPLE USING FUNCTIONS

The characteristics of C functions will be explained by way of an example. The program listed in Figure 3.1 has two functions. This program reads integers from the keyboard and prints out all their prime factors. A *factor* of an integer is another integer that will divide it exactly. When an integer has no factors other than itself and one, it is a prime number. If a number is not prime, there are smaller prime numbers that are factors for it: the *prime factors*. Finding prime factors can be useful in the design of data encryption, error-correcting codes, and databases.

In this program, the **main** function reads in numbers to be factored. Entering a number less than 2 is interpreted as a direction to end the program. For any other number, **main** repeatedly invokes a function named **smallest_factor** to find the factors, one after another. This function finds the smallest factor of a given value. Each time a new factor is found, the original number is divided by the factor, until it has been reduced to a value of one.

```
#include <stdio.h>
main( )
{
    int test_number ;          /* number to be factored*/
    int factor ;               /* factor found          */
    int smallest_factor( ) ;
                               /* continue until stop   */
    while ( 1 )
    {                          /* ask for number        */
        printf( "Enter number to factor:  " ) ;
        scanf( "%d", &test_number ) ;
        if ( test_number < 2 )
            break ;            /* stop if less than 2   */

                               /* until no more factors*/
        while ( test_number > 1 )
        {                      /* get smallest factor   */
            factor = smallest_factor( test_number ) ;
                               /* print the factor      */
            printf( "  %d", factor ) ;
                               /* divide by the factor  */
            test_number = test_number / factor ;
        }
        printf( "\n" ) ;       /* print an end-of-line  */
    }
}

                               /* function to find smallest
                                  factor of integer     */
int smallest_factor( integer_value )
int integer_value ;            /* value to be factored  */
{
    int factor_limit ;         /* largest factor to try*/
    int trial_factor ;         /* trial factor          */
    int quotient ;             /* result of dividing    */
                               /* set limit of factors  */
    factor_limit = integer_value / 2 ;
    trial_factor = 2 ;         /* first trial factor 2  */
                               /* continue up to limit  */
    while ( trial_factor <= factor_limit )
    {                          /* divide by trial fact.*/
        quotient = integer_value / trial_factor ;
                               /* see if division exact*/
        if ( trial_factor * quotient == integer_value )
                               /* if so, return factor  */
            return trial_factor ;
                               /* if not, next trial    */
        trial_factor = trial_factor + 1 ;
    }                          /* if no factor found,   */
    return integer_value ;     /*   return integer value*/
}
```

Figure 3.1: *A program using two functions.*

□ PROGRAM NAMES AND COMMENTS

Variable and function names in C must be made up of letters, digits, and the underscore character (_). The factoring program uses underscores in the names **test_number** and **smallest_factor**. The underscore can make the names in your programs easier to understand. Although names can be of any length, compilers may use as little as the first eight characters to distinguish between them. Names of functions processed by a linker may be subject to even shorter limits. Some compilers and some linkers, however, will distinguish between much longer names.

The factoring program includes comments, which can be added to any C program. A comment begins at /* and ends at */ and includes these characters and everything between them. A comment can be placed anywhere except inside a variable name, a constant, a keyword, a symbol with more than one character, or another comment. (Some C compilers permit comments inside comments.) A comment can occupy part of a source line, all of a source line, or many source lines. The two characters that begin and the two characters that end a comment must be written together; there can be no spacing between them. Keeping comments to the right side of a page will often help readability, as will blank lines.

□ FUNCTION ARGUMENTS AND RETURN VALUES

Look now at the **smallest_factor** function. Notice that this function is found completely outside the **main** function. Although the **main** function was written first, this order is not required. The approach of C to the role of functions might be summarized by the old saying, "Every tub on its own bottom." C functions are generally independent of one another.

The **smallest_factor** function is designed to be invoked with one argument. Within the function, the value of this argument will be available from **integer_value**, which is one of the **smallest_factor** function's variables. It is a special type of variable, called a *parameter*. It receives an initial value from a corresponding argument that was supplied when the function was invoked.

Function parameters are named in the argument list of the function definition, between parentheses following the function name, separated by commas. Immediately after the parameter list, declaration statements for the parameters can appear. Any parameter not declared at this point is assumed to have a data type of **int**.

In the smallest_factor function, the integer_value parameter is explicitly declared to be **int**. When the main function invokes smallest_factor, it supplies the **int** variable test_number as an argument. The smallest_factor function obtains the current value of test_number as the value of its parameter integer_value.

Each C function may return a value. Functions are not required to return values, and the parts of programs that call functions are free to ignore any value returned. The smallest_factor function does return a value. The word **int** appearing just before its name at the start of the function definition indicates that the value returned will have that data type:

```
int smallest_factor( integer_value )
```

If a return values data type is not specified, the C language assumes that it is **int**. For the smallest_factor function, the value returned is the smallest integer, larger than one, that divides exactly into integer_value.

□ LOCAL VARIABLES IN FUNCTIONS

Inside the smallest_factor function, three local variables are used. They are declared after the opening brace and before any of the executable statements of the function:

```
int factor_limit ;
int trial_factor ;
int quotient ;
```

These variables can be used only within the smallest_factor function. Their values are not retained after return from the function; they are unpredictable each time the function is entered, until the function has assigned values.

□ THE OPERATION OF A FUNCTION

The smallest_factor function continually divides integer_value by trial_factor, trying to find an integer that will divide integer_value exactly. It tries values for trial_factor that start at 2 and go up through factor_limit:

```
trial_factor = 2 ;
while ( trial_factor <= factor_limit )
```

When the value of trial_factor becomes greater than the value of factor_limit, the repetition controlled by **while** ends.

In the block controlled by **while**, integer_value is first divided by trial_factor; the result is assigned to quotient:

```
quotient = integer_value / trial_factor ;
```

When integers are divided, any remainder is ignored. To see if such a division was exact, quotient is then multiplied by trial_factor, and the result is compared to integer_value:

```
if ( trial_factor * quotient == integer_value )
    return trial_factor ;
```

If the two values are equal, the division was exact. When the division is exact, the smallest_factor function stops, returning the value of trial_factor.

The **return** statement causes a function to terminate. It means "Stop the function that is currently executing and go back to the function that invoked it." Whatever expression appears after the word **return** is the value returned. For the **return** that appears inside the **while** block, the return value is the value of trial_factor, which has just produced an exact quotient.

When division is not exact, the value of trial_factor is increased by one, and the **while** repetition continues to seek an exact quotient:

```
while ( trial_factor <= factor_limit )
{
    quotient = integer_value / trial_factor ;
    if ( trial_factor * quotient == integer_value )
        return trial_factor ;
    trial_factor = trial_factor + 1 ;
}
    return integer_value ;
```

If trial_factor becomes larger than factor_limit and no factor has been found, the **while** repetition stops. The next statement returns a value equal to integer_value, because no smaller number was found that could be divided into integer_value exactly.

A function is not required to have a **return**. At the end of any function, control automatically returns to the function that invoked it.

However, a **return** statement is required if you want a function to return a value or to stop before reaching the end.

Now look at the main function of the program. This function uses two variables, named test_number and factor:

```
int test_number ;
int factor ;
int smallest_factor( ) ;
```

The third declaration tells a C compiler that the main function will use a function named smallest_factor, which returns an integer value.

□ INDEFINITE REPETITION

Next in the main function comes a statement that may seem curious at first:

```
while ( 1 )
{
    . . .
}
```

The control expression for this **while** is just the number, 1. This is a repetition that continues indefinitely. Each time a repetition ends, the control expression is tested again. It is always nonzero, so a new repetition begins. The integer 1 is often used to indicate an indefinite repetition, because it is the number assigned by C when a relation is TRUE.

If the **while** (1) repetition in the main function is ever to stop, something inside the statement or block being repeated must stop it. The factor function used one such type of statement, **return**. The main function uses another:

```
if ( test_number < 2 )
    break ;
```

The **break** statement will be executed when the value of test_number is less than two. A **break** can appear anywhere inside a repetition. It means "Stop the repetition and proceed with the next statement following it." In the main function, there are no more statements, so when **break** is executed, the program ends. If an "inner" repetition lies inside another, "outer" repetition, a **break** within the inner repetition will stop only the inner repetition.

□ USING FUNCTIONS TO READ AND PRINT

The statements repeated by **while** (1) in the **main** function include the following:

```
{
    printf( "Enter number to factor: " ) ;
    scanf( "%d", &test_number ) ;
    if ( test_number < 2 )
        break ;
    . . .
}
```

The **printf** message tells the user to type in a new number. The next statement uses a similar function, called **scanf**. This function obtains input from some standard device, generally the user's terminal. The notation **%d** says that a decimal integer is expected. There is a second argument, **&test_number**, which causes the value of the decimal integer to be assigned to the variable **test_number**. The *ampersand* is required by **scanf**, as explained in later chapters.

If the value of **test_number** is less than 2, the **main** function will end, as explained before. If not, the statements that were omitted from the excerpt above will print the prime factors of **test_number**. Here are those statements:

```
while ( test_number > 1 )
{
    factor = smallest_factor( test_number ) ;
    printf( " %d", factor ) ;
    test_number = test_number / factor ;
}
printf( "\n" ) ;
```

Inside the main **while** repetition, there is a second **while** repetition, this one continuing as long as the value of **test_number** is greater than one.

The inner **while** block obtains factors of **test_number**, one at a time. The first statement inside the **while** block invokes the **smallest _factor** function, to obtain one factor of **test_number**. The current value of **test_number** is sent to **smallest_factor** as an argument. The value returned is assigned to the variable **factor**:

```
factor = smallest_factor( test_number ) ;
```

After obtaining a factor, the **main** function invokes **printf** to print the factor. When **%d** is used with **printf** its effect is similar to that of the same notation use with scanf; that is, the value of factor is to be printed as a decimal integer. Notice that with printf no ampersand is placed before a variable name in an argument. The character string '' %d'', causing printing of a decimal number, contains two blanks before the percent sign. It will thus cause two blanks to appear before each number that is printed.

After printing whatever factor was obtained, the main function reduces the value of test_number, dividing it by the value of factor:

    test_number = test_number / factor ;

If test_number has not yet been reduced to one, the inner repetition will continue, and another factor will be obtained. When all factors have been found, test_number has been reduced to a value of one, and the repetition ends. Finally, printf is invoked again, to end the line of output with a newline character.

□ THE CONTENTS OF THE C LIBRARY

Except for specialized control programs and parts of operating systems, most C programs use functions from the C library. These functions provide the following types of program services:

- keyboard input and display output

- file input and output

- data conversion

- character string manipulation

- dynamic memory allocation

- mathematical functions

This chapter will discuss the most often used input, output, and string manipulation functions. Dynamic memory allocation is discussed in Chapters 8, 9, and 10. All the C library functions are described in detail in Chapters 18 and 19.

Any program that uses the C library's input or output functions must start with the statement

    #include <stdio.h>

For some systems, you may need one of two slightly different forms of this statement:

```
#include "stdio.h"
#include stdio
```

The number sign (#) must be in the first column of the line. Consult manuals or personnel for your system to determine which form of the statement your system requires. This type of statement is explained in more detail in later chapters. It causes certain symbols, needed for the C library functions, to be defined.

The C language is designed so that, in general, the only functions linked to a program are the ones it specifically invokes, plus additional functions that those may require. There are minor exceptions for certain C compilers, such as functions to perform operations that are not provided by machine instructions. Unlike other high-level languages, C has no hidden infrastructure of library functions. That is what makes it easy to combine C functions with programs written in another language. The C language does not carry along a baggage of support code, conventions, and restrictions.

The C library usually has a only few "layers" of functions to provide its services. The functions that a program invokes call on other library functions to perform data conversions and to coordinate access to operating system services for the user terminal, data files, and dynamic memory. When you use certain library functions, the linker automatically includes some of these common service functions.

□ INPUT AND OUTPUT FUNCTIONS

The program example for this chapter employs two frequently used C library functions, **printf** and **scanf**, which transmit "formatted" data to and from the user's terminal. The first argument for each is a string that defines a format. Characters in a format string are transmitted literally, except for format codes, preceded by a percent sign (%), and "escape characters," preceded by a backslash (\). Format strings for **scanf** generally consist only of format codes.

Each format code in a format string transmits data to or from a variable that must appear in an additional argument for **printf** or **scanf**. These arguments must be in the same order as their corresponding format codes. A format code consists of one letter that tells how to convert data for output or interpret data for input. The most commonly needed format codes are these:

d	decimal number
o	octal number
x	hexadecimal number
c	printed character
s	character string

Between a percent sign and the format code there can be a decimal integer, giving a "field width." This is the number of character positions corresponding to data as it appears at the user's terminal. Other uses of format codes are explained in Chapter 19.

The arguments for printf, other than the format string, are not limited to variables; they can also be expressions. Arguments for scanf, however, can only be variable names; and each must be preceded by an ampersand. The meaning of this notation will be explained in later chapters.

In general, the C library's input and output functions transmit data literally. Unlike those of some other languages, they do not automatically insert line markers or other control information. You have already seen examples of output that explicitly transmit \n to start a new line; this is an escape character used for control information. The most common escape characters are these:

\n	new line marker
\t	tab marker
\'	single quote
\"	double quote
\\	backslash

Each escape character corresponds to a single character code and can be used in a character constant or as part of a quoted character string.

The C library includes two functions commonly used for single character input and output at the user's terminal, as shown in the following examples:

```
putchar( output_character ) ;

input_character = getchar( ) ;
```

The function putchar writes to the user's display; getchar reads from the user's keyboard. The getchar function does not require an argument, but parentheses must be included to show that a function is being invoked.

In many C implementations, input from a user's terminal is not transmitted to a program until the user types "ENTER" or "RETURN." If your system works this way, both scanf and getchar will be affected. The scanf function normally scans over the newline marker you generate when you type "ENTER" or "RETURN." However, if newline is the next input character available to read, either getchar or scanf (with the %c format code) will transmit it literally.

□ INPUT AND OUTPUT USING DATA FILES

When a program uses a data file through the C library, it must explicitly *open* and *close* access to the file. When access to a file is opened, the name of the file is provided by a character string argument. In a second argument, the program must also specify whether the file will be read or written. The following example opens a file named FX23.DAT for reading:

```
#include <stdio.h>

FILE *input_file ;
FILE *fopen( ) ;

input_file = fopen( "FX23.DAT", "r" ) ;
```

The fopen function returns a special type of value, called a *file pointer*. You declare a variable with the file pointer data type as shown in the example:

```
FILE *input_file ;
```

Asterisks are required, as shown, in file pointer declarations. Their meaning will be explained in later chapters. They are not otherwise used with a file pointer name. The symbol FILE is defined when stdio.h is included. If access cannot be opened to the file you request, fopen will return a zero value. You can test for this value by using statements such as:

```
input_file = fopen( "FX23.DAT", "r" ) ;
if ( !input_file )
{
    printf( "Unable to open input\n" ) ;
    . . .
}
```

To open a file for writing, you use "w" instead of "r" as the second argument for fopen. A new file will be created. If there is an existing file of the same name, in some systems the existing file is deleted. In others, a new "version" of the file will be created. You should determine how your system responds. Instead of a quoted string, an **fopen** argument can also be the name of a character array containing a character string.

The most common functions using files to read and write data are named **fscanf**, **fprintf**, **fgetc**, and **fputc**. These functions operate like **scanf**, **printf**, **getchar**, and **putchar**, except that they require an additional argument, which must be a file pointer for an open file. Some examples follow:

```
#include <stdio.h>

FILE *input_file ;
FILE *output_file ;
FILE *fopen( ) ;

input_file = fopen( "FX23.IN", "r" ) ;
output_file = fopen( "FX23.OUT", "w" ) ;

fscanf( input_file, "%d", value ) ;
fprintf( output_file, "%d", result ) ;
control = fgetc( input_file ) ;
fputc( '\n', output_file ) ;
```

You can use a value returned by any of the input functions to determine whether the end of data has been reached. It is equal to the symbol **EOF**, defined when **stdio.h** is included, if no more data are available to read. Statements that check for this value look like the following:

```
control = fgetc( input_file ) ;
if ( control == EOF )
{
    printf( "End of input\n" ) ;
    . . .
}
```

When your program has finished reading or writing a data file, it should close access to the file using the **fclose** function, as in:

```
fclose( input_file ) ;
```

This ensures that the operating system's records of the file are correct.

The data type returned by all the input and output functions except **fopen** is **int**. If you do not declare the data type returned by a function, the C language automatically assumes that it is **int**. While you must declare the data type returned by **fopen**, you can omit declarations for the other functions.

□ CHARACTER STRING FUNCTIONS

Most C programs use character strings. The C library provides several functions to perform commonly needed string operations. Although it is easy to write C statements that perform these operations, using the library functions is usually more efficient. Where a character string is required as an argument, it will most often be the name of a character array. A quoted character string can also be an argument, but you must not try to copy anything into it. The most commonly used functions are shown in the following examples.

```
int length, cmp ;
char string[ 80 ] ;

strcpy( string, "Sally" ) ;
strcat( string, " forth" ) ;
length = strlen( string ) ;
cmp = strcmp( string, "Sally Forth" ) ;
```

All of these functions rely on the C convention of placing a null character (with a code value of zero) after the data characters in a string. The **strcpy** function copies all the characters in the second argument, up to and including the null, into corresponding positions in the first argument. The **strcat** function locates a null in the first argument and then, beginning at that position, copies all characters from the second argument up to and including the null.

The **strlen** function counts the number of characters in a string, up to but not including the null. The value of **length** in the example above will be 11. The **strcmp** function compares two strings, character by character, until it finds unequal characters or a null in either string. The result is the code value at that position from the first string, minus the code value at that position from the second string. This value is zero only if the strings are identical. The **strcmp** comparison is sensitive to case; **cmp** in the example above will be nonzero.

The data type returned by all the string manipulation functions is **int**. The functions shown are *unbounded;* they stop only when they find a null character. It is thus essential to use them only with strings that observe the C language convention of ending a string in a terminating null. Some C libraries provide additional functions that can operate on arbitrary character strings.

□ EXERCISES

3.1: Most of the "work" of the factoring program (Figure 3.1) is done by the smallest_factor function. Each time it is invoked, it looks for possible factors of test_number, starting at 2 and going up through test_number / 2 in increments of one. Although this form of the function will do the job, it is not at all efficient.

    (a) Since smallest_factor always obtains the smallest factor of the number, once it has found a factor, that factor can serve as a starting point for the next search. Modify the program, adding a second argument to the smallest_factor function. This argument should give the value of the first trial factor. For each new number to be factored, the main function should start this trial factor at 2. Each time main gets a new factor for the number, this last factor obtained should be supplied to smallest_factor as the starting point for its next search.

    (b) It is wasteful to increase the trial divisor by one for each trial; this is only necessary when trying a factor of 2. Once trial_factor gets beyond 2, all the factors of 2 have been extracted, so that only odd numbers can be factors. Modify the smallest_factor function to try only odd values for trial_factor, once it has passed a value of 2. Your modification should not include a division, since this operation could take as much time as the testing of an even factor that it would replace.

3.2: In the smallest_factor function, factor_limit, the highest factor tried, is set to integer_value / 2. Actually, there is no need to try factors beyond the square root of integer_value. If integer_value can be divided exactly by some number larger than its square root, then the quotient, which is smaller than the square root, must also be a factor. If there is no integer factor either larger or smaller than the square root, then either the square root is itself an integer (and thus the only prime factor), or, if it is not, integer_value is prime.

(a) Unfortunately, it takes a little work to calculate a square root. Start with this simple approach. Begin with factor_limit at the smallest factor that will be tried. Find the square of factor_limit, multiplying factor_limit by itself, and test whether that is larger than integer_value. If not, double the value of factor_limit, adding factor_limit to itself, and keep testing until its square becomes larger. This change will greatly reduce the number of factors to be tried but should add only three or four lines to the program.

(b) The result of (a) is a value of factor_limit that is not more than a factor of 2 greater than the square root of integer_value. With only slightly more work, you can find an integer that is within one of an exact square root. From the equation

$$y = x^2$$

you can obtain the formula

$$x = ((y / x) + x) / 2$$

Create an approximate square root function. Begin with y as the quantity for which a square root is needed and x equal to one. Repeatedly evaluate this formula (known as the Newton-Raphson formula) until the value of x no longer changes. How does the number of iterations required vary with the size of the squared quantity? Do the results come out larger or smaller than the exact values of square roots? Can you show why?

3.3: Certain easily defined sequences of numbers behave quite erratically. They vary wildly, then eventually lose their steam and settle into a pattern. One such type of sequence has been called the "hailstone numbers." The most common procedure for generating hailstone numbers is this:

Pick a starting number.
If it is odd, triple it and add 1.
If it is even, divide it by 2.
Use the result to get the next number.

Write a program that obtains a starting number from the user's terminal, then generates and prints the first 60 hailstone numbers that begin with it.

It is believed (but has not been proven) that any hailstone number series will eventually settle into the sequence 1, 4, 2. Once this is reached, the sequence cycles through only these numbers. Expand your program for generating hailstone numbers, so that it automatically tries 1, 2, 3, and so on as starting numbers. For each starting point, find out how many hailstone numbers you can generate before getting the value, 1, that acts as a "trap."

Adapt your automatic hailstone program to find the largest number that you generate for each starting number. Be prepared for a surprise when you start with 27. If you go as far as a starting number of 703, you may find that some numbers generated exceed values your computer can use for normal integers.

3.4: Create a program to accept a (decimal) number from the user's terminal and print out its equivalent in Roman numerals. This is not especially hard. Recall that the common Roman numerals have these values:

M	1000
D	500
C	100
L	50
X	10
V	5
I	1

Begin by subtracting away thousands, printing M as long as the result does not go below zero, then progress to the lower values of Roman numerals. With this approach, you can convert all numbers up to 4999.

True Romans, of course, would write 4 as IV, rather than IIII (certain antique clocks notwithstanding). This family of special cases includes the following:

4000	MU[1]
900	CM
400	CD
90	XC
40	XL

[1] The Roman numeral for 5000 is $\overline{V}$, but since that is not an ASCII character, U makes an acceptable substitute.

```
9   IX
4   IV
```

Find a way to add this wrinkle to your Roman numeral converter.

3.5: Computers often keep track of dates by the year and day of the year (that is, 1 to 365 or 366). This arrangement is more convenient for computers than for the people who use them. Write a program that obtains from the user's terminal first a number for a year, then another number for a day of the year. Print the equivalent date in a conventional form. For example, day 321 of year 1954 becomes

November 17, 1954

(a) In addition to "Thirty days hath September . . . ," note that leap years are skipped when the year is a multiple of 100 but not of 400.

(b) Now make your date converter into a universal calendar, by adding the day of the week. The easiest way to do this is probably to find the number of days since some particular day, then take the remainder when divided by 7. With this feature, day 321 of year 1954 becomes

Wednesday, November 17, 1954.

MASTERING

CHAPTER 4

PLANNING
SOFTWARE FOR C

Getting the most out of any software effort requires planning. This chapter describes planning techniques that are particularly useful for writing programs in C, including the following topics:

- the stages of software development
- defining requirements
- designing software
- software segments
- sharing software conventions
- design methods and principles
- planning for validation
- the software outline
- documenting a design

☐ THE STAGES OF SOFTWARE DEVELOPMENT

While some software is still produced for personal use, most software is now produced for use by other people. Its users rarely know who produced it or how it works. As a result of these circumstances, the development of computer software has become a discipline. It shares with other professional disciplines these characteristics:

- Clients and employers expect both performance and reliability from the work.
- Personnel are specialized, by field of application and by customary type of work.

Many people think that software development is mainly "programming," by which they mean writing in some computer language. However, software development is usually organized in projects, with explicit goals, assignments, and schedules. Software projects typically include the following stages:

1. definition
2. design

3. implementation

4. validation

5. maintenance

Definition is concerned with the external operation of software. *Design* is concerned with internal organization. *Implementation* produces testable programs. *Validation* detects and corrects their initial defects. *Maintenance* corrects latent defects and adapts software to changes in requirements. Of these stages, only implementation resembles "programming" in the conventional sense of the word.

Over the lifetime of a software system, it is common to find the following distribution of development efforts:

Definition	10 percent
Design	15 percent
Implementation	5 percent
Validation	20 percent
Maintenance	50 percent

For simple systems, validation and maintenance may be less than these percentages. For complex systems, however, they are often greater.

The major objectives of most software projects are to achieve performance and reliability and to control the potentially high costs of validation and maintenance. Good software planning—the definition and design stages—is critical. To anyone who has seen a badly planned project, wandering into trouble or lurching toward disaster, the need for good planning becomes all but unforgettable.

Software planning means writing. Unwritten plans count for little, because they are of use only to their creators (and only when the creators can remember them). Clear writing is a necessary skill for software personnel. Good ideas poorly written are likely to result in costly misunderstandings.

□ DEFINING REQUIREMENTS

The objective of the definition stage of software development is to designate the services that software should deliver. The end product of definition is a *software specification,* describing those services in realistic detail. Usually, a specification does not describe the organization of programs or data, unless that organization is an essential part of the services themselves (for example, a device controller for a particular operating system or a processor to be used with an established database).

The requirements definition specifies external characteristics—that is, exactly what the software will do, as seen by its users. It includes the following items:

- services the software will deliver

- data to be received from or prepared for other software

- physical devices to be used or managed

- interactive commands and data entry procedures

- contents of messages, displays, and reports

- secondary features, such as default actions, help messages, and automatic data backup

- speed of processing required

- requirements for communication or coordination with other simultaneous programs

- restrictions imposed by other software

Many developers start defining requirements by writing a "wish list," describing capabilities that seem most important. For interactive software, "prototype" programs can be helpful. These simulate major features of displays, messages, and data entry. For time-critical or pattern-recognizing programs, it may be necessary to create a mathematical model of software performance and estimate the response to different demands.

The choice of a computer language will often follow, not precede, the definition stage of a project. For projects likely to be implemented in C, however, it can help to observe these guidelines when writing a specification:

- Give explicit directions for all commands, data entry procedures, data displays, and messages.

- If software is expected to provide automatic or default actions, state when and how they are to be performed.

- Describe the content of data and the relations among data items.

- Unless data sources and destinations are critical to performance, leave their details to the design stage.

- Avoid dependence on features of particular equipment and operating systems unless they are essential to performance.

- Consider errors that can be detected by software, and specify what to do when they are detected.

- Outline the major priorities in performance clearly. State minimum acceptable factors.

- Consider how to test the software. Describe how to verify an acceptable level of performance and reliability.

- Try to forecast future requirements. Estimate the likelihood and usefulness of possible requirements.

□ DESIGNING SOFTWARE

If the definition stage of software development plans what to do, the design stage plans how to do it. The end product, a *software design*, explains in detail how software will be organized. Several books are available on software design; this discussion presents an overall approach likely to be of use when software will be implemented in C.

Software design usually begins with a general plan of how the software will work. Such a plan will usually aim to divide a complex task into simpler tasks. After you are satisfied that your overall approach is workable, you should apply the same process to the lower-level tasks. Subdividing tasks, filling in detail, and reviewing consequences are the basic work of software planning. Eventually, a level will be reached that is nearly as detailed as program code.

While this approach will provide some kind of plan for software, it will not necessarily result in a design. As a plan is developed, it becomes detailed, but the details do not make it a design. What most characterizes a design is *coherent organization*. The designer provides a clear pattern for a program; the pieces of the pattern fit together; the pattern fits the requirements.

Most successful designs are developed around some carefully chosen organizing principles. Identifying these core elements is a crucial step in a project. Sometimes they may be obvious to an experienced designer, but often they are not. A design usually requires more than one attempt to describe an organization, review the consequences, and revise the plan. You should be especially willing to revise a plan when working on its upper levels. There, the benefits of sound design are greatest, while the costs of revision are least.

Just as a design is developed in levels of detail, it should also be explained in levels; a program of practical scale may require several levels of detail. An hour or two spent with the top level of a design should give a thorough understanding of all major software components. Further levels of detail should be easily identified and should require only reasonable amounts of further study. A consistent style should be used to explain each software component.

A software design may be difficult to work out, but it should be easy to explain. One useful test of a design is to present it to another software developer. Many organizations formalize this process as "design review." The designer explains the principles of a proposed design; the reviewers look for inconsistencies and potential conflicts.

While making a design is work, it must not become drudgery. You should maintain a balance of detail during the process; don't overcommit to details in some areas while remaining sketchy in others. As a plan is worked through, new ways of organizing data, arranging controls, or performing computations may emerge. When you maintain balance in your effort, you will be able to reconsider program segments affected by new ideas, rearrange your plan, and make it more coherent. However, if you have an imbalance of commitment to details, it can be painful to reorganize your work, even though reorganization would bring benefits.

□ SOFTWARE SEGMENTS

All software systems of substantial scale are divided into *segments,* each performing some particular type of work. The segments may be planned, and will often be developed, by different people. It is essential to have a clear understanding of boundaries between segments, responsibilities of each segment, and the means for communicating between them. These topics are often referred to as *software interfaces.* As soon as you can identify different segments of a software system, you should plan software interfaces.

The smallest segment is the individual *procedure,* corresponding to a C function. A procedure has some specific task to perform. To accomplish this, it can manipulate specific information, through arguments and return values. In addition, it may share access to data and may share conventions, such as organizations of data, with other parts of software. Methods for sharing data and conventions in C will be explained in later chapters.

A larger segment of software is a *module,* consisting of a group of procedures that perform closely related tasks. For example, a module might maintain lists of elements and labels for a graphics image, or it might read, write, and sort the data for a retail inventory. In the C language, a module consists of everything contained in one source file. C allows functions grouped together in a module to share data and conventions that are limited to that particular module and also to share data and conventions that are potentially accessible to all modules in a program.

Many software systems need still larger types of segments. For example, a manufacturing test system might be divided into sectors that operate equipment, maintain test records, and communicate with personnel. Each sector would probably be composed of several modules.

As a design effort progresses, you will often find some segments forming an administrative hierarchy that includes

- a main segment, controlling actions that occur when the program starts and ends

- one or more additional levels of control, directing the performance of the program's major functions

- one or more levels of operations, performing details of the work to be accomplished

A diagram can be made to show the flow of control in such a program structure. Each box in the diagram represents one software segment. It has an path entering it, showing the segment from which it gets control. Most boxes have one or more paths leaving them, showing the segments to which they pass control in order to obtain the services needed. Such a structure, illustrated in Figure 4.1, suggests a pyramid, with a "main control" segment at the apex, "higher" levels of control near the top, and segments performing detailed operations near the bottom.

For most practical programs, this organization is not sufficient. There are usually essential services—for example, reading or writing data files, inspecting tables, or sorting lists—that are needed in different parts of the program. One goal of program design is to organize such services consistently and efficiently. These services, in turn, often require still more "basic" services that are ultimately few in number. A diagram of these parts of a program, illustrated in Figure 4.2, may resemble an orchard, with a few tree trunks and many twigs.

Most programs need a combination of a service and an administrative structure. As an analogy, you might think of this as an organization combining "labor" and "management." In actual designs there are sometimes conflicts that mimic those seen in business disputes: a program fails when one of the service segments becomes overloaded and "goes on strike."

□ SHARING SOFTWARE CONVENTIONS

It is often necessary to share control and organizational information, the "conventions" of software, among different software segments. This information includes:

• lengths of arrays

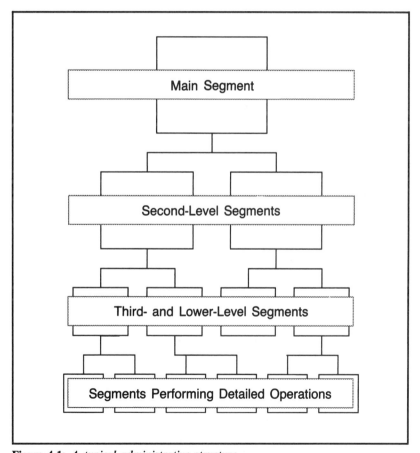

Figure 4.1: *A typical administrative structure.*

- values of control constants
- ranges of allowed values
- details of data organizations
- data types used for variables

Some languages, such as BASIC and FORTRAN, do not provide any organized method for sharing such information. The Ada language, by

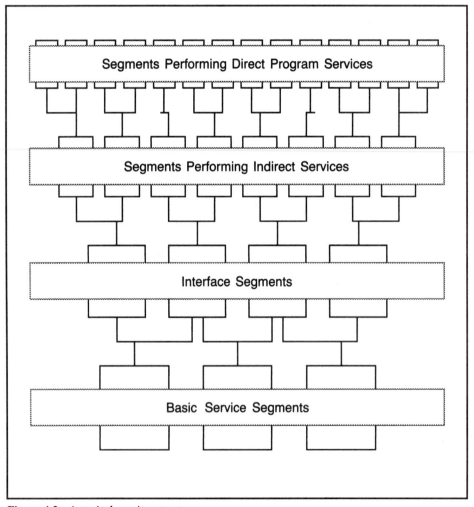

Figure 4.2: *A typical service structure.*

contrast, provides a complex infrastructure in which conventions are automatically passed from one software segment to another.

C allows the programmer to define symbolic constants and to create symbols for data organizations and data types that are similar to those of Pascal. However, it uses a peculiar mechanism to transmit conventions from one software segment to another, called *preprocessor* facilities. This section covers only the most common uses of data type definitions and the preprocessor facilities. Complete explanations of these topics are found in Chapters 9, 10, and 17.

The most common C statement for recording software conventions is the **#define** statement, which assigns values to symbols. The example shown in Figure 4.3 uses this statement.

Once a symbol has been named in a **#define** statement, its value is available to all succeeding statements in a module. Although a **#define** statement can be used for other purposes, good programming practice restricts its use to assigning constants to symbols.

A symbol name must begin with a letter. C programmers generally name symbols using either all uppercase letters or a combination of uppercase letters and digits. This helps to distinguish symbol names from the names of variables and functions. The **#define** statement

```
#define  LENGTH   20
#define  FIRST  'A'
#define  LAST   'Z'

int inspect( options, number )
char options[ LENGTH ] ;
int number ;
{
    int i, count ;

    if ( number > LENGTH )
        number = LENGTH ;
    count = 0 ;
    i = 0 ;
    while ( i < number )
    {
        if ( options[ i ] >= FIRST )
            if ( options[ i ] <= LAST )
                count = count + 1 ;

        i = i + 1 ;
    }
    return count ;
}
```

Figure 4.3: *Designating software conventions with #define.*

must start in the first column of a source line, may occupy only a single source line, may define only one symbol, and may contain only spacing as shown in Figure 4.3. It has no semicolon at the end.

Another common C statement for designating program conventions is **typedef**. It provides a symbol that can be used in place of a data type, as shown in Figure 4.4.

The **typedef** statement is used mainly with the more complex data organizations, as illustrated in Chapters 8, 9, and 10.

It is common practice in C to collect the software conventions needed in connection with a particular module in what are called *header* files. With an #include statement, a header file can be inserted into the source code for any module. The following shows how header files might have been used with Figure 4.4:

```
#include "decode.h"
#include <stdio.h>

SIZE significance( command, length )
```

 . . .

```
            typedef char TEXT ;
            typedef int SIZE ;

            SIZE significance( command, length )
            TEXT command[ ] ;
            SIZE length ;
            {
                SIZE pos, sgf ;
                TEXT chr ;

                pos = 0 ;
                sgf = 0 ;
                while ( pos < length )
                {
                    chr = command[ pos ] ;
                    if ( !chr )
                        break ;
                    if ( chr != ' ' )
                        sgf = sgf + 1 ;
                    pos = pos + 1 ;
                }
                return sgf ;
            }
```

Figure 4.4: *Designating software conventions with* typedef.

A header file named decode.h would be expected to include at least the following statements:

typedef char TEXT ;
typedef int SIZE ;

Like #define statements, #include statements must start in the first column of a source line, may occupy only a single source line, may include only one file, and may contain only spacing as shown in the examples above. They have no semicolon at the end. These statements are normally placed at the beginning of a module. Where the file-naming conventions of an operating system permit, a header file is usually given the same name as the source file for its module, except that .h is used for the file name suffix.

The C library has header files; a file named stdio.h will normally be included whenever its input and output functions are called. For many implementations, these system-supplied header files must be designated by placing angle brackets around the file name, as shown in the previous example. For some systems, quotation marks are used in the same way as with other file names. A few systems require a special format, such as this:

#include stdio

□ DESIGN METHODS AND PRINCIPLES

The literature of software engineering includes several highly structured approaches to design. While these approaches can be useful in some situations, they often fail to provide practical guidance. This section addresses methods likely to be helpful for software implemented in C.

Once software reaches the scale at which it is written by several people or developed over an extended time, software design faces problems of communication. A design cannot be completed unless each designer maintains an accurate understanding of the overall goals and of his or her individual contribution. The software itself needs a consistent approach to communication between its segments.

Two complementary approaches to these issues are *design standards* and *robust design*. Design standards deal with such matters as

- content of critical control data

- procedures for access to data

- use of program services

- naming of variables and functions

- use of language features

- program formats and documentation

Robust design builds insurance against mistakes directly into a program and helps it cope with departures from and misunderstandings about design standards.

One common type of design standard is an insistence that access to program services follow only certain prescribed paths. For example, it may be necessary to construct control data in such a way that every function potentially has direct access to the data. This makes accidental changes to data extremely difficult to detect. A design standard might thus require that access to control data be obtained by calling certain C functions. This would make it possible to monitor the use of control data and prevent many possible problems.

Robust design builds checks against departures from standards into modules and procedures. In C, these checks are generally performed by the functions that will be called from outside a module. They check to see that data values supplied through arguments are consistent and fall within valid ranges. They may also check to see that operations are being performed in a valid sequence. Once such tests have been passed, other functions that may be used within the same module will generally not repeat the tests.

A program that uses exception checking extensively will need a consistent way to handle the exceptions it detects. This is essential for real-time and interactive programs, so that critical services are not cut off and users do not become confused. Software of this type will often include a specialized segment that records exceptions and controls corrective actions.

A general principle effective in all software design is to keep the connections between software segments as simple and direct as possible. There are three major types of connections between segments:

- flow of control

- shared access to data

- shared conventions

For software implemented in C, control flow means invoking functions. Data are shared through global declarations, and conventions are shared through #include files, both explained in later chapters.

The major principle for managing control connections is simple: avoid cross-connections. Within an administrative structure like that shown in Figure 4.1, a function located in one branch must not directly invoke a function located in a different branch. Instead, control must flow through a segment that has access to both branches. For a service structure, as shown in Figure 4.2, only functions at the top level should be invoked from outside the service structure.

Most designers using C find it necessary to limit data sharing to functions located in the same module. Otherwise, it becomes extremely difficult to ensure software reliability. It is impractical to limit the sharing of conventions so narrowly; they need to be managed through standards.

Most conventions that can be shared through C mechanisms define data types and data organizations. Each software segment can be described as either an *producer* or a *consumer* of such conventions. Two principles are generally used in managing shared conventions:

- Dependencies created by shared conventions should parallel the flow of control.

- Shared conventions should be kept independent of one another.

Details of these issues will be discussed in Chapter 17, which presents the C language preprocessor facilities that are generally used to share conventions.

□ PLANNING FOR VALIDATION

Validation represents a substantial proportion of every software project. This is the stage of a project at which the design has been completed, and the inital code to implement the design has been written. The job of validation is to make an entire software system work and to prove that it works reliably.

Software validation usually involves the following sequence of activities:

- unit testing

- integration testing

- system testing

- performance testing

Unit tests are performed on individual procedures and modules, to verify that they perform as designed. *Integration* tests are performed as modules are linked together, to verify that they continue to operate correctly when they are assembled into a system. *System* tests verify the ability of a completed system to handle correctly both normal demands and errors. Finally, *performance* tests assess the ability of a system to meet time-critical demands, to process complex data, or to cope with a heavy work load.

Planning a validation strategy helps keep the effort consumed at this stage of development within bounds. A successful approach in many projects has been to determine a *backbone* for a software system, build and validate that part of the system first, and then graft additional segments onto the backbone, validating each one as it is added. To carry this out requires a sound design, one that clearly identifies the organizing principles of the system.

The advantages of the backbone approach to validation include the following:

- As soon as the backbone is completed, the developers have a system to demonstrate.

- Each subsystem is tested in place. Problems caused by a new subsystem can be traced quickly.

- Testing becomes more productive. Except for the backbone, unit tests are conducted as integration tests. There is no need to build complex code simply to perform unit tests.

This approach is not without its costs, however. Its limitations include the following:

- Planning and coordination are essential. Subsystems of the software must be added to the backbone in a well understood sequence.

- The software system needs to include features, such as test modes and the capability to run and record tests, that make it possible to repeat tests when needed.

- As new subsystems are added, previously added subsystems must be retested, to ensure that they continue to operate correctly.

- Revisions to subsystems that have been integrated must be carefully controlled. They may have to be postponed until a system is complete. Good test records are essential.

Whether or not the backbone approach is used, software planning has a major effect on validation. Good control of the dependencies in a software system can simplify the test procedures. Minimizing the complexity of decisions made by software also tends to minimize the complexity of testing those decisions. Unambiguous specifications help to produce thorough and straightforward tests.

□ THE SOFTWARE OUTLINE

A technique known as *software outlining* becomes useful as a software plan reaches a substantial level of detail. This technique condenses written language, revealing key points and relationships. It is particularly appropriate for software to be implemented in a *structured* procedural language such as C, because the flow of control provided by a structured language closely resembles an outline.

An outline is a structured form of the language that you write and speak. Its main advantages, as compared to narrative prose, are these:

- obvious grouping of related items
- an easy way to show dependencies
- abbreviations that emphasize content

An outline rarely describes anything that could not be shown in some other way; its purpose is to encourage organization. Unlike graphical notations, an outline is easy to compose. You can use pen and paper, a typewriter, or a text editor. An outline also provides components that are simple to break apart, change, and recombine.

The main principles for writing software outlines are the following:

- The steps in an outline are to be carried out in the order written, unless they are governed by a conditional or a repetition.

- A group of steps can be executed, omitted, or repeated under the control of a condition. The condition is written first; the steps it governs are indented underneath it.

- The steps governed by a condition may themselves involve conditions. Levels of control, shown by indenting, can be carried to any depth necessary.

Conditions in software outlines are described using certain words in special ways. The words "if" and "else" have the same meanings as in C language conditionals. The word "for" is used when repeating steps in some way that can be counted. Use "while" to continue a repetition as long as a condition is satisfied. Use "until" to stop a repetition after a condition is satisfied. Unlike "for" and "while," the use of "until" implies that the steps it governs will be executed at least once.

The following outline shows procedures that might be used to collect overdue fines for parking tickets:

```
For each ticket found in the active list
    If the ticket has not been paid
        If the ticket is more than 90 days old
            Remove the ticket from the active list
            Place the ticket in the tow-and-hold list
        Else if the ticket is more than 60 days old
            If a letter has not been sent
                Send a warning letter
                Indicate that a letter was sent
        Else if the ticket is more than 30 days old
            If a notice has not been sent
                Send an unpaid ticket notice
                Indicate that a notice was sent
    Else (the ticket has been paid)
        Remove the ticket from the active list
        Place the ticket in the completed list
```

All statements in this outline except the first are repeated until the active list is exhausted. For unpaid tickets in the list, there is a conditional cascade, providing actions when the ticket is more than 90, 60, and 30 days old.

□ DOCUMENTING A DESIGN

The software outline is an efficient way to document the operation of a single procedure. It is not adequate for any larger software segment, however, because it lacks information about the connections between segments. For each procedure in a module, at least the following information should be made part of the design documentation:

- the name and purpose of the procedure

- input data, usually function arguments
- output data, including a return value
- a general description of the operations
- assumptions, including sequences of usage
- exceptions that will be detected
- other procedures that are used
- a software outline for the operations

For a module containing several procedures, design documentation should contain additional information, describing the type of service provided by the module. It should include at least the following:

- the name and purpose of the module
- the overall operation of procedures in the module
- sequences for the use of procedures, if any
- data files and formats used or generated
- data and conventions shared within the module
- data directly shared outside the module
- conventions originated for use by other modules
- conventions used from other modules
- a list of procedures in the module
- a list of modules used by these procedures

Software segments larger than a module are generally documented in a similar manner. The documentation should emphasize what holds the segment together, how its services are related. It should also describe the connections to other software segments, particularly dependencies that involve shared data or conventions.

Aside from its use in planning a software project, the documentation for a software design is an investment made to reduce the cost of maintenance. When software must be changed to correct latent defects or adapt to new requirements, the changes are often far easier if good documentation is available to explain how the software is organized. If design documentation is not adequate, maintenance is often required to create or correct it. When software has to be changed, the documentation must also be kept up to date.

□ EXERCISES

4.1: Write a software design for some ordinary task for which you might find a small computer useful. Write a general description of what the program should do. Work out the modules that you would need. Make a diagram to show which modules will call on which other modules, and see if you can identify the administrative and service sectors that seem to work best. Here are some suggestions for programs:

    (a) household inventory

    (b) personal address and telephone list

    (c) weekly budget and expense account

    (d) notecard organizer

    (e) automobile maintenance log

    (f) list of technical literature

    (g) mailing list for a small organization

    (h) log of sales contacts

4.2: Choose one of the designs you developed for the previous exercise. Expand parts of this design with some of the details needed to write a program.

    (a) Write a *lexicon,* explaining exactly what each specialized term or data item relevant to your program and design means.

    (b) Select an area of the program requiring critical decisions. Write a software outline for this part of the program, describing the methods by which the program will make those decisions.

    (c) Examine your software outline, and see if your description of what the program should do contains all the details needed to specify the program's capabilities in the area you outlined.

PART 2

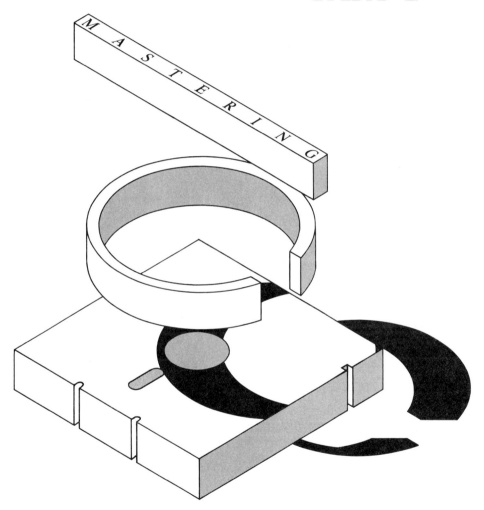

MASTERING

PORTABLE DATA

CHAPTER 5

TYPES OF DATA ELEMENTS

This chapter presents the fundamental data types available in the C language. C is parsimonious in this area. Its power is based not on a wealth of data types but on flexible organization of a limited number of types of data. This chapter deals with machine independent data types, which you can use in all environments. In it, you will read about:

- data types and values
- integer data
- character data
- binary representations
- type conversions
- string conversions

□ DATA TYPES AND VALUES

Items of data in the C language are classified as *variables* or *constants*. A program can change the value of a variable but not that of a constant. The *type* of a data element is a characteristic restricting it to a particular range of possible values. A variable of type **int**, for example, may have an integer value greater than or equal to some lower limit and less than or equal to some upper limit.

Variables always have names. In C, variables must be declared. A declaration statement identifies the variable's name and associates it with a data type. When the name of a variable appears in any other C statement, that means for the computer either to use or to set the current value. Variables generally do not have predictable values until a program has assigned them. Declaration statements, which are covered in detail by Chapter 10, must appear in a program before variable names are used in any other way.

Constants always have definite values, but they may or may not have names. A constant that is identified only by value is called a *literal* constant. You include literal constants in program statements by writing their values. For example, − 137 identifies an integer constant with the indicated value (in decimal). A literal constant may appear anywhere in a C program and will always be correctly interpreted.

A *symbolic* constant has a name. The only way to create a symbolic constant in C is to use a **#define** statement, like this:

```
#define PROTON 1836
```

Such a statement associates a name with a literal value. A symbolic constant will be recognized only after it has been defined in this way. The definition will apply throughout the remainder of a source file, unless a subsequent definition for the same name overrides it.

□ INTEGER DATA

Integer data have values that can be used for counting. You have been working so far with the main fundamental data types of C, **int** and **char**. Variables of type **int** take on positive and negative integer values. Variables of type **char** also take on integer values, but their values are associated with particular printable and control characters.

Variables of type **int** are the main working data of many C programs. The minimum and maximum values of **int** variables are not the same from one computer to another. The C language guarantees that **int** variables will be implemented efficiently, not that they will have some specific range of values. For all common implementations of C, **int** variables will accept positive and negative values whose magnitudes are less than 2^{15} (or 32,768 in decimal).

Constants of type **int** can be specified in decimal, octal, or hexadecimal numbering. Any sequence of decimal digits that does not begin with zero specifies an integer constant with the indicated value in decimal. An octal integer constant in C is a sequence of octal digits (0–7) that begins with zero. A hexadecimal integer constant consists of the notation 0x or 0X followed followed by a sequence of hexadecimal digits (0–9, A–F). The letters that represent hexadecimal digits may be in either upper- or lowercase. Any integer constant may be preceded by a minus sign to indicate a negative value.

The following are all valid integer constants, in decimal, octal, or hexadecimal:

0	10	−11
1	35	−129
00	012	−013
01	043	−0201
0x0	0xA	−0Xb
0x1	0X23	−0x81

The following are invalid constants, for the reasons noted:

1A	hexadecimal value doesn't start with 0x
049	octal value has a non-octal digit

| 0x | hexadecimal value has no digits |
| +8 | preceding plus sign is not allowed |

Although the value − 0 is allowed, if a variable assigned this value is compared with another assigned the value 0, they will be found to be equal.

Three *modifiers* can be applied to the data type **int**: they are **long**, **short**, and **unsigned**. A variable of type **long int** may have a greater range of possible values than one of type **int**; a variable of type **short int** may have a smaller range. The uses and ranges of these types are strongly machine dependent. They are discussed in Chapter 16, on implementation features. A variable of type **unsigned int** accepts only positive values.

The data type **int** is the default data type of the C language. When a statement contains enough information to indicate that a data type is being specified but does not include the name of a type, **int** is assumed. You may, for example, specify an **unsigned int** variable named count, as:

    unsigned count ;

When you make any comparison, such as level == 3, the result of the comparison has the value 0 or 1 and the type **int**. An integer constant of the forms previously described automatically has the data type **int**.

□ CHARACTER DATA

Character data have integer values that are associated with particular printable and control characters. The association is governed by your computer and terminal equipment. In the United States, there are two common associations, or *character codes:* ASCII, an acronym for American Standard Code for Information Interchange, and EBCDIC, for Extended Binary Coded Decimal Interchange Code. EBCDIC was defined by IBM; it is used mainly on large computers. ASCII was defined by ANSI, the American National Standards Institute. It is used on most minicomputers, microcomputers, and computer terminal equipment.

The ASCII code comprises 94 printable characters and 34 nonprinting control characters. There are standard two- and three-letter abbreviations for the names of control characters. The table in Figure 5.1 presents the ASCII character codes, by integer values (in decimal).

In the ASCII code, the control character abbreviated as SP is used to print a space. The other control characters are based on signals for teletypewriter machines. A few are used to control printing and displays,

Code	Character	Code	Character	Code	Character	Code	Character
0	NUL	32	SP	64	@	96	`
1	SOH	33	!	65	A	97	a
2	STX	34	"	66	B	98	b
3	ETX	35	#	67	C	99	c
4	EOT	36	$	68	D	100	d
5	ENQ	37	%	69	E	101	e
6	ACK	38	&	70	F	102	f
7	BEL	39	'	71	G	103	g
8	BS	40	(	72	H	104	h
9	HT	41	)	73	I	105	i
10	LF	42	*	74	J	106	j
11	VT	43	+	75	K	107	k
12	FF	44	,	76	L	108	l
13	CR	45	-	77	M	109	m
14	SO	46	.	78	N	110	n
15	SI	47	/	79	O	111	o
16	DLE	48	0	80	P	112	p
17	DC1	49	1	81	Q	113	q
18	DC2	50	2	82	R	114	r
19	DC3	51	3	83	S	115	s
20	DC4	52	4	84	T	116	t
21	NAK	53	5	85	U	117	u
22	SYN	54	6	86	V	118	v
23	ETB	55	7	87	W	119	w
24	CAN	56	8	88	X	120	x
25	EM	57	9	89	Y	121	y
26	SUB	58	:	90	Z	122	z
27	ESC	59	;	91	[	123	{
28	FS	60	<	92	\	124		
29	GS	61	=	93	]	125	}
30	RS	62	>	94	^	126	~
31	US	63	?	95	_	127	DEL

Figure 5.1: *The ASCII character codes.*

particularly CR or carriage return (move to start of line), LF or line feed (move to next line), HT or horizontal tab (move to next tab stop), BS or backspace (move one character width toward the left), and FF or form feed (move to next page or screen). Program statements of the C language use 91 printable characters (all the printable characters in ASCII except those for values 36, 64, and 96).

Character data are defined in C by the **char** data type. The C language does not specify a range of integer values for the **char** data type. For all common implementations of C, **char** variables will accept values of 0 through 127, in decimal. All characters required for writing C program statements will have positive character values.

Constants of type **char** are defined by placing a character between single quotes. Nonprinting characters may be designated by the backslash (\) followed by one to three octal digits, giving the integer value to be assigned. For example, you might assign values to character variables by writing

```
vowel = 'a' ;
finis = '\15' ;
```

Note that a numerical character value is expressed in octal, not decimal, and that it need not start with zero. There are also eight standard forms for frequently used special values, as follows:

\r	carriage return (CR in ASCII)
\n	line feed, or newline (LF in ASCII)
\t	horizontal tab (HT in ASCII)
\b	backspace (BS in ASCII)
\f	form feed (FF in ASCII)
\\	the backslash character
\'	the single-quote character
\"	the double-quote character

The following are all valid character constants, using one of the forms previously described:

'a'	'A'	'\40'	'\n'
'r'	'R'	'\101'	'\\'
'&'	' '	'\0'	'\' '

The following are invalid constants, for the reasons noted:

' '	no character between single quotes
'\9'	octal form has a non-octal digit

'\z'   undefined special value
\n   single quotes missing
'AB'   more than one character

Note that the integer value zero differs from the numeral character zero. In ASCII, the numeral character zero has an integer value of 48, in decimal. A character whose integer value is zero is often called a *null character.* In C, null characters have special uses. C requires that no printing or normal control character have zero integer value.

The C language does not specify whether **char** data are *signed,* that is, whether their integer values may be negative. In practice, the choice is whatever will be the most efficient for a particular computer. Some implementations that provide signed characters allow the programmer to specify an **unsigned char** data type, but this is not standard. To keep your programs portable, either do not use the integer values of **char** data or use only positive values between 0 and 127, inclusive.

□ BINARY REPRESENTATIONS

The C language was designed to give efficient performance on computers that can store data as binary integers. The binary number system, whose base is two, has two *binary digits,* 0 and 1. Each digit of a binary integer is usually called a *bit.* A binary integer, as represented in a computer, has some fixed number of bits, each of them either a one or a zero. Knowledge of binary integers will help you understand the number conversions performed when using C.

A binary integer can be pictured by using a bit map, as illustrated in Figure 5.2, which shows the two common methods of numbering the bits. In this figure, the "most significant" bits are those with the highest numerical values. Arithmetic numbering assigns to each bit in an integer a bit number equal to the power of two for the multiplier of its corresponding binary digit. Positional numbering uses the same bit numbers, but in the reverse order; as shown, the most significant bit has the lowest position number.

Figure 5.2 illustrates integer data elements with n bits. If these are restricted to hold only positive integers, the range of values they can hold is 0 through $2^n - 1$. Both numbering methods use bit numbers from 0 through $n - 1$. Most modern computers have standard integers with a length, measured in bits, that is a power of two. A few use older designs with a length in bits that is a multiple of six. The most common standard integers have 16, 24, 32, and 36 bits.

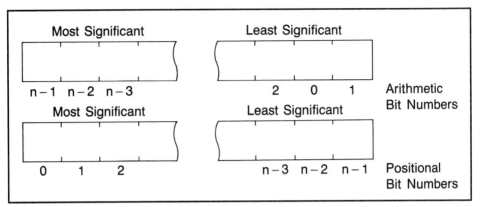

Figure 5.2: *Bit maps of integers.*

Modern computers also have a special small integer, called a *byte*, that is designed to hold a character code. The common sizes of bytes are 7, 8, and 9 bits. Most minicomputers and microcomputers produced in the United States since the middle 1970s have standard integers of 16 bits and bytes of 8 bits. Some of the more powerful machines have standard integers of 32 bits.

For negative integers, modern computers use a representation called *twos complement*. To make a quantity negative, first all the bits are inverted: ones become zeros and zeros become ones. Then the value 1 is added, ignoring any carry from the high-order bit position. Some older computers use *ones complement* (bit inversion) or *sign-magnitude*, in which the high-order bit is 1 to indicate a negative value, and the low-order bits give the magnitude of the value. While the older machines provide a special representation for -0, trying to force a zero value negative in twos complement will result in the same value: a representation with all zero bits.

C programmers use *octal* and *hexadecimal* numbers as a compact way of writing binary values. Each octal digit corresponds to three binary bits, each hexadecimal digit to four bits. The C language measures sizes of data in bytes. It assumes that all larger data elements have a length in bits that is a multiple of the number of bits in a byte. The ranges of integer data values are determined by the sizes of elements implemented on a particular computer. When integer values are signed, one bit is used for the sign. If there are n bits in a signed value, then the magnitude is held in $n-1$ bits, with a range of 0 to 2^{n-1}. If the same data element is used for unsigned values, with no bit reserved for a sign, then the available magnitude range doubles.

□ TYPE CONVERSIONS

C provides automatic conversion between data types. An **int** value may be assigned to a **char** variable; a **char** value may be assigned to an **int** variable. In performing data type conversions, C simply follows a set of rules, as explained in Chapters 10, 13, and 14. There is no check to see whether a value being converted can actually be represented correctly in its destination data type. When the validity of a type conversion is questionable, you must check it by statements in a program.

Conversion from **char** to **int** and from a smaller to a larger integer is performed by "padding," which preserves a correct numerical value. If the starting value is positive or unsigned, it is extended with high-order zero bits. If it is negative, the required high-order bits are generated to preserve the same negative value. Conversion from **int** to **char** and from a larger to a smaller integer is performed by truncation; high-order bits are dropped and low-order bits are used. The result of truncation may be a different value.

Conversion between signed and unsigned values of the same type is performed by copying binary bits without regard for numerical value. If a value is positive and within the range of the signed type, it will not change. Otherwise, a converted value will depend on the representation of negative numbers that is used by your computer.

Data type conversions are reviewed in detail in Chapters 14 and 16. One particular conversion, however, can prove troublesome unless it is well understood. Whenever the value of a **char** constant or variable is used for any purpose, including its appearance in an expression or as an argument for a function, the value is immediately converted to **int**. In other words, the C language actually provides no operations that act upon **char** data. They are defined only for purposes of data storage; all data manipulation uses **char** values as though they were **int** values.

To keep your programs portable and robust, do not convert from a larger to a smaller integer type or from an integer to a character unless you can be sure the smaller integer or the character will hold the required value. Do not convert between signed and unsigned types unless you can be sure the values being converted are positive and are within the range of the signed data type.

□ STRING CONVERSIONS

C library functions such as **printf** will convert data from character strings representing numbers to their binary equivalents. However, the use of these functions can make an executable program much larger than necessary, because the linker will bring in other functions to perform all types of string conversions. When the only conversions needed are between strings and integers, it may be more efficient to write conversion functions.

Figure 5.3 shows a function, named **decint**, that will convert a string representing a decimal integer to the equivalent binary value. This function does not depend on the code values of characters. Instead, it compares each character from the string against the ten characters for decimal digits. When a string character matches one of these, the value of the digit is added to the integer result. The function stops when it encounters a null character or any other character that is not a digit. Then the integer result is returned.

Notice that the length of **string** was not declared. For a function argument, only the brackets to indicate that it is an array are required.

```
int decint( string )
char string[ ] ;                    /* string to convert    */
{
    static char digit[ 10 ]      /* decimal characters    */
        = { '0', '1', '2', '3', '4',
            '5', '6', '7', '8', '9' } ;

    static int value[ 10 ]       /* decimal values        */
        = { 0, 1, 2, 3, 4, 5, 6, 7, 8, 9 } ;

    char chr ;                       /* string character      */
    int ival ;                       /* integer value         */
    int i, j ;                       /* counting variables    */

    ival = 0 ;                       /* inspect string chars */
    for ( i = 0 ; string[ i ] ; ++i )
    {
        chr = string[ i ] ;      /* compare decimal chars*/
        for ( j = 0 ; j < 10 ; ++j )
            if ( chr == digit[ j ] )
            {                             /* add value to result  */
                ival = 10 * ival + value[ j ] ;
                break ;               /* get next string char */
            }
        if ( j == 10 )               /* stop at strange char */
            break ;
    }
    return ival ;                    /* return result         */
}
```

Figure 5.3: *A function converting numeric character data to binary values.*

The decint function uses two internal arrays, declared **static char** and **static int**. The contents of each are specified by a list of values. Use of the **static** keyword and initialization of arrays will be explained in detail in Chapters 6 and 11.

The decint function uses a particularly powerful type of repetition, which is introduced by the keyword **for**. In this construction, the parentheses after the keyword enclose three expressions, separated by semicolons. The first expression is evaluated only once, before any repetition begins. The last is evaluated after each repetition is finished, unless a repetition is interrupted by **break** or **return**. The middle expression controls whether the repetition will proceed. As with **while**, a **for** repetition proceeds when the value of the expression is TRUE, or nonzero, and stops when it is FALSE, or zero. The inner **for** loop in the example, using j, controls only the following **if** statement. There is no need for braces to show the scope of control. Chapter 15 explains the **for** repetition in detail.

The **for** repetitions of the decint function each use in their third control expressions a convenience of the C language, the incrementing operator. Placing two plus signs before the name of a variable causes it to be incremented. The expression ++j is equivalent to j = j + 1. Chapter 13 explains this operator in more detail.

The example shown in Figure 5.3 is a primitive conversion function. It does not convert negative values, it does not handle octal or hexadecimal representations, and it does not test whether a value can be accommodated within the range of values allowed for a standard integer. These refinements are left to the reader.

□ EXERCISES

5.1: The following exercises involve determining the properties of data types:

(a) Write a program that will determine the ranges of values allowed by your computer and C compiler for **int** and **char** data.

(b) Extend the program from part (a) to handle **unsigned int**, **long int**, and **short int** data.

(c) Write a program that will determine whether the **char** data type is signed or unsigned.

5.2: You can make a program check the validity of data type conversions by writing an #include file, as introduced in Chapter 4.
Such a file should define symbols for the ranges of data types, for
example:

```
#define IMAX 32767
#define IMIN -32768
#define UMAX 65535
```

A module can then use these symbols after an #include statement
that gives the name of this file. When you take the program to a new
computer, only the symbol definitions will need to be rewritten.

(a) Find out the ranges of data types supported by your computer and C compiler. Write a file named dtype.h, containing definitions for them.

(b) How would you use the symbols defined in dtype.h to determine whether the **char** data type is signed or unsigned?

(c) Consider the following variables, of several different data types:

```
int limb, branch ;
char leaf, bark ;
unsigned int root ;
long int canopy ;
short int twig ;
```

Using your dtype.h definitions, write **if** conditions that check
whether the following conversions will be valid:

```
bark = twig ;
limb = root ;
branch = canopy ;
leaf = bark ;
twig = limb ;
canopy = leaf ;
root = branch ;
```

5.3: Expand the string-conversion function shown in Figure 5.3 to provide a more useful set of services:

(a) Make the function accept negative integers, by allowing a
minus sign as the first character.

(b) Make the function accept octal integers, by detecting whether
the first digit is zero.

(c) Make the function accept hexadecimal integers, by detecting whether the first digit is zero followed by **x**. Allow **x** and the digits represented by letters to occur in either upper- or lowercase.

(d) Make the function detect whether the string represents a value that is within the range allowed for a standard integer by your computer and C compiler. If it is not in that range, return the largest allowed value that has the same sign.

5.4: Write a function with two arguments, one an integer, the other a character array, that converts the integer to a decimal representation that is stored in the array. The function should handle negative values by placing a minus sign at the start of the character string. The string should end in a null character.

(a) Modify the function so that it can produce octal representations.

(b) Modify the function so that it can produce hexadecimal representations.

(c) Modify the octal and hexadecimal functions so that they use **unsigned** integers and produce only positive values as output.

5.5: Most implementations of C provide a function named **getchar**, introduced in Chapter 3, which returns one character at a time obtained from a standard source of input, generally your interactive terminal. The data obtained by **getchar** include a newline character to mark the end of a line. Suppose a function is needed that obtains input as integers, using **getchar** to get character input and performing the required conversions. Call this function **int_input**. It has no arguments and returns as its value the next number in the input stream.

(a) Write **int_input**, assuming that input values are limited to positive decimal integers, ended by null characters.

(b) Make **int_input** handle numbers that begin with a minus sign, returning negative integers.

(c) Modify **int_input** by providing an **int** argument that is zero, greater than zero, or less than zero, to specify conversions based on decimal, octal, or hexadecimal digits.

(d) Eliminate the argument to **int_input** and make it recognize the form of integer value, using the same conventions for integer constants found in C.

(e) Make int_input more robust, by checking to see that input characters are valid for the type of conversions the function is to perform. When beginning to read a value, ignore any invalid characters until a valid character is read. After that, treat the first invalid character as the end of a value.

(f) Provide data value checking. Test the values read by int_input to see that they are within the range allowed for an **int** variable. Whenever the input would produce an invalid **int**, skip to the end of a value and read the next value.

5.6: Consider the following sets of statements, based on the variables declared for Exercise 5.1. Suppose you are working with a computer using ASCII characters, which provides the following data characteristics:

char	8 bits, unsigned values
int	16 bits, twos complement
long int	32 bits, twos complement
short int	16 bits, twos complement
unsigned int	16 bits, unsigned values

What integer value is assigned by the last statement in each of the following sets of statements?

(a)

```
leaf = 'A' ;
branch = leaf ;
```

(b)

```
limb = '#' + 32 ;
bark = limb ;
```

(c)

```
root = 'U' + ( 'z' − 'Z' ) ;
```

(d)

```
twig = 1200 / 37 ;
leaf = twig ;
```

(e)

```
canopy = 30 * 500 * 12 ;
limb = canopy ;
```

(f)

```
twig = 'A' - 'a' ;
root = twig ;
leaf = root + 320 ;
```

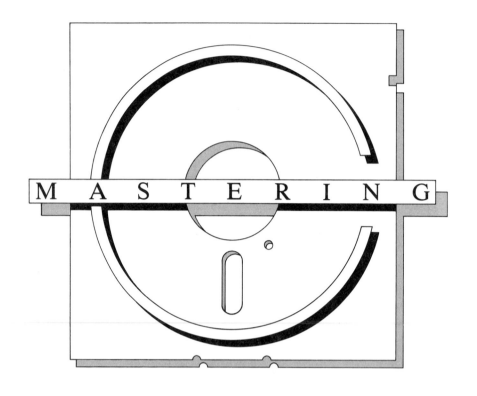

CHAPTER 6

STORAGE CLASSES

The C language enables a programmer to control the ways in which data are stored and made accessible. Each data element belongs to a storage class, which can either be declared along with a data type or determined by default. In this chapter, you will read about:

- organization of main storage
- data allocation and span
- storage-class specifiers
- sharing data among program modules
- effective use of storage
- dynamic storage

□ ORGANIZATION OF MAIN STORAGE

Space in main storage, or "memory," is an important computer resource. Data normally reside there when your program is working with them. Space in main storage is normally required for each variable or constant that appears in a program. In most computers, the same storage used to hold data is used to hold program instructions.

Main storage is divided into separately addressable units. Computers differ in the choice of these units. Most modern computers provide a small, independently addressable storage unit—the byte, discussed in Chapter 5. They construct other types of data out of contiguous bytes. Some older computers use storage units larger than a byte; often there are restrictions on how the available storage units can be used.

A data element held in main storage has four major properties:

1. *location,* specifying exactly where in main storage it begins

2. *size,* specifying how much storage it occupies

3. *format* or *mapping,* stating how the information in storage is arranged

4. *content,* the specific information stored at any particular time

Size and format are specified in the C language by declaring a data type, such as **int** or **char**. Content is established by assigning a value and by certain other operations. This chapter is primarily concerned with the ways in which storage is allocated and its location determined.

□ DATA ALLOCATION AND SPAN

Main storage is controlled by allocating specific data locations and by making them known to parts of a program. Storage is implicitly allocated when you use a constant by stating its value and when you use a variable by stating its name. Your program does not have to request storage for these data or know their locations. Instead, storage is allocated and its locations determined by the combined actions of your C compiler, your linker, and your operating system. A program written in C can explicitly allocate storage by using library functions and can explicitly manipulate data locations by using pointers, as described in Chapters 8, 9, and 12.

Programs in C implicitly allocate storage in either of two ways, called *fixed* and *automatic*. Fixed storage is allocated for the duration of a program's running time. Both the content and the location of a fixed data element remain predictable. Automatic storage is allocated on entry to and released on exit from a part of a program where it is used. The content and location of an automatic data element can change unpredictably each time it is allocated.

The program statements with potential access to a named data element are referred to as its *span*. The span of an automatic data element in C is restricted to the block within which it is declared, unless its location is disclosed by some program action. This is known as *local span*. With fixed data, the programmer has three options for span:

- *local span,* following the same rules that apply to automatically allocated data

- *module span,* potentially usable by all functions within a single module

- *global span,* potentially accessible to all the modules in a program

The span of accessibility does not determine an exact area of actual data use. Chapter 10 explains in detail the distinctions between *span, reach,* and *scope.*

An explicit way of allocating storage, often used in C programs, is called *dynamic.* Dynamic storage is allocated at the request of a program and manipulated through its data locations, using pointers. The C language does not provide forms of program statements to supply dynamic storage. However, the function libraries available in most C programming environments include functions that allocate and release dynamic storage.

□ STORAGE CLASS SPECIFIERS

Allocation and span are specified for fixed data in C programs partly by storage class specifiers and partly by the locations of data declaration statements. Four storage class specifier keywords can be included in your declaration statements; defaults apply when they are not included. The storage class specifiers are:

auto
register
static
extern

For example, to declare an **int** variable named valence, with **static** characteristics, a program would contain the following declaration statement:

static int valence ;

A variable that is declared without a storage class specifier has these characteristics:

- if declared inside a C function, automatic allocation and local span

- if declared outside a C function, fixed allocation and global span

A variable declared as a parameter to a C function has automatic allocation and restricted span. Only the **register** storage class specifier may be used in a parameter declaration.

The **auto** and **register** storage class specifiers both provide automatic allocation. They can only be used inside a C function. The **auto** specifier adds no other information. Since automatic allocation is the default inside a C function, **auto** is unnecessary; it is rarely used.

The **register** specifier is used to identify a variable that will be heavily used. If high-speed machine registers are available, many C compilers will try to hold the value of such a variable in a register. The practical effects of this specifier vary with the computer, the compiler, and the other requirements of program statements.

The effect of the **static** storage class specifier depends on the context in which it appears. When it appears inside a C function, the **static** specifier affects allocation, making allocation fixed instead of automatic. When it appears outside a C function, **static** affects span, producing module instead of global span.

The **extern** storage-class specifier gives a C function access to global data specified outside the function. It is not required for global data that have been defined within the same module before the points of use. When an **extern** declaration appears outside a function, all subsequent statements in a module can use the data declared.

All data declarations that do not include the **extern** specifier will cause storage to be allocated; they are called *definitions*. There can be only one definition for any global data element in a program, although there may be many **extern** references to it. A module that defines a global data element is allowed to contain a separate **extern** declaration for the same element,[1] provided the specifications are otherwise consistent. It is a programmer's responsibility to ensure that any **extern** data declaration matches its corresponding data definition.

The **static** and **extern** storage class specifiers are also used in declaring C functions. Use **extern** to declare the existence of a named function, returning a specified type of value, located outside the function or module in which the declaration appears. For example, the declaration

    extern int mat_trace( ) ;

states that there is a mat_trace function, which will return an **int** value.

A function declared inside another function is assumed to be an external reference; **extern** can be omitted. However, **extern** is required if you locate the declaration of an external function outside any other function. Without it, a C compiler may assume you are beginning the definition of the function you named! When you are, in fact, beginning a function definition, you can declare it **static** to produce module span instead of global span. Details of these uses of storage-class specifiers are discussed in Chapter 10, on data declarations, and Chapter 12, on functions.

☐ SHARING DATA AMONG PROGRAM MODULES

Global data definitions and **extern** declarations that refer to them allow a program to share data among modules without passing the data as arguments to functions. This capability disrupts modular design and tends to reduce the robustness of a program. It should be used

[1] Brian W. Kernighan and Dennis M. Ritchie, *The C Programming Language* (Englewood Cliffs, N. J.: Prentice-Hall, 1978), p. 77. Unfortunately, some C compilers violate this standard and reject a definition that follows an **extern** declaration.

with reluctance and caution, for the following reasons:

- Global data must have fixed storage allocation and cannot be allocated only when needed.

- Inconsistent data declarations can lead to corruption or misinterpretation of data.

- Globally shared data are more susceptible to accidental misuse than local data.

- It may become difficult to trace the flow of data during software testing and maintenance.

- You will need to maintain documentation about which modules and functions set and which of them use the values of each data element.

One solution to the problems of consistent data-declarations is data-declaration or *header* files, as discussed in Chapters 4 and 17. Each module that defines global data becomes a *producer* module and has a corresponding header file. A header file should contain an **extern** declaration corresponding to each global data definition in its producer module. A header file also contains any other information required to describe its data. All modules that need access to global data are *consumers*. Declarations in a header file are added to both the producer module and each consumer module by **#include** statements, located before any of the other program statements in each module.

For example, a producer module named **RXV** might have the following global data definitions:

```
int rxv_status ;
char rxv_option[ RXV_SIZE ] ;
int rxv_length ;
```

A header file named **RXV.H** could have the corresponding external data declarations:

```
#define RXV_SIZE 40
extern int rxv_status ;
extern char rxv_option[ RXV_SIZE ] ;
extern int rxv_length ;
```

At the start of the **RXV** module and any consumer module using these data would appear the following:

```
#include "RXV.H"
```

For all modules, this line brings in a symbolic definition of the array size. The **extern** declarations should match global data definitions in the producer module. For consumer modules, the #include statement provides access to data that the producer module has defined.

It is good programming practice, particularly helpful for maintenance and documentation, to name your modules, header files, C functions, and global data consistently. An effective method, recommended in Chapter 17, is to use two or three characters for the name of each source module and its header file, if any, and to prefix these characters to the names of all C functions that the module defines and all global data and symbols that it produces. Also helpful in the management of shared data is a consistent organization of your program modules, using the following sequence:

1. #include statements for global data

2. definitions for global data, if any

3. #define and data-type-specifying statements for the module

4. definitions for the module's data, if any

5. functions contained in the module, each with local data declarations

A header file should should have a consistent organization, using the following sequence:

1. #define and data-type-specifying statements for global data

2. **extern** declarations for global data defined in the producer module

3. **extern** declarations for the values that are returned by producer module functions

You should be wary of placing #include statements in a header file. This practice, which is permitted in C, can lead to a chain of dependencies that is extremely difficult to trace, test, document, and maintain.

□ EFFECTIVE USE OF STORAGE

Programmers sometimes think that using fixed data will increase the speed of their programs, because that way the data will be allocated only once. Usually, however, the practice does not result in a faster program. The reason has to do with the method of storage management on most modern computers, which uses a mechanism called a *stack*.

Each time a C function is entered, it allocates a block of space, including space for locally defined data. The stack mechanism accomplishes this task efficiently. The time needed to get stack space does not depend on the size of a block. Even when a stack is not used, the time needed to allocate storage does not depend strongly on the amount allocated.

Because of these characteristics of C programs, there is usually no speed gained by using fixed instead of automatic data. In fact, on some computers, using fixed global data slows down a program, because extra work must be performed to access them. Storage efficiency is lost when you use fixed data, because space must be allocated for the entire duration of a program, instead of only while it is needed.

Fixed allocation should therefore be used only where it is clearly needed. When data values must be preserved for the duration of a program, the need is obvious. When time-consuming calculations have been performed and their results will be used repeatedly, fixed data can prevent duplicate work. When a large amount of array space is a major program feature, fixed storage may be advisable; then the program will run only if the necessary space is available. Finally, as explained in Chapter 11, fixed data may be needed to provide initial values for variables.

In Chapter 2 the reader was cautioned against assuming that a variable contains any particular value until a program statement has assigned one. This rule can now be stated more precisely. Until they are changed by a program, the C language guarantees that fixed data will have values of zero. For characters, this means integer values of zero. The programmer may designate different initial values, as explained in Chapter 11. For automatic data, specific initial values are provided only for the parameters of a function. For other data, unless the programmer has designated initial values, the storage allocated will have unpredictable contents.

□ DYNAMIC STORAGE

A program can manage its data space by using *dynamic* storage. If you use fixed allocation and there is not enough memory, your program won't run at all. If you use automatic allocation and at some point there's not enough memory to satisfy a demand, your program will be abruptly terminated. A stack-oriented computer "blows its stack," sometimes with obscure symptoms. If you use dynamic allocation, your program can release storage when it is no longer needed; it may also be able to adapt to the limits of a computing environment. Most aspects of dynamic storage will be covered in Chapters 8, 9, 10, and 18, after the use of pointers has been discussed.

```
extern int length, sort ;     /* ordering parameters  */
int switch( ) ;               /* decision function    */
int sort( addr, length )
int addr[ ] ;                 /* list of addresses     */
int length ;                  /* length of list        */
{
    int i, j ;                /* counting variables    */
    for ( i = 0 ; i < length - 1 ; ++i )
        for ( j = i + 1 ; j < length ; ++j )
            if ( switch( addr[ i ], addr[ j ] ) )
            {
                next = addr[ i ] ;
                addr[ i ] = addr[ j ] ;
                addr[ j ] = next ;
            }
    return length ;
}


int next ;                    /*  control parameter    */
int switch( first, second )
int first ;                   /* first address         */
int second ;                  /* second address        */
{
    extrn int next ;          /* last address switched*/
    if ( first < next )       /* switch if first addr */
        return 1 ;            /*  less than next addr */
    else if ( length < 10 )   /* no switch if length   */
        return 0 ;            /*  was less than 10     */
    return second ;           /* else switch if second*/
}                             /*  addr is nonzero      */
```

Figure 6.1: *Some code that may contain storage class errors.*

□ EXERCISES

6.1: Write two functions, called **val_max** and **val_min**, that each receive an **int** as an argument and return an **int** as a value. The val_max function should return the value of the largest argument it has received, and the **val_min** should return that of the smallest. You will need to use data with fixed allocation.

(a) Make sure that your functions respond correctly to negative arguments.

(b) Write a third function, called **val_reset**, that discards the extreme values previously recorded by **val_max** and **val_min**, restarting these functions. You will need data shared among functions.

6.2: Use of storage class specifiers sometimes leads to problems in C programs. Look over the code listed in Figure 6.1, which was written to sort addresses, and identify errors associated with storage class specifiers.

CHAPTER 7

DATA ARRAYS

A program in C can use ordered collections of identical data elements, called *arrays*. Arrays are commonly used to hold character strings, control information, and numerical matrices. In this chapter, you will read about:

- array types, elements, and indexes
- arrays for character strings
- arrays with more than one dimension
- naming and declaring arrays
- arrays as function parameters
- using arrays in programs

☐ ARRAY TYPES, ELEMENTS, AND INDEXES

In Chapter 2 of this book, you encountered arrays of integers and characters. An *array* is a countable collection of data elements, each of the same type. The data elements are known as *members* of an array. The C language distinguishes between an array and its members. Whereas each member of an array has all the properties of any other data element, as discussed in Chapter 7, an array itself has the following three properties:

1. *type,* that is, the data type of its members, which determines their size and format
2. *location,* that is, the location of the first member
3. *length,* the number of data elements for which storage is allocated

The members of an array are identified by means of an index, with integer values that begin with zero. Thus, an array with N members has the following index values:

$$0, 1, 2, \ldots, N-2, N-1$$

The limits of allowed index values are known as the *bounds* of an array. The first member of every array has an index value of zero; the last member of an N-member array has an index value of $N-1$. A valid index must have a value that is either between these bounds or equal to one of them.

To designate a particular member of an array in a program statement, use the name of the array followed by a pair of brackets enclosing an integer expression for the index. For example, if **motion** has
been declared an array and **next** has been declared an integer, your
program might use the following array members:

```
motion[ 0 ]
motion[ next ]
motion[ 3 + next ]
motion[ next / 5 ]
```

Any expression appearing between brackets must be convertable to an
integer value.

Any array must have at least one member. A C compiler will limit
the valid range of an array index to some maximum. For a **char** array,
that maximum will be at least as great as the range of positive values
for an **int** variable. As noted in Chapter 5, for all common implementations of C, this range extends to at least $2^{15}-1$ or 32,767. An index
for an array of larger data elements may be further restricted. The fact
that an array index is within an allowed range does not necessarily
mean that a computer or an operating system can allocate that much
storage.

No index expression should at any time have a negative value or a
value that is equal to or greater than the length of an array. However,
the C language does not automatically check the bounds of array use.
To make your programs robust, always check the value of an array
index before using it, whenever the characteristics of a program make
it possible to exceed the bounds of the array. The omission of bounds
checking is among the most common causes of errors in C programs.

□ ARRAYS FOR CHARACTER STRINGS

In C programs, arrays of type **char** are frequently used to store character strings. Character string constants are the only array constants
available in C. A character array is declared in the same format used
for other array declarations, for example:

```
char text[ 160 ] ;
```

This statement defines **text** as an array of type **char** data elements and
causes an allocation of storage for elements from **text[0]** through
text[159].

A character string constant is a sequence of characters between double quote marks. These characters can include the numerical and special values available as **char** constants (for single characters); they were

described in Chapter 5. Each of the following is a valid character string constant:

```
"Now is the time for all good people?"
"\14string with numerical characters\15"
"This sentence ends with a linefeed!\n"
"This string uses \"quote\" characters."
```

The following are invalid character-string constants, for the reasons noted:

```
"xyz        no terminating double quote
"\"         final quote is part of string
"A\8B"      octal form has non-octal digit
```

The double quotes that enclose a character string constant do not become part of the string. However, the data stored for a character string constant include an additional character with integer value of zero immediately after the last character specified. The use of a *null* terminating character to indicate the end of a character string is a convention of the C language. You may use a *null string*:

```
" "
```

The data stored for a null string consist of only the null terminating character.

When you use a numerical character value in a character string constant, the numerical value must include at least one octal digit, and it will continue for as many as three octal digits, up to the first character that is not an octal digit. You may therefore be required to supply leading zeros as part of the numerical value. For example, to make a string with integer value 8 followed by the numeral character "2," you must write it as "\0102", not as "\102". The latter would specify a string with a character of integer value 66, in decimal, followed by a null terminator. Because of the null terminator, the length of a character-string constant is always one character greater than the number of characters represented between double quotes.

□ ARRAYS WITH MORE THAN ONE DIMENSION

The C language allows arrays of arrays; this can be continued to any extent, to create arrays of multiple *dimensions*. For example, an array declared as

```
char grid[ 10 ] [ 20 ] ;
```

is an array of 10 arrays of 20 characters each. You use the members of such an array by writing integer expressions in brackets after the array name, for example:

grid[vertical] [horizontal]

You can also use *subarrays*. For example, when invoking a function, you might supply as a parameter the following:

grid[vertical]

This refers to a one-dimensional array of 20 characters, starting with the element grid[vertical] [0] and continuing through the element grid[vertical] [19].

In order to support subarrays the C language stores the members of multiple dimension arrays in an order with the last index varying most rapidly and the first index varying least rapidly. When an array of multiple dimensions has been defined, the storage required for all its members will be allocated. There is no provision for allocating only part of an array.

In C, constants must be specified for the bounds of all indexes of a multidimensional array except the first. There is no way a program can adjust the "inner" dimensions of such an array, but you can easily create the effects of a fully adjustable array by defining a linear (one-dimensional) array and calculating the values of its index in your program.

Suppose, for example, you have available a linear array called locus and you want a three-dimensional array with lx by ly by lz members. Provided the length of locus is at least lx * ly * lz, you can calculate an index value for the [ix] [iy] [iz] member of a three-dimensional array as an expression, using the array element

locus[lz * (ly * ix + iy) + iz]

The index expression shown provides the same order of array elements that C would use, but a different order can be generated by changing the expression. Using such an approach, you can also create efficient triangular matrices and some kinds of sparsely populated arrays.

□ NAMING AND DECLARING ARRAYS

To declare an array in the C language, write a declaration in the same form that you would use for one of its data elements, followed by one or more constant expressions, in brackets, specifying the length of each array dimension. For example, if you need an array of **int** data named **local** that has **static** allocation and span, and it is to be two-dimensional with dimensions 16 by 32, the declaration would be

static int local[16] [32] ;

The **register** storage class specifier cannot be used with an array declaration.

All array declarations without the **extern** storage class specifier, except for function parameters, define elements of an array and cause storage to be allocated. When an array is defined, the lengths of all dimensions must be specified as constant expressions. When an array is declared as **extern** or as a function parameter, the first (or only) dimension length can be left out. When an array defined elsewhere is being processed, the C language permits its first dimension to be *indeterminate*. You must, however, indicate the number of dimensions for an array by including square brackets for the omitted dimension.

For example, the following specifies an array of type **char**, named txt_buffer, that is defined elsewhere:

extern char txt_buffer[ ] ;

The following shows how this array might be declared as a parameter of a function:

char txt_buffer[ ] ;

In such cases, the dimension length of the array might be supplied through a **#define** symbol, as the value of a global variable, or in a separate function parameter.

When you define a **char** array with fixed allocation, you may assign initial values to the array with a character-string constant. After the last bracket in the declaration, add an equals sign, followed by the character string constant that you want to assign. Such a definition might look like this:

static char txt_buffer[80] = "Empty" ;

In this example, the first five characters of **txt_buffer** will contain the characters in the string shown; the sixth character will be a null terminator. Because of the C convention that fixed data, unless otherwise specified, begin as zeros, all the remaining characters will also be null. The array length must be great enough to accommodate all the string characters, including the null terminator. You may omit a dimension length in such a definition; it will be made just large enough for the string.

In the C language, arrays are not regarded as a fundamental data type, like **int** or **char**. Instead, they provide an organization for data elements, creating a *data aggregate*. Chapter 9 presents the other major data organization in C, the data structure. It is possible to combine these data aggregates, creating structures that contain arrays and arrays of structures. In later chapters you will also encounter arrays of additional data types, particularly arrays of pointers in Chapter 8.

□ ARRAYS AS FUNCTION PARAMETERS

When you specify an array as a function parameter, you must declare the data type and the lengths of the minor dimensions. The first dimension can either be specified as a constant or left indeterminate. To invoke a function with an array argument, supply only the array name, with partial dimensions of a subarray. As explained in the next chapter, a function can return a pointer to an array, but not an array itself.

The following is an example of a linear array defined in one function and supplied as an argument to another:

```
char file_name[ 40 ] ;
. . .
status = file_check( file_name ) ;
. . .
int file_check( name_of_file )
char name_of_file[ ] ;
{
```

The name_of_file parameter in file_check has been declared to be of the same array type as the argument file_name, which is used when the function is invoked. A dimension length is not declared for name_of_file. The file_check function will manipulate the actual data in file_name when invoked as shown.

A second example shows a three-dimensional array, from which a two-dimensional subarray is passed to a function:

```
int event[ 10 ] [ 40 ] [ 40 ] ;
. . .
top = evn_total( event[ k ] ) ;
. . .
int evn_total( scatter )
int scatter[ 40 ] [ 40 ] ;
{
```

The **scatter** array declared by **evn_total** will address the members of **event**, beginning at **event[k] [0] [0]** and going through **event[k] [39] [39]**.

□ USING ARRAYS IN PROGRAMS

Figure 7.1 shows an **int** function, called **lim_minimum** that finds a minimum value in a two-dimensional **int** array called **limit**, for values of the first index between **lower** and **upper.**

```
int lim_minimum( limit, lower, upper )
int limit[ ] [ EXTENT ] ;    /* array of limit values   */
int lower ;                  /* lower bound, first index */
int upper ;                  /* upper bound, first index */
{
    int minimum ;            /* minimum value found    */
    int value ;              /* value being compared   */
    int started ;            /* starting value flag    */
    int i, j ;               /* counting variables     */

    started = 0 ;            /* look at values in array */

    for ( i = lower ; i <= upper ; i = i + 1 )
        for ( j = 0 ;      j < EXTENT ; j = j + 1 )
        {
            value = limit[ i ] [ j ] ;
                             /* get starting minimum   */
            if ( !started )
            {
                minimum = value ;
                started = 1 ;
            }                /* compare other values   */
            else if ( value < minimum )
                minimum = value ;
        }
    return minimum ;         /* return lowest value    */
}
```

Figure 7.1: *Finding the minimum value in a two-dimensional array.*

The bounds of an array must somehow be made known to those parts of a program that use the array. In the foregoing example, the minor dimension length of **limit** is a symbol, **EXTENT**, defined somewhere before this function. The function assumes that the values of **lower** and **upper** are within the major dimension bounds of **limit** and that **lower** is less than or equal to **upper.** If the design of the program allows any possibility for an error in these assumptions, then the index values should be checked, either in **lim_minimum** or before this function is invoked.

Another example, listed in Figure 7.2, shows an **int** function, named **str_search**, that examines one character array to see if it contains a copy of the data in a second character array.

```
int str_search( unknown, pattern )
char unknown[ ] ;              /* array with unknown text */
char pattern[ ] ;              /* array with pattern text */
{
    char cu, cp ;              /* comparison characters   */
    int i, j ;                 /* counting variables      */

    for ( i = 0 ; 1 ; i = i + 1 )
        for ( j = 0 ; 1 ; j = j + 1 )
        {
            cp = pattern[ j ] ;
            if ( !cp )         /* reached end of pattern  */
                return i ;
            cu = unknown[ i + j ] ;
            if ( !cu )         /* reached end of unknown  */
                return -1 ;
            if ( cu != cp )
                break ;
        }
}
```

Figure 7.2: *An* int *function that examines a character array.*

If the **str_search** function finds the **pattern** data in the **unknown** array, it returns the index value of the starting character in the **unknown** array. Otherwise, it returns a value of −1. The **str_search** function receives the dimension length of neither array; it relies on the presence of null terminator characters. When it performs a character match, these terminators are not compared, but if either were missing, the function could continue indefinitely. An invoking function must therefore ensure that each argument string has a null terminator.

A final example, Figure 7.3, shows arrays used to implement a decision table. The **opt_step** function inspects a *vector* (that is, a linear array) of current conditions. It compares the values of these conditions with members of a decision table array. There are **CLENGTH** different conditions considered, and the decision table has entries for **CEXTENT** combinations of them. If a member of the decision table is negative, this indicates that the corresponding condition should be ignored. If **opt_step** is able to find a match to one of the combinations in the decision table, it invokes a function called **opt_action**, transmitting to it a corresponding subarray of actions. If there is no match, **opt_action** receives an array for default actions. There are **ALENGTH** members in the action array sent to **opt_action**.

```
#define CLENGTH 12           /* number of conditions    */
#define CEXTENT 30           /* number of combinations  */
#define ALENGTH 8            /* number of actions       */

int opt_step( condition )
int condition[ CLENGTH ] ;   /* current condition vector */
{
                             /* external condition table */
    extern int opt_tb_condition[ CEXTENT ] [ CLENGTH ] ;
                             /* conditional action table */
    extern int opt_tb_action[ CEXTENT ] [ ALENGTH ] ;
                             /* default action table    */
    extern int opt_tb_default[ ALENGTH ] ;

    int opt_action( ) ;      /* the action function      */
    int cond ;               /* condition table element  */
    int match ;              /* condition match flag     */
    int status ;             /* status of action         */
    int i, j ;               /* counting variables       */
                             /* test all combinations    */
    for ( i = 0 ; i < CEXTENT ; i = i + 1 )
    {
        match = 1 ;          /* match combination i      */
        for ( j = 0 ; j < CLENGTH ; j = j + 1 )
        {
            cond = opt_tb_condition[ i ] [ j ] ;
            if ( cond >= 0 )
                if ( cond != condition[ j ] )
                {
                    match = 0 ;
                    break ;  /* stop when match fails    */
                }
        }
        if ( match )         /* quit if match was found  */
            break ;
    }
    if ( match )             /* conditional actions      */
        status = opt_action( opt_tb_action[ i ] ) ;
    else                     /* default actions          */
        status = opt_action( opt_tb_default ) ;
    return status ;          /* return status of action  */
}
```

Figure 7.3: *Arrays used to implement a decision table.*

□ EXERCISES

7.1: A character array can be used to represent sequences of genetic molecules. DNA molecules are chains of four components, often labeled "G," "C," "A," and "T," after the first letters of the chemical names of their nucleotide components. In analyzing these molecules, it is often necessary to search for sequence matches and other patterns. An important pattern is a "genetic palindrome," a short sequence that is followed immediately by a sequence in the opposite order, in which G and A from the first sequence are matched by C and T, respectively, from the second, or vice versa.

(a) Write a function that searches a character string, assumed to contain only GCAT codes, for a genetic palindrome. This function should receive as its arguments:

- a character array to be searched
- the length of data in the array
- the length of a palindrome

The function should search only for palindromes of the specified length (an even integer) and return either an index to the first character or a negative integer.

(b) Write a program, using your searching function, that reads an input string and prints all palindromes up to some maximum length.

(c) Modify the program to find "partial palindromes," in which one or more matches can be incorrect, up to some specified limit.

(d) Adapt the program to find "split palindromes," in which the two halves of a palindrome are separated by an intervening sequence of up to some specified maximum length.

7.2: Multidimensional arrays are useful for many types of problems. It is common for these to use an *array descriptor,* giving details of the array structure. An array descriptor is often constructed as a small, separate **int** array, with the first member specifying the number of array dimensions and succeeding members giving the dimension lengths. The following exercises assume a multidimensional array that has such a descriptor.

(a) Write functions that

- calculate the overall length of the array, based on the descriptor.

- calculate the length of a subarray, given the number of dimensions.

(b) Invent a descriptor for an *array section*. A section is equivalent to an array of lower dimension, whose contents are taken from the main array by designating constant index values for some dimensions.

(c) Invent a descriptor for a member of an array section. Write a program that obtains a value from an array section, given the main array, the descriptor for the section, and the descriptor for the section member.

(d) How can you make a descriptor that minimizes the multiplications required to address a member of an array section?

7.3: Two-dimensional arrays are often involved in automated pattern recognition. A **char** array that contains only 0 or 1 can approximate a high-contrast image. Write a program that searches such an array for outlines of characters. Try a 5 × 7 matrix, such as one that represents "I" and "D" by these patterns:

```
0 1 1 1 0          1 1 1 1 0
0 0 1 0 0          0 1 0 0 1
0 0 1 0 0          0 1 0 0 1
0 0 1 0 0          0 1 0 0 1
0 0 1 0 0          0 1 0 0 1
0 0 1 0 0          0 1 0 0 1
0 1 1 1 0          1 1 1 1 0
```

(a) Build "tolerance" into your search, so that recognition will succeed even when there is some level of mismatch.

(b) Construct a way to describe an "alphabet" of primary patterns that you will search for.

(c) Invent a way to scale patterns, so that they can be recognized when the image being scanned contains copies of a different size. It is advantageous to start with fine-grained originals.

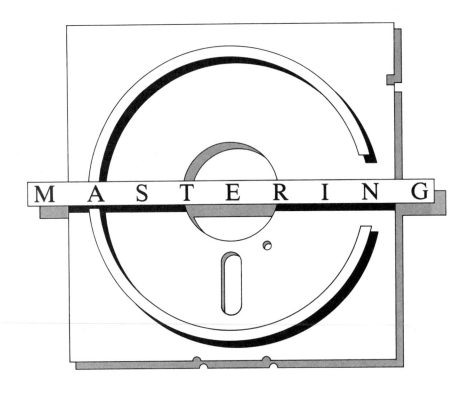

CHAPTER 8

POINTERS

A program in C can manipulate data through their *locations,* using *pointers.* A pointer is a data element that specifies the location of another data element. For each data type, there is a corresponding pointer type. In this chapter, you will read about:

- operations with pointers

- pointer arithmetic

- using pointers with arrays

- using pointers with functions

- declaring pointers

- precautions when using pointers

☐ OPERATIONS WITH POINTERS

As noted in Chapter 7, C does not treat as fundamental data types its arrays or its data structures, which are covered in the next chapter. In most implementations of the language, there are no operations that affect whole arrays or whole data structures; these data aggregates are manipulated through their data elements. In many programs, pointers help to do this work. Pointers also allow programs to create arbitrary extensions of their data.

In the C language, data can be manipulated either by name or by location. To use or set the current value of a data element by name, you write its name into a program statement. There is no need to be concerned with the location of the data element. However, there are circumstances in which it is necessary or convenient to address the locations of data. In C, the most common purposes are these:

- to return more than one value from a function

- to manipulate character strings

- to indicate connections between data

- to construct arrays with members of different sizes, lengths, or data types

For each type of data that can be declared in C, it is possible to declare a corresponding type of pointer. To indicate that a data element contains a pointer to a specified type of data element rather than the data itself, include an *asterisk* before the name of the data element in a declaration statement. For example, the declaration

extern char *txt_buffer ;

specifies that there is a pointer named txt_buffer, defined elsewhere, whose value is the location of a character.

To use or set the value of a data element whose location has been specified by a pointer, write the name of the pointer preceded by an asterisk. In terms of the above example, to place the character "A" into the **char** data element whose location is given by txt_buffer, a program would have this statement:

*txt_buffer = 'A' ;

The appearance of a data element name Z in a C program can be interpreted as "the value of the data element named Z." Using the same approach, the appearance of *Z in a program would be interpreted as "the value of the data element at the location given by the value of Z." The asterisk is sometimes called an *indirection operator,* because a pointer provides an indirect way to use data that might have been used directly, that is, by name.

What you store in a pointer itself, rather than in the data element to which it points, should be the *location* of an element of the pointer's data type. To get the location of a data element, prefix its name with an *ampersand.* Continuing the previous example, if your program has another **char** variable named symbol, you could set the value of the pointer txt_buffer so that it points to the character named symbol by using this statement:

txt_buffer = &symbol ;

The ampersand is sometimes called a *reference operator.* You can interpret the appearance of &Z in a program as "the location of the data element named Z." The ampersand generates a reference to a data element.

The indirection operator can be applied repeatedly. It is thus possible to create a pointer to a pointer to a data element. If ppval is such a pointer, then **ppval gets the value of the data element. The reference operator, on the other hand, can be applied only once. It must operate on the name of a variable and cannot be applied to a constant of any kind. The reference operator can be applied to a member of an array. For example, &pool[8] will get the location of the ninth member of the pool array. You may write, if you insist, a weird combination such as *&datum, where datum is any data element. The indirection operator will cancel the reference operator, producing the same result as writing datum.

The contents of pointers are highly machine-dependent, and the C language provides no particular format or size. However, it does guarantee the following special properties:[1]

1. You can set a pointer to the integer value zero.

2. When the value of a pointer is tested, as in an **if** or a **while** statement, it will be found zero only after it has been set to the integer value zero.

3. No location of an actual data element will have the integer value zero.

A pointer that has been set to the integer value zero is often referred to as a *null pointer*. Statements such as the following will set a pointer named **dot** to zero and will test whether it has a zero value:

> **dot = 0 ;**
>
> **if** (dot)
>   . . .
>
> **while** (!dot)
>   . . .

Note that a pointer with fixed allocation, unless specified otherwise, will have the integer value zero as its initial value, making it a null pointer.

□ POINTER ARITHMETIC

The C language provides several operations, besides referencing and indirection, that are performed with pointers. Because they involve addition, subtraction, and comparison, these operations are sometimes called *pointer arithmetic*. If **ivalue** is an **int** value and **pvalue** and **qvalue** are pointer values for the same data type, then the following expressions are permitted in C:

> **pvalue + ivalue**
> **pvalue − ivalue**

---

[1] Brian W. Kernighan and Dennis M. Ritchie, *The C Programming Language,* (Englewood Cliffs, N.J.: Prentice-Hall, 1978), p. 192.

qvalue − pvalue

qvalue < pvalue
qvalue > pvalue
qvalue <= pvalue
qvalue >= pvalue
qvalue == pvalue
qvalue != pvalue

The first two expressions yield pointer values of the same type as **pvalue**; the third has an **int** value that can be positive or negative; and the others produce **int** values that are either 0 or 1.

Pointer arithmetic is used most often within arrays. If a pointer holds the location of an array member, the addition of the integer value 1 gives the location of the next member of the array. Likewise, subtraction of the integer value 1 gives the location of the previous member of the array. The C language provides this behavior for arrays of all compositions and data types.

If two pointers both hold locations of members of the same array, subtracting the pointers gives an integer value equal to the offset, counted in array members, of the first pointer value from the second. Comparing pointers to members of an array gives the same result as comparing the corresponding index values for a linear array. When one pointer is "ahead" of the other, its value will be greater. If both pointers point to the same location, their values are equal. In physical terms, pointer arithmetic manipulates a pointer value in unit steps whose size is governed by the amount of storage required for an element of the pointer's data type.

□ USING POINTERS WITH ARRAYS

As already indicated, many common uses of pointers involve arrays. The C language interprets the name of an array, written without indexes, as a pointer constant. The data type of an array name constant is a pointer to an element with the data type of the array. The value of an array name constant is the location of the first array element.

The reference operator cannot operate on an array name, since an array name is a constant. The indirection operator can; the result will be to get the value of the first array member. In fact, pointer arithmetic may be used in place of array indexes. For an array **wire** and **int k**, the following three expressions have exactly the same effect:

    wire[k]

  *(wire + k)

  *(&wire[0] + k)

The correspondence between array indexing and pointer arithmetic is sometimes used for multidimensional arrays. Functions operating on multidimensional arrays can allocate the arrays in dynamic storage and perform all subscript calculations explicitly in program statements. For access to a particular element, such functions will calculate an integer offset and add it to a starting pointer.

The processing of character data is often written in terms of pointer arithmetic. This choice is partly a matter of programming style. Often, exactly the same results can be obtained by writing array operations. The following example shows two program fragments, side by side, that will copy characters from an orig array to a dest array, through and including a null terminator character:

```
/* using arrays */              /* using pointers */

char orig[ ] ;                  char orig[ ] ;
char dest[ ] ;                  char dest[ ] ;
int i ;                         char *p, *q ;

                                p = orig ;
i = 0 ;                         q = dest ;
while ( orig[ i ] )             while ( *p )
{                               {
   dest[ i ] = orig[ i ] ;         *q = *p ;
   i = i + 1 ;                      p = p + 1 ;
                                    q = q + 1 ;
}                               }
dest[ i ] = 0 ;                 *q = 0 ;
```

Each fragment has "utility" variables. The array side has an array index i; the pointer side has character pointers p and q. Which is better? In Chapter 13, you will see a popular condensation of the pointer approach that is written in one line. If the computer increments pointers quickly, this way may be preferable. The array approach, however, makes it simple to compare positions in the dest array with the array bounds. When you are writing a robust program, you will probably want to make these comparisons.

☐ USING POINTERS WITH FUNCTIONS

In previous chapters, you were advised to supply array names as arguments for the arrays when invoking functions. As this chapter shows, the value conveyed by stating the name of an array is the location of its first member. You can interchange pointers and arrays as the arguments and parameters of functions, provided that data element types are otherwise specified identically. The difference between these methods is whether a program obtains access to data elements through indexes or through pointer arithmetic.

Figure 8.1 shows the use and the definition of a function named **scattergram**, which compiles a two-dimensional distribution of paired

```
#define VL 50
. . .

    int plot[ VL ] [ VL ] ; /* distribution array    */
    int ix, iy ;             /* data values           */
    int weight ;             /* data weight           */
    int scattergram( ) ;     /* accumulation function */

    . . .

    weight = scattergram( plot, ix, iy ) ;

    . . .

int scattergram( count, k1, k2 )
int *count ;                 /* distribution counts   */
int k1, k2 ;                 /* data values           */
{
    int *site ;              /* count to increment     */
    int value ;              /* accumulated count      */

    if ( k1 < 0 )            /* check lower bounds     */
        return 0 ;
    if ( k2 < 0 )
        return 0 ;
    if ( k1 >= VL )          /* check upper bounds     */
        return 0 ;
    if ( k2 >= VL )
        return 0 ;           /* get location of count  */
    site = count + VL * k1 + k2 ;
    value = *site + 1 ;      /* read and increment count */
    *site = value ;          /* store incremented count */
    return value ;
}
```

Figure 8.1: *A function invoked with a two-dimensional array, but manipulating the array using pointers.*

quantities. The function is invoked with a two-dimensional array, but it manipulates the array using pointers.

Although the **scattergram** function is invoked with the name of an **int** array, it manipulates the contents of this array as though it had received a pointer to an **int** variable. The pointer arithmetic it performs to get the location of a **count** element duplicates what might have been done by array indexes. With array indexes, however, this work would have been done twice. With pointers, the calculation is done only once, and the result is used to obtain and then change the value of an array member.

You may sometimes need to return more than one value from a function. Athough it is possible to supply an array as an argument and let the function place whatever is necessary in the array, that approach can be cumbersome. A simple way to have multiple values returned is to supply pointers to variables as function arguments. Figure 8.2 is a function that will count the zeros in an array and return the number of zeros and also the minimum and maximum values in the array.

```
int val_check( value, length, minimum, maximum )
int value[ ] ;              /* array of values        */
int length ;                /* length of array        */
int *minimum ;              /* minimum value found     */
int *maximum ;              /* maximum value found     */
{
    int datum ;             /* value from array        */
    int zeros ;             /* number of zeros found   */
    int i ;                 /* counting variable       */

    zeros = 0 ;
    *minimum = value[ 0 ] ;
    *maximum = value[ 0 ] ; /* inspect each value      */
    for ( i = 0 ; i < length ; i = i + 1 )
    {
        datum = value[ i ] ;
        if ( !datum )       /* count zeros             */
            zeros = zeros + 1 ;
                            /* check for new minimum   */
        if ( datum < *minimum )
            *minimum = datum ;
                            /* check for new maximum   */
        if ( datum > *maximum )
            *maximum = datum ;
    }
    return zeros ;          /* return number of zeros  */
}
```

Figure 8.2: *A function that counts the number of zeros in an array.*

This function returns the minimum and maximum values using pointer indirection. The function would be invoked by a statement of the following form:

```
zeroct = val_check( spot, len, &smin, &smax ) ;
```

The additional values to be returned are obtained by supplying, as function arguments, pointers to the variables where the values are to be stored. The pointers are created by using the reference operator and the variable names.

Functions can return pointer values. For example, the following declaration states that a function named **select** returns a pointer to an **int**:

```
int *select( ) ;
```

A definition for **select** as a function returning an **int** pointer might look like the following:

```
int *select( result, k )
int result[ ] ;
int k ;
{
  if ( k % 5 )
    return result ;
  else
    return result + k ;
}
```

If the value of **k** is a multiple of 5, this function returns a pointer to member **k** of the **result** array; otherwise, it returns a pointer to the first member of the array.

Pointers can be used to invoke functions. You can declare a variable as a pointer to a function. For example, the following declaration states that a pointer named **test** holds the location of a function returning an **int**:

```
int ( *test )( ) ;
```

The parentheses around *test are needed so that this declaration won't refer to a function that returns a pointer to an **int**, like the declaration shown above for the **select** function. The function pointed to by **test** could be invoked by a statement such as this:

```
mark = ( *test )( cases, conditions ) ;
```

The function pointer is also enclosed in parentheses here. Otherwise, the statement would mean "apply the indirection operation to a return value (which should be a pointer)."

Using pointers to functions, you can build decision tables that specify different functions to be invoked according to the conditions a program encounters. Function pointers also provide a means of writing a general-purpose routine that receives a pointer to a data-specific function when it is executed.

In most implementations of C, functions cannot return arrays. However, functions can return pointers to arrays. For example, the following function returns a pointer to a **char** array:

```
char ( *choose( name, k ) )[ ]
char name[ ][ NLEN ] ;
int k ;
{
  if ( k % 5 )
    return name[ 0 ] ;
  else
    return name[ k ] ;
}
```

If the value of k is a multiple of 5, this function returns a pointer to subarray k of the name array; otherwise, it returns a pointer to the first subarray of the name array. An example of how the choose function could be used, printing the name it picks, is shown in Figure 8.3. Notice that the pointers to arrays are enclosed in parentheses, to make the indirection operators act before indexing.

□ DECLARING POINTERS

Pointers are declared in C by writing the form of use that will give the value of a fundamental type of data element. When you write a declaration such as this:

```
char *txt_buffer ;
```

you are stating that the appearance of *txt_buffer in a program statement will have a **char** value. Since the name txt_buffer is prefixed with an indirection operator, then to produce a **char** value, txt_buffer itself must be a pointer to a **char** data element.

This approach to pointer declaration may seem obscure at first. Its advantage is that pointers can be declared flexibly, without needing a

```
extern char ( *choose( ) )[ ] ;
char namelist[ NTOT ] [ NLEN ] ;
char ( *tag )[ ] ;
char c ;
int kn, i ;

. . .

tag = choose( namelist, kn ) ;
for ( i = 0 ; i < NLEN ; i = i + 1 )
{
    c = ( *tag )[ i ] ;
    if ( !c )
        break ;
    putchar( c ) ;
}
putchar( '\n' ) ;
```

Figure 8.3: *The* choose *function in use.*

complex method of description which would be used only in their declarations. You can create pointers that point to data elements of the
fundamental types and pointers that point to data aggregates or to
other pointers. In any pointer declaration, you write what has to be
done to the pointer to get a data value that has a particular data type.

For example, a variable called synapse that contains a pointer to a
pointer to an int can be declared as

int **synapse ;

Your program will then have a variable, synapse, whose value is a
pointer. Your program will expect this to point to a second pointer, which
then points to an int. If your program also contains pint, declared as a
pointer to an int, it might include the following statements:

int *pint ;

synapse = &pint ;

An array named title that consists of 40 pointers to **char** data elements can be defined as follows:

char *title[40] ;

As always, when an array is defined, in the place where an index
would be used the length of the array is stated. To understand this declaration fully, you need to know something about the priority of operations in C statements, a subject that will be covered in detail in

Chapters 13 and 14. In particular, when both an array index and an indirection operator are attached to a data name, indexing is done first. The indirection operator is applied to an array element. The indexing operation is said to have *priority* over the indirection operator.

Sometimes a declaration will need *parentheses*. When what you want to describe differs from the usual priorities of C operations, use parentheses to tell what is done first. For example, suppose that instead of an array of 40 pointers to **char** data elements, you wanted **title** to be a pointer to an array of 40 characters. You would write

```
char ( *title )[ 40 ] ;
```

With this data definition, you can get character **k** from this array by using the expression

```
( *title )[ k ]
```

Because pointer arithmetic can always be used in place of array indexing, this expression could also be written as

```
*( *title + k )
```

Pointers can be used in place of certain array declarations. The foregoing declaration of a pointer to an array of characters could also have been written entirely in terms of pointers, that is, as either of the following:

```
char ( *title )[ 40 ] ;
```

```
char * *title ;
```

How might such a variable be used in program statements? If **grid** is an array of **char**, you might think of writing

```
char grid[ 40 ] ;
```

```
title = &grid ;
```

This won't work; the reference operator can't be applied to an array name, because it is a constant (a pointer constant). However, using **tloc**, a pointer to **char**, your program could include the following consistent statements:

```
char *tloc ;
```

```
tloc = grid ;
title = &tloc ;
```

Function pointers have similarities to array pointers. Like the name of an array, the name of a function is also interpreted as a pointer constant; you may not apply the reference operator to it. Like array brackets, function parentheses also have priority over the indirection operator. If you specify

```
int *aliquot( ) ;
```

you declare a function that returns a pointer to an **int**. To declare a pointer to a function returning an **int**, you need to keep the function parentheses away from the name with a pair of isolating parentheses. For such a declaration, the following would be consistent statements in a program:

```
int ( *sample )( ) ;
int residue, vial ;
extern int contaminated( ) ;

sample = contaminated ;
residue = ( *sample )( vial ) ;
```

The foregoing statements will invoke the **contaminated** function, because its location was most recently assigned to the **sample** pointer variable.

Function pointers make it possible to write, for example, a sorting function for character strings that takes as an argument a pointer to a string comparison function. The sorting function sends the comparison function two strings at a time, and the comparison function decides which belongs first. By writing only a comparison function, you can sort such diverse information as personal names, chemical formulas, or street addresses. The sorting function would be invoked by statements such as

```
char *name_list[ LEN ] ;
extern int sequence( ) ;

nsort = str_sort( name_list, LEN, sequence ) ;
```

A character string sorting function based on this approach is shown in Figure 8.4.

This example uses a method originated by Donald Shell.[2] The function pointed to by **swap** will receive two strings, as pointers to **char**.

---

[2] For an analysis of this sorting method, see Robert Sedgewick, *Algorithms* (Reading, Mass: Addison-Wesley, 1983).

```
int str_sort( string, count, swap )
char **string ;                   /* array of strings      */
int count ;                       /* number of strings     */
int ( *swap )( ) ;                /* comparison function   */
{
    int span ;                    /* comparison span       */
    int i, j ;                    /* counting variables    */
    char *member1, *member2 ;     /* strings to compare    */

    for ( span = 4 ; span <= count ; )
        span = 3 * span + 1 ;
    for ( span = span / 3 ; span ; span = span / 3 )
        for ( i = span ; i < count ; i = i + 1 )
                                                             {
            member2 = *( string + i ) ;
            for ( j = i span ; j >= 0 ; j = j span )
            {
                member1 = *( string + j ) ;
                if ( !( *swap )( member1, member2 ) )
                    break ;
                *( string + j + span ) = member1 ;
            }
            *( string + j + span ) = member2 ;
        }
    return count ;
}
```

Figure 8.4: *A sorting function that uses function pointers.*

Its responsibility is to compare them and return a value of 1 if they should be interchanged, a value of 0 if not. The pointers passed to the comparison function are obtained by using pointer arithmetic on the parameter **string**. Since **string** points to a pointer, integer offsets to it have units of pointers; thus the program moves through an array of pointers. Notice that when an exchange occurs, the strings themselves are never directly involved; only the pointers to them are shifted.

As noted in Chapter 7, a quoted character string is the only array constant provided in C. The value of such a string is of the same type as the name of a character array: it is a pointer constant. When you use such a string as a function argument, the effect is the same as naming a character array containing the identical characters.

A function that receives a character string can declare the corresponding parameter as either an array or a pointer. For example, suppose you invoke a function as follows:

```
int length ;
extern int str_count( ) ;
```

```
length = str_count( "#bes" ) ;
```

The parameter of the **str_count** function could be defined in either of the following ways:

```
int str_count( string )
char *string ;
```

```
int str_count( string )
char string[ ] ;
```

When you write a function that may receive a quoted character string as an argument, keep in mind that a string is a constant; the function must not store any characters in it.

□ PRECAUTIONS WHEN USING POINTERS

Pointers must be used with care. The consequences of a corrupted pointer value resemble those of an invalid array index. Storing data outside the locations reserved for it can have long-range effects on a program's behavior; these effects may be extremely difficult to trace and correct. As with array indexes, the C language provides no validity checking for pointer values. Unfortunately, there is sometimes no simple method to test the validity of a pointer value, nothing that might correspond to the checking of array bounds.

We've seen that a common use of pointers is to pass data to and return values from a function. A convention found in many C programs is to supply a null pointer when there are no data to be passed or returned. The convention is useful, but a function receiving a pointer should always check that it has a nonzero value before using it in any other way. There is no provision in C for determining from a pointer argument any of the following:

- the data type of the pointer

- the validity of a particular location value

- the amount of space reserved at that location

Special caution is necessary when a function receives a **char** pointer. As stated, this is the data type of a quoted character string constant. A program in C should never store data in a constant. Since the reference operator cannot be applied to constants, doing so is ordinarily impossible. A quoted string is the one exception, since it produces a pointer to constant character data. A function that receives such a pointer will not be able to tell whether is it a pointer to a constant. On some computers, quoted string characters are placed in protected storage, and a machine error will occur if a function attempts to store data into their locations.

The only way to make robust programs that use pointers is by design. A design for a program using pointers should ensure that each pointer value will be valid. In some circumstances, the time when a pointer is generated will be the only time when all the necessary information is available. In other circumstances, the values of data elements will determine a pointer value; those values must be properly controlled.

A common error in C programs involves the use of pointers to copy null-terminated character strings. An *unbounded* string-copy function, which receives no array dimension and recognizes the end of a string only when it finds a null character, will continue indefinitely if the terminator is missing. A robust C program can use such functions, but then its design should require that:

- every part of the program which originates a character string ensures that the string is terminated by a null character

- before a string is copied, the program checks to see that the number of characters, including the terminator, is less than or equal to the length of the destination array

- when a string is copied, the terminator is copied as part of the string

It is often easier (and generally safer) to rule out the use of unbounded string functions and, instead, always to transmit array lengths and check indexes against them.

The results of certain kinds of pointer operations depend on details of a computer, compiler, and operating system. These system-dependent operations include:

- assigning a pointer value for one data type or organization to a pointer declared for a different data type or organization

- assigning the value of a pointer to an integer

- assigning an integer value other than zero to a pointer

- comparing the values of pointers for different data types or organizations

- subtracting the values of pointers that do not both hold locations within a single array

The first type of operation is sometimes known as "pointer punning." The second and third are sometimes used to manipulate machine-dependent data. All are undesirable programming practices. They are not portable, and their results are often unreliable. As this chapter has shown, pointers provide complex and powerful techniques in C. Treat them with respect.

□ EXERCISES

8.1: Comparison functions are needed for Shell's sort, as listed in the text of this chapter. These functions must be adapted to different types of data. You can test such functions by initializing arrays of pointers to **char** with strings, as in this example:

```
char *stew[ 3 ] =
{
   "One potato",
   "Two potato",
   "Three potato"
} ;
```

(a) Write a comparison function for surnames, sorting on name prefixes before the remainder of a name, so as to sort the following list as shown:

Day
De la Roux
DeSmet
Delavier
Du Pont
M'Bow
MacDonald
MacDonnell
McIntosh
Macdonald
O'Day
O'Donnell
Oboe

(b) Write a function for street addresses, sorting first on street name, second on compass direction, third on street number, and last on subnumber, so as to sort the following list as shown:

6 Old Saybrook Ave.
27 Saddlewraith Lane
123A Saddlewraith La.
570 Saddlewraith Lane
9 Saybrook Place
108r North Saybrook Road
304 SW Saybrook Rd.
23 St. Severnius St.
East Sleaverly Cove

8.2: As implemented in most C programming environments, a function named **main** receives arguments from the command line that started a program. The characters of a command line are divided into strings, separated by blanks or tabs in the command line. These strings are supplied to a **main** function by a pointer array:

```
int main( argc, argv )
int argc ;
char *argv[ ] ;
{
```

In some environments, **main** can return an **int** value that gives a program-completion status. The value of **argc** gives the number of members of **argv**. The first member of "ragged array" **argv** holds the program name from the command line; on some systems it will be a null string. Any remaining members of **argv** are the strings from the command line.

(a) Write a parsing function. Interpret "option" arguments beginning with a virgule (/) and check them against an array of option names. Record selected options in a selection array, and remove these options from the arguments, by decrementing the value of **argc** and compressing the pointers in **argv**.

(b) The Unix convention is to begin option names with a hyphen (-) and generally to use single-character names. Some Unix commands provide a "condensed" option format, in which several characters follow one hyphen to indicate several options. Write a parsing function, as in part (a), that will handle both of these formats, even when combined in the same command.

8.3: Pointers provide an efficient way to manage lists of strings. You can start assembling a dictionary as a list of pointers to **char**. Word strings themselves can be placed in a large array of **char**, while a smaller array of pointers to **char** gives the starting locations of the words.

This exercise is to build a dictionary-maintenance module. Start with these lines:

```
#define DX_WORD_SPACE 10000
#define DX_TABLE_SIZE 1000
#define DX_WORD_LIMIT 31

static char dx_word_space[ DX_WORD_SPACE ] ;
static char *dx_word_table[ DX_TABLE_SIZE ] ;

int dx_table_size = DX_TABLE_SIZE ;
int dx_word_limit = DX_WORD_LIMIT ;

static char *dx_next_word = &dx_word_space ;
static int dx_next_entry = 0 ;
```

This code gives your DX module a 10,000-character space for word strings and a pointer array sufficient to hold the locations of 1000 words in the string space. Outside users of the module have access to global variables that indicate a maximum number of words and a limit on the length of any word. The value of **dx_next_word** is the location of the next available character in the **dx_word _space** array. The value of **dx_next_entry** gives an index to the next available member in **dx_word_table**. Details of assigning such initial values are explained in Chapter 11.

(a) Write **dx_lookup**, a function that searches the word table for a matching string. If an exact match is found among the words in the table, it should return a value of 1; otherwise, it should return 0.

(b) Write **dx_add**, a function that adds a word to the dictionary. This function should check the word length and should look up the word. It should return a value of 1 if the word was added, 0 if the word is already in the table, and −1 if the word string is too long.

(c) Write **dx_locate**, a searching function like **dx_lookup**, except that it ignores spaces and punctuation, and it treats lower- and uppercase letters as equivalent. If there is a match, this function returns a pointer to the word that was found; otherwise, it returns a null pointer.

(d) Modify **dx_add** so that the word table is maintained in ascending order. Let the order be determined by character values. When inserting a word, you will shuffle pointers in **dx_word_table** but should not move the characters stored in **dx_word_space**.

(e) Modify **dx_lookup** to exploit the sorted word table by using a binary search technique, as explained in the following software outline:

> Set upper search limit to start of table
> Set lower search limit to end of table
> Until word is determined present or absent
> Set test point midway between limits
> Examine word at test point
> If test word matches search word
>   Search word is present in table
> Else
>   If search word less than test word
>   Lower limit = test point minus 1
>   Else upper limit = test point plus 1
>   If lower limit above upper limit
>   Search word is absent from table

8.4: Review Exercise 7.3, a pattern-recognition exercise. Describe how pointers could be used for primary patterns of different sizes. Write a software design for this problem. Assume that you will want to use pointers in data management.

8.5: Consider the following function definition, which uses pointers as arguments:

```
int c ;
int f( a, b )
int *a, *b ;
{
    c = *a ;
    *a = *b ;
```

```
    *b = c ;
    return c ;
}
```

Suppose c, d, and e have just been set to 1, 2, and 3. What is the value of c after each of these statements:

(a) d = f(&c, &e) ;
(b) c = f(&e, &d) ;
(c) e = f(&d, &d) ;

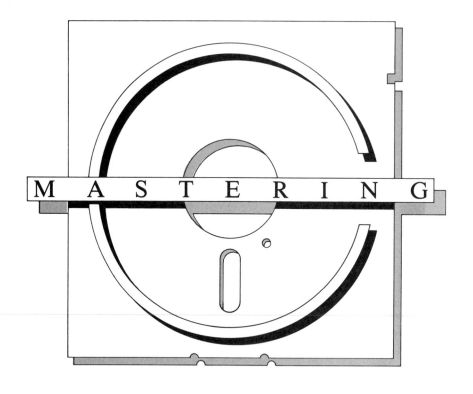

CHAPTER 9

DATA STRUCTURES

A program in C can collect data elements in *structures,* giving elements within structures unique identities. Unlike an array, a data structure may include elements of different types. In this chapter, you will read about:

- declaring and using data structures
- structure tags and substructures
- arrays and data structures
- pointers and data structures
- connective data organizations
- using data structures with functions
- data structures for software design

☐ DECLARING AND USING DATA STRUCTURES

Data structures are the most general form of data organization provided in C. They can contain elements of the fundamental data types, arrays of data elements, and pointers. The components of a data structure are called *members.* The members of a data structure, unlike the members of an array, are given individual names. The names are part of a structure declaration, as in the following example:

```
struct
{
    int rcd_part_number ;
    int rcd_quantity ;
    char rcd_description[ 20 ] ;
    char rcd_supplier[ 20 ] ;
}
    part_record ;
```

This statement declares a structure named part_record. The structure has two **int** members, named rcd_part_number and rcd_quantity. It also has two members, rcd_description and rcd_supplier, that are **char** arrays with 20 members each. Unless such a declaration has the **extern** storage class or describes an array parameter, it will act as a definition for the structure, causing storage for these members to be allocated.

The declaration of a data structure uses the keyword **struct**, followed by declarations of its members enclosed in braces. The **struct** keyword and the member declarations occupy the same position in a structure declaration that a keyword for one of the fundamental data types takes in a data element declaration. In this sense, a data structure becomes a type of data element. However, the analogy is limited. In most implementations of C, there are no operations on entire structures, only operations involving individual structure members.

Individual members of data structures are referred to by a composite of a structure name and a member name, using a period between the two names. For the example shown, program statements would refer to the two integers as

    part_record.rcd_part_number

and

    part_record.rcd_quantity

For arrays that are contained within structures, array names and array members can be written in the usual ways, except that a name must be prefixed by its structure name and a period, as in these examples:

    part_record.rcd_description[3]
    *(part_record.rcd_supplier + k)

You can prefix to these composite names either a reference operator or an indirection operator, as required. The effects of one of these operators will apply to the specified member, not to the structure or the structure name.

Early C compilers required all names in a program to be distinct. By the mid-1970s this requirement was made less stringent, allowing member names in structures to be identical with names of data variables, on the principle that the different uses could be distinguished by context. However, except for special cases, member names in different structures were required to be distinct.[1] Most C compilers produced since the early 1980s maintain a separate list of member names for each structure. These compilers determine the meaning of a member name by considering the structure name with which the member name is used.

For maximum portability, it is necessary to maintain distinct names of structure members. An effective way of doing this is to follow the

[1] Brian W. Kernighan and Dennis M. Ritchie, *The C Programming Language* (Englewood Cliffs, N. J.: Prentice-Hall, 1978), p. 197.

methods presented in Chapters 10 and 14 for naming functions and global data. The definer or "producer" of a structure should add a two- or three-character prefix to each structure member name. Sometimes this prefix can be the same as a module name or, as discussed in the next section, a structure tag. Such a practice has been observed in the examples presented.

□ STRUCTURE TAGS AND SUBSTRUCTURES

Programs frequently need more than one structure of a particular type. For this purpose, a *structure tag* can be declared. A structure tag preserves information about the organization of a data structure, including the order, type, and member name of each component. It does not include information about the storage class, which must be declared separately for each structure. Using the first example of this chapter, you could designate the structure tag RCD with the following declaration:

```
struct RCD
{
    int rcd_part_number ;
    int rcd_quantity ;
    char rcd_description[ 20 ] ;
    char rcd_supplier[ 20] ;
}
    part_record ;
```

This declares both a structure organization, named RCD, and a particular structure using the RCD organization, named part_record.

Once it has been declared through a tag, a structure organization can be reused. For example, another structure using the RCD organization above could be declared as:

```
struct RCD
    repair_record ;
```

A declaration statement may declare only a structure tag, if you wish. Simply omit the name of any structure. (Remember to supply the semicolon that ends the declaration.) Once a tag has been declared, other declarations can refer to it and create specific structures using its organization.

A structure tag is a programmer-defined symbol, resembling in some ways the symbols you can create with #define statements. However, the scope of a tag resembles that of a variable. When a structure tag is declared inside a function, it should be recognized only within that function.[2] If declared outside a function, it should be recognized by all subsequent statements in a module. It is helpful to distinguish tags as symbols by writing them in uppercase.

Structures can include other structures within them; these are sometimes called *substructures.* There are two basic approaches to declaring such structures. One, called *nesting,* is shown in Figure 9.1. In this example the **warranty_record** structure has two members that are themselves structures, each of the **DT** organization, and two data element members.

```
struct WR
{
    struct DT
    {
        int dt_month ;
        int dt_day ;
        int dt_year ;
    }
        wr_service_date ;

    struct DT
        wr_sale_date ;
    int wr_authorization ;
    int wr_shop_minutes ;
}
    warranty_record ;
```

Figure 9.1: *A declaration of nested substructures.*

The declaration in Figure 9.1 specifies and uses a structure organization that is given the tag **DT.** This organization is used for date information. An element from one of the dates can be used by prefixing its member name with the member name of its substructure—either **wr_sale_date** or **wr_service_date**—and then that of the main structure. The entire list of named components from this structure and its substructures, in the order declared, is as follows:

warranty_record.wr_service_date.dt_month
warranty_record.wr_service_date.dt_day
warranty_record.wr_service_date.dt_year

---

[2] Ibid., p. 206. Unfortunately, a few C compilers violate this standard and treat all structure tags as though they were declared outside a function.

warranty_record.wr_sale_date.dt_month
warranty_record.wr_sale_date.dt_day
warranty_record.wr_sale_date.dt_year
warranty_record.wr_authorization
warranty_record.wr_shop_minutes

As you can see, the names of elements quickly become long and cumbersome. When you need to express complete element names, the practical depth to which substructures can be nested is about three or four levels.

A nested structure declaration has **struct** declarations, with their braces and components, inside other **struct** declarations. Nesting can be carried to any level. As the complexity of a nested declaration grows, however, it quickly becomes difficult to understand.

To express complex data organizations, use the other method— separated structure declarations. Define your inner organizations first, using structure tags, and then progress toward outer levels. Each declaration statement should specify only one structure organization. It can include substructures using other organizations, referring to their tags. The example from Figure 9.1 can be expressed in separated declarations by the statements shown in Figure 9.2. The information is the same, but it is presented in a more easily understood form. The difference in intelligibility becomes even more marked as the complexity of data grows.

```
struct DT
{
    int dt_month ;
    int dt_day ;
    int dt_year ;
} ;
struct WR
{
    struct DT wr_service_date ;
    struct DT wr_sale_date ;
    int wr_authorization ;
    int wr_shop_minutes ;
}

    warranty_record ;
```

Figure 9.2: *The same structure as in Figure 9.1, declared separately.*

□ ARRAYS AND DATA STRUCTURES

As the examples have shown, data structures may contain arrays as components. You can use array components of a structure in the same ways as other arrays. If you omit an index after the name of an array component, you have specified an array name. As with other arrays, this name will be treated like a pointer constant.

An array that is contained in a structure can be used for pointer arithmetic or as a function argument, just as other arrays can. The following example shows a structure declaration containing an array, followed by a statement invoking a function with the name of the array, used as an argument, and another statement with pointer arithmetic:

```
struct
{
    int vx_form ;
    char vx_label[ 32 ] ;
}
    vector_exam ;
    . . .
    vkrn = vec_iden( vector_exam.vx_label ) ;
    . . .
    if ( *( vector_exam.vx_label + vkrn ) == '#' )
        . . .
```

It is possible to create arrays of structures. The following example uses a structure to make a list of references for a research paper:

```
struct
{
    int rl_ref_number ;
    char rl_author[ 40 ] ;
    char rl_citation[ 80 ] ;
}
    ref_list[ 200 ] ;
```

This declaration specifies **ref_list** as an array of structures. Each member of this array has two structure members, **rl_author** and **rl_citation**, which are **char** arrays.

To specify an element from one of the **ref_list** array members, the name **ref_list** must be followed by an array index. For example, the **rl_ref_number** component from member **index** in the **ref_list** structure array would be written as

```
ref_list[ index ].rl_ref_number
```

When one of the components is an array, to specify a member of that array you will need another array index. Using the above example, to specify rl_citation character xchr from member index of ref_list, you would write

ref_list[index].rl_citation[xchr]

The name of a structure has the same behavior as other variable names in C. If the name denotes an array of structures, you have the same capabilities and restrictions that apply to other array names:

- The name is treated as a pointer constant.

- You can designate a particular member by pointer arithmetic.

Because array brackets have priority over the indirection operator, you may need to add parentheses to get the right result. The previous example, naming a particular data element from an array within an array of structures, could have been written as any of the following expressions:

```
ref_list[ index ].rl_citation[ xchr ]
*( ref_list[ index ].rl_citation + xchr )
( *ref_list + index ).rl_citation[ xchr ]
*( ( *ref_list + index ).rl_citation + xchr )
```

In the second example above, pointer arithmetic is used with the **char** array. In the third, it is used with the array of structures. In the last, it is used with both. The C language correctly identifies the selection of structure members from a structure array, regardless of whether array indexing or pointer arithmetic is used to designate an element of the structure array.

□ POINTERS AND DATA STRUCTURES

So far in the discussion of arrays and structures, you have seen pointers and pointer arithmetic used to select members of structure arrays. You can also use pointers themselves as structure components, and you can create pointers to data structures and to all structure components, including substructures. To understand the capabilities of C in this area, keep in mind that for the purpose of defining data, a structure behaves like a data element, as does any substructure it may contain.

In programs that use large amounts of data, allocating space efficiently for arrays and character strings can become a problem. The

solution is usually *storage management,* which allocates space from
a pool of available storage. In response to requests for storage, a storage manager module supplies other modules with pointers. These designate locations where data can be stored in the space controlled by the
storage manager. Instead of containing string and array data, many
data structures of a program set up this way will contain pointers to
spaces allocated by the storage manager.

The following example uses pointers as components of arrays. It is a
different organization for a list of references in a research paper. This
version of the data structure uses **char** pointers, rather than **char**
arrays, to designate character strings:

```
struct
{
    int rl_ref_number ;
    char *rl_author ;
    char *rl_citation ;
}
    ref_list[ 200 ] ;
```

When a program using this type of structure needs to add a new reference, it determines actual lengths of the strings for rl_author and
rl_citation. Space for these items is obtained from a storage manager,
which furnishes pointers to their locations. The pointer values are
stored in the above data structure, and the strings are stored in the
spaces allocated by the storage manager.

C programming environments usually provide a simple storage-
management function, named malloc, that returns a **char** pointer.
This function is invoked with an argument giving the number of characters of storage needed. If the requested space is not available,
malloc returns a null pointer. A program using this function might get
space for citation kref, of length lcit, by the following:

```
extern char *malloc( ) ;
char *string ;
. . .
string = malloc( lcit ) ;
if ( string )
    ref_list[ kref ].rl_citation = string ;
else
    . . .
```

Statements following **else** would react to a null pointer returned by
malloc, indicating that malloc does not have enough space available
to satisfy the request.

Pointers to structures provide powerful techniques for describing cross-references. Structures with some of the data describing the items of interest can contain pointers to structures that give other characteristics. Data about the other characteristics can be stored in structures that are separately described and maintained. Thus, a program can use a single copy of data that might otherwise need to appear in several places.

For example, a program to analyze manufacturing requirements might need to compare information about:

- manufacturing components

- component vendors

- specification documents

- quality standards

The program could define an array of structures, with each member describing some particular manufacturing component. The structure for a manufacturing component could include pointers to members of other structure arrays, which contain the rest of the information.

The declarations listed in Figure 9.3 show how data about manufacturing components might be connected to data about vendors. In this figure, each structure in the **component** array has a pointer to a structure in the **vendor** array, where information about the supplier of the component can be found.

```
struct VND                    /* vendor structure    */
{
    char *vnd_name ;
    char *vnd_address ;
    char *vnd_location ;
    int vnd_zipcode ;
    int vnd_company_size ;
}
    vendor[ VND_LEN ] ;

struct CMP                    /* component structure  */
{
    int cmp_identifier ;
    char cmp_description[ CMP_DES_LEN ] ;
    struct VND *cmp_vendor ;
}
    component[ CMP_LEN ] ;
```

Figure 9.3: *Declaration of separate data structures linked by pointers.*

In Figure 9.3, note how a pointer to a **VND** structure was declared, within a **CMP** structure:

    struct VND *cmp_vendor ;

A structure tag is commonly used when declaring a structure pointer. This declaration says that **cmp_vendor** will have as its value the location of a structure of type **VND**. A program could assign **vendor** array member **kvn** to provide the **cmp_vendor** data for **component** array member **jcm** by the following statement:

    component[jcm].cmp_vendor = &vendor[kvn] ;

The reference operator is used to obtain the location of the appropriate structure in the **vendor** array of structures. Having done this, a program could retrieve the **vnd_zipcode** value for the vendor of component **jcm** as:

    (*component[jcm].cmp_vendor).vnd_zipcode

The part of this expression between parentheses is equivalent to naming a **VND** structure; the last part selects a member of that structure.

The operation of naming a structure by applying the indirection operator to a structure pointer and then selecting a member of that structure, is so common in C programs that there is a special operator for indirect structure member selection. Using it, the selection of a **vnd_zipcode** value above could have been written:

    component[jcm].cmp_vendor->vnd_zipcode

Like == and !=, the -> operator has two characters, which should be immediately adjacent. This operator says, "For name on the left (which must be a pointer to a structure), get the current value of the pointer and use the name on the right to select a member from that structure."

In the earlier discussion of structure tags and substructures it was recommended that you separate the declarations of your substructure types both from each other and from the declaration of an enclosing structure. With structure pointers and the indirect structure member selection operator, you can separate the substructures themselves. You don't need to fit everything under one roof. It is easy to travel from one structure to another by means of structure pointers.

Just as you can use the direct structure member selection operator (.) more than once in an expression, to get to more than one level inside a single structure, you can use the indirect structure member selection operator (->) more than once, to traverse separated structures. Using the structures shown in Figure 9.3, suppose that a program also has a structure for the components needed to make a subassembly:

```
struct SUB                          /* subassembly structure*/
{
    int sub_identifier ;
    char sub_description[ SUB_DES_LEN ] ;
    struct CMP *sub_component[ SUB_CMP_LEN ] ;
}
    subassembly ;
```

The **SUB** structure has a member, **sub_component**, that is an array of pointers to **CMP** structures. They describe the components used in the subassembly. To obtain the **vnd_zipcode** value of the vendor for subassembly component **isb**, you would write this expression:

```
subassembly.sub_component[ isb ]->
cmp_vendor->vnd_zipcode
```

Expressions such as the foregoing tend to run off the edge of the paper. To keep them manageable and easy to understand, you may want to define structure pointers as utility variables. For example, the following lines declare a pointer for a **CMP** structure, set it to the location of a particular subassembly component structure, and then use the pointer value to obtain the vendor ZIP code:

```
struct CMP *subcomp ;
int zip ;
. . .
subcomp = subassembly.sub_component[ isb ] ;
. . .
zip = subcomp->cmp_vendor->vnd_zipcode ;
```

In this example, the pointer to the **component** structure for subcomponent **isb** is assigned to the **subcomp** structure pointer variable. Then the ZIP code value is picked up, using indirect structure member selection with the utility variable **subcomp**.

Statements using indirect structure selection will appear often in programs that have connected structures. When you declare utility variables for pointers, remember that a structure pointer must have a structure type. Usually, it will be specified by a tag. In your program statements, be careful to observe the structure type; don't try to use the same pointer for structures of different types.

□ CONNECTIVE DATA ORGANIZATIONS

The previous section showed how to connect data structures that describe an assembly made out of parts. This is a typical example of one kind of regular connection between structures. A *connective* organization of data has paths, following some general pattern, that link one component to another. The C language does not automate this type of data organization, as do languages like Lisp, Snobol, and Sail. However, C pointers and data structures make it easy to construct such an organization. Many sophisticated programs written in C use a connective data organization to represent or analyze patterns.

For a C program using connective data organization, most data components will reside in structures, and most connections between components will consist of pointers to structures. Without knowing the contents of structures (aside from the fact that they will have pointers to one another), you can represent a connective data organization as a diagram of boxes and arrows. Each box represents a structure; each arrow represents a connection, effected by a pointer, from one structure to another. Figure 9.4 shows an example.

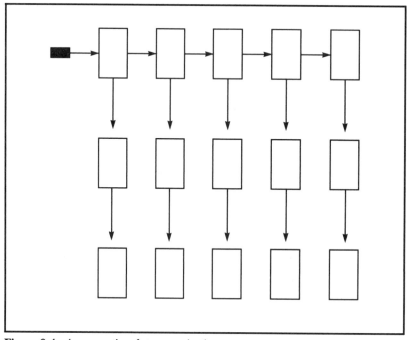

Figure 9.4: *A connective data organization.*

There are two classes of links in Figure 9.4. One class goes horizontally, across the top row of boxes. The other goes vertically, down the columns. The boxes in the top row have both types of links; those below have only the vertical links. Differences in *connectivity*—the overall pattern of connection—are often related to differences in information. For example, you might represent a manufacturing assembly with the type of connections shown in Figure 9.4. The boxes in the top row would represent subassemblies; those below would represent the components of the subassemblies.

The simplest type of connective data organization is a *linked list*. This is a chain of data components, with links between each member and the next, as shown in Figure 9.5.

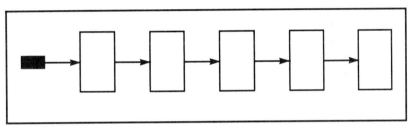

Figure 9.5: *A linked list.*

The links in a connective organization are directional; a pointer points in one direction only. As shown in Figure 9.5, a link takes you from one component to another. There is not necessarily any way to get back. An organization like the one shown in Figure 9.5 is sometimes called a *unidirectional* linked list. Of course, it is easy to create pointers in both directions. Figure 9.6 shows such an organization, a *bidirectional* linked list.

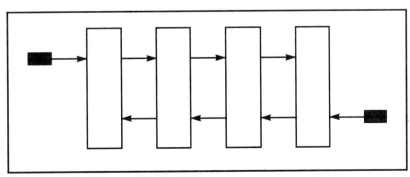

Figure 9.6: *A bidirectional linked list.*

All three organizations shown so far have a link that starts outside the organization and connects to one of its elements. These are often called *origin* links. An origin link provides a path for entering a connective data organization. Look again at Figure 9.4, and you will see that it represents a list of lists. The "outer" list, along the top row, has an origin link outside it. Each component of the outer list contains an origin link to one of the "inner" lists. Such an organization can be expanded to many levels, when necessary.

To construct a linked list using structures and structure pointers, reserve a pointer in the structure to hold the location of the next structure in the list. The usual convention in C programs is to store a null pointer value to indicate the end of the list. A structure declaration for a linked list will look like this example:

```
struct SUB                          /* subassembly structure*/
{
    struct SUB *sub_next ;
    int sub_identifier ;
    char sub_description[ SUB_DES_LEN ] ;
    struct CMP *sub_component[ SUB_CMP_LEN ] ;
}
```

Notice that this structure has a pointer to another structure of the same type. This form of self-reference is permitted in C; other forms are not.

Using the structure example just shown, program statements to search through the list of structures would have the following appearance:

```
struct SUB *sub_first ;             /* start of list */
struct SUB *sub ;                   /* current item */
int ident;                          /* current ident. */
. . .
for ( sub = sub_first ; sub ; sub = sub->sub_next )
{
    ident = sub->sub_identifier ;
    . . .
```

These statements provide a pointer, **sub_first**, that holds the location of the first structure in the list. Another pointer, named **sub**, holds the location of the structure currently being examined. If the list is empty, **sub_first** should contain a null pointer.

At the start of the **for** loop, **sub** is set to the location of the first structure in the list. Before each iteration, **sub** is tested to see whether it holds a null pointer value. If so, the end of the list has been reached and the loop terminates. Otherwise, indirect structure member selection is used with the value of sub to obtain access to values in the current structure. At the end of each iteration, the value of sub is replaced with the location of the next structure in the list. If the list is empty, the loop will terminate before its first iteration.

Any organization that is connected as a list, or a list of lists, and so on, might be constructed as an array, or an array of arrays, and so on. It usually takes more work to manipulate linked lists than arrays. Linked lists are preferable only when at least one of the following applies:

- Items are added one at a time, and the total number cannot be determined in advance.

- Items must be frequently inserted, deleted, or rearranged.

- Lists must be split up or combined.

Always consider arrays as an alternative to list structures, whenever the demands of a task permit.

The use of lists to illustrate *recursive functions* has become something of a cliche in programming books. These are functions that invoke themselves or cause some other function to invoke them. When processing a single, otherwise unconnected list, list of lists, or similar organization of data, recursive functions fail to deliver any new capability; instead, they add confusion, consume extra storage, and slow down your program. Avoid them.

A connective organization that cannot easily be constructed without the use of structures and structure pointers is a *tree*. Each component of a tree can contain links to two or more additional components. A tree has the following characteristics:

- From exactly one component, called the *root,* it is possible to reach any other component by a path of links.

- There is exactly one path from the root to any other component.

A tree organization is illustrated in Figure 9.7. The root component is at the bottom. Beneath that is shown an origin link from outside the organization. All the links are in the upward direction.

Tree organizations are often found where details of information can be expanded to an arbitrary degree. For example, a set of specifications for an industrial process, a set of drawings to describe a manufactured assembly, and a set of topics in a book all often have tree

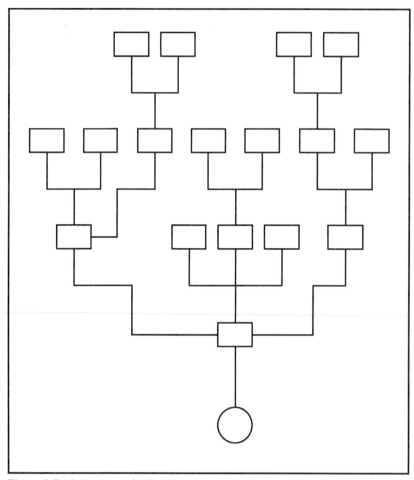

Figure 9.7: *A tree organization.*

organizations. To represent a component of a tree, a data structure in C will have an array of pointers or a linked list, linking it to other components, as well as data elements providing information for one level in the tree.

A useful type of tree for many applications, called a *binary tree,* has two links for each component. The components are called *nodes,* the two links, the *left* and *right branches*. A common application of a binary tree is to maintain data in an order determined by some parameter. For this use, one data element of each node determines the order of nodes. Lower-collating nodes are reached through the left branch, higher-collating nodes, through the right branch.

Figure 9.8 illustrates a binary tree for composers of music. The ordering parameter is the composer's last name. At each node, additional information gives the year of birth for the composer whose name appears at the node. In this example, left branches are shown above and right branches beneath the nodes.

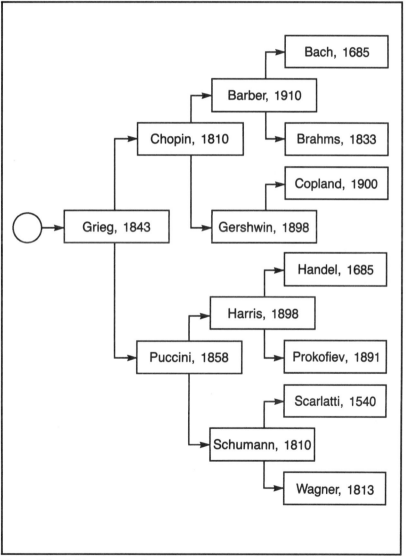

Figure 9.8: *A binary tree of composers.*

The branching of the tree in Figure 9.8 obviously has nothing to do with musicology. The primary use of such a tree is to facilitate rapid searches of data for the occurrence of particular items. The following software outline shows the search procedure for this tree:

Locate the first node, from the origin
Until the desired composer has been found
    If the desired composer's name collates lower
        than the name at the current node
    If there is no left branch
        The composer is not in the tree
        Break
    Go to the node on the left branch
    Else if the desired composer's name collates higher
        than the name at the current node
    If there is no right branch
        The composer is not in the tree
        Break
    Go to the node on the right branch
    Else the desired composer has been found

If a binary tree is well balanced, so that at any node the number of other nodes that can be reached through the left and right branches is about the same, a search goes through about $\log_2 n$ links to reach a particular node, where n is the total number of nodes. For a linked list, the average number of links would be about $n/2$. A binary tree is usually faster to search than a linked list when n is more than 10.

If data are in an array, you can also perform a binary search. At each step, divide the range of data in half and examine the center item. A binary search is possible because the members of an array can be reached at random, without going through any one of them. You may want to use a binary tree when you need a list organization, for one of the reasons stated earlier, but you need to perform searches quickly.

A binary tree has different connectivity from a linked list, but it also provides a single level of organization. As with linked lists, you can make *tiers* of binary trees—that is, trees of trees—and so on. The price of this data organization, as compared to a linked list, is two links for each data component and more complex data management.

□ USING DATA STRUCTURES WITH FUNCTIONS

The capabilities of C functions complement those of C data structures. To make functions that manipulate data structures, you need to understand how to pass data contained in structures to and from a function.

The C language interprets the name of a structure, written without any member selection, as a data element—that is, as a data value, not a data location. Notice that this interpretation differs from that of array and function names, which are treated as pointer constants. Most implementations of C provide no operations for an entire structure. Some compilers, however, particularly those produced since the early 1980s, provide the following extensions:

- An entire structure can be transmitted as an argument when a function is invoked.

- An entire structure may be returned as a value by a function.

- All the data values contained in an entire structure may be assigned to the members of another structure of the same type.

When these extended structure facilities are provided, you can name structures as function arguments and return values, and you can transfer the data from one structure to another, using statements such as the following:

```
struct
{
    int knives ;
    int forks ;
    int spoons ;
}
    head_table, end_table ;

end_table = head_table ;
```

For maximum portability, however, you should not employ structure assignments, and you should not designate structures as the arguments and return values of functions.

Without extended facilities, structure data are usually passed between functions by structure pointers. Note that the indirection operator cannot operate on a structure name; a structure does not have a location value. The reference operator can; use it to create a pointer to a structure or a substructure. The example in Figure 9.9, taken from a program for architectural detailing, declares two structure types and a pointer to one of them. It shows how to assign a substructure location to the pointer.

```
struct DES
{
    char des_pattern[ 20 ] ;
    int des_era ;
} ;

struct FAC
{
    struct DES fac_design ;
    int fac_finials ;
    int fac_pilasters ;
}
    facade ;
struct DES *design ;

design = &facade.fac_design ;
```

Figure 9.9: *A declaration of two structure types and a pointer to one of them.*

A structure pointer can be used as a function argument. Within a function, the structure pointer is used with indirect structure member selection to obtain access to structure data. Figure 9.10 uses the structure types from Figure 9.9 to invoke **facade_check,** a function that receives a pointer to a **FAC** structure and returns a pointer to a **DES** structure. It also shows a definition for the **facade_check** function.

```
    extern struct DES *design_check( ) ;
    struct DES *design ;

    design = design_check( &facade ) ;
    .   .   .
struct DES *design_check( visual )
struct FAC *visual ;
{           .   .   .
    return &visual->fac_design ;
```

Figure 9.10: *A function that uses the structure types declared in Figure 9.9.*

Programs that use data structures often include modules related to each structure type that perform basic operations. Many programs allocate dynamic storage for their structures. Among the functions in a structure handling module will be a function to create a structure using dynamic storage and, sometimes, a function to release the storage that had been allocated for a structure. Figure 9.11 shows a function to create structures for the binary tree of composers, which was illustrated in the discussion of connected data organizations in Figure 9.8.

```
struct CMP                          /* composer structure   */
{
    struct CMP *cmp_left ;       /* left branch           */
    struct CMP *cmp_right ;      /* right branch          */
    char cmp_surname[ CMP_NLEN ] ;
    int cmp_birthyear ;
} ;

struct CMP *cmp_create( surname, birthyear )
char surname[ CMP_NLEN ] ;       /* composer's name       */
int birthyear ;                  /* composer's birth year*/
{
    extern struct CMP *malloc( ) ;
    struct CMP *composer ;
    int cmp_size ;               /* size of CMP structure*/
    int i ;
                                 /* allocate structure    */
    cmp_size = sizeof( struct CMP ) ;
    composer = malloc( cmp_size ) ;
    if ( composer )              /* if allocated,         */
    {
                                 /* store name and date */
        for ( i = 0 ; i < CMP_NLEN - 1 ; i = i + 1 )
            composer->cmp_surname[ i ] = surname[ i ] ;
        composer->cmp_surname[ i ] = 0 ;
        composer->cmp_birthyear = birthyear ;
    }
    return composer ;            /* return CMP structure */
}
```

Figure 9.11: *A function to create structures.*

This preceding example uses two features of C that ought to be clarified. Both relate to the **malloc** function, which is used to obtain dynamic storage. The first of these is the expression **sizeof(struct CMP)**. As the next chapter explains, the value of this expression is the number of bytes required for an instance of the **CMP** structure type. This information is required by the **malloc** function to determine the amount of storage to allocate. The second feature is the declaration of the type of value returned by the **malloc** function, in this example a pointer to a **CMP** structure. In all ordinary implementations of C, it is possible to have a pointer value that can be used for any type of data element, although a pointer with these characteristics cannot be specified in the C language. The **malloc** function will return such a pointer. You may therefore declare it to return any single type of pointer that is needed.

The **cmp_create** function checks to see whether **malloc** returned a null pointer. If not, it stores a string for the composer's name and an integer for the year of birth in the structure. A null character is stored at the end of the name array, to insure that it is correctly terminated. The value returned is either a pointer to a completed **CMP** structure or a null pointer, indicating that the structure could not be created.

A final example of a function for structure manipulation is called **cmp_add**, listed in Figure 9.12. This function adds a new **CMP** structure to a binary tree of these structures. It receives as arguments a pointer to the origin of the tree (which is a pointer to the first structure in the tree), and a pointer to the component that is to be added. It returns an integer value of 1 if the addition was completed, and 0 if it was not performed because an existing component was found with the same name.

The **cmp_add** function invokes a string comparison function named **cmp_compare**. This function receives two **CMP** structure pointers. It is required to compare **cmp_surname** strings of these structures and return an integer value:

- -1, if the first string collates before the second string

- 0, if the strings are the same

- 1, if the first string collates after the second string

The **cmp_add** function first checks to see whether the tree is empty. If so, it installs the new structure as the first component in the tree. Otherwise, it searches the tree until it finds either a component with the same name or a null branch. On finding a null branch, it links the new component from that branch.

☐ DATA STRUCTURES FOR SOFTWARE DESIGN

As explained in Chapter 4, the most important early step in software design is to develop an organizing principle for the job at hand.

```
struct CMP                          /* composer structure  */
{
    struct CMP *cmp_left ;          /* left branch          */
    struct CMP *cmp_right ;         /* right branch         */
    char cmp_surname[ CMP_NLEN ] ;
    int cmp_birthyear ;
} ;

struct CMP *cmp_add( cmp_tree, cmp_new )
struct CMP **cmp_tree ;             /* origin of tree       */
struct CMP *cmp_new ;               /* node to be added     */
{
    extern int cmp_compare( ) ;
    struct CMP *cmp ;               /* structure in test    */
    struct CMP *cmp_next ;          /* next one to test     */
    int compare ;                   /* comparison of names  */
    cmp_new->cmp_left = 0 ;         /* clear new branches   */
    cmp_new->cmp_right = 0 ;
    if ( !*cmp_tree )
    {                               /* if tree is empty,    */
        *cmp_tree = cmp_new ;       /*   install first node */
        return 1 ;
    }                               /* start search         */
    cmp = *cmp_tree ;               /*   from first node    */
    while ( 1 )
    {                               /* compare names        */
        compare = cmp_compare( cmp_new, cmp ) ;
        if ( !compare )             /* if the names match,  */
            return 0 ;              /*   don't add the node */
        if ( compare < 0 )          /* if new collates low, */
        {                           /*   check left branch  */
            cmp_next = cmp->cmp_left ;
            if ( !cmp_next )        /* if branch is empty,  */
            {                       /*   link the new node  */
                cmp->cmp_left = cmp_new ;
                return 1 ;          /* node was added       */
            }
        }
        else                        /* if new collates high,*/
        {                           /*   check right branch */
            cmp_next = cmp->cmp_right ;
            if ( !cmp_next )        /* if branch is empty,  */
            {                       /*   link the new node  */
                cmp->cmp_right = cmp_new ;
                return 1 ;          /* node was added       */
            }
        }
        cmp = cmp_next ;            /* continue the search  */
    }
}
```

Figure 9.12: *A function that adds a new structure to a binary tree.*

Because of the high cost of software development, there is an increasing trend toward flexible programs that can be adapted to a wide range of tasks. This software is then customized by its users, through control data. The construction of such a program is largely driven by the plan for managing its data. Its organizing principle is more likely to be a way of characterizing and partitioning data than a method of controlling the flow of procedures.

Sometimes, data can be organized around a central "spine," upon which all data relationships are based. For library management software, for example, this central organization would most likely be the catalog of holdings; a funds management program would probably be based on an investment portfolio. As software services become better integrated and more comprehensive, however, this single line of descent fails.

As an example of how the scope of software services can affect data organization, consider the organization of printed circuit layout programs. The basic service of these programs is to map the geometry of metallic traces on one or more surfaces of a printed circuit board. The first such programs were purely geometrical; their data consisted of positions, shapes, and orientations. The dimensions of a board surface could and did provide a central organization.

A subsequent generation of programs was based on a combination of a logical description of a circuit and a set of physical descriptions of components. These programs could physically reorient components to improve the efficiency of a layout. In this stage, data split into three broad categories:

- a permanent library, containing physical descriptions of circuit components

- a list of connections for a particular circuit

- the geometrical patterns for circuit surfaces

More recent programs can redesign portions of a circuit itself, to achieve a compact physical form. In addition to the foregoing data, these programs must work with:

- the electrical characteristics of circuit components

- the graphical representation of components, in order to draw a schematic of a final circuit

The most advanced programs of this type can evaluate effects of circuit geometry on electrical performance and create control data to drive automated manufacturing.

The succeeding generations of software for printed circuit layout have had to cope with substantial increases in:

- volume of information

- variety of information

- relationships among information

The experience of software developers in this area is not at all unusual. A similar course of evolution can be found in software for text processing, business management, financial records, engineering design, image analysis, and many other applications; it is a mark of success.

Since this pattern of development is so common, a good software design will anticipate it. The key to a flexible design is modularity. Chapter 4 of this book showed how to design modular procedures; modular data design is equally important. It rests on:

- clusters of data that are internally cohesive, sharing similar characteristics and serving similar uses

- connections between clusters of data that are easy to define, create, break, trace, use, and understand

No abstract principle of design will by itself provide a sound basis for your work. There is no substitute for foresight and knowledge of a subject.

The C language's data structures and structure pointers make it possible to organize modular data that complement good procedural design. They provide critical capabilities for:

- explicit grouping of data that are related by content and use

- composition of larger, more general data groupings from smaller, more specific ones

- creation of connections between data groupings of different compositions

To use these capabilities effectively, you need to understand the content of, and the relationships among, the data you work with and the patterns of operations in which these data will be employed.

A robust approach to the design of data structures will be firmly grounded on an analysis of the information that is relevant to an application and the uses that will be made of it. It should observe the following guidelines:

- Data that will be used together should be grouped together within a structure.

- If data do not serve a common purpose, do not create a data structure for them.

- When future demands on your software may require that data be processed separately, put them in separate structures.

- Try to keep your data structures small.

- If the items grouped in a structure will sometimes be used in different combinations, make substructures for the combinations.

- If some operations on the data in a structure require only a portion of the data, place that portion in a substructure.

- Keep the connections between your data structures as simple and regular as the work to be accomplished will permit.

Remember that data structures are an internal organization of data. Their groupings, boundaries, and pointer connections ordinarily exist only inside a computer, while your program is running. Most programs require a means of storing data outside a program and of recreating an organization when it is retrieved. While the use of data files will be covered in Chapter 19, it is related to the design of internal structures. In general, the simpler and more orderly your data structures, the more effective your external data organization can become.

□ EXERCISES

9.1: As discussed in this chapter, the design of data structures should reflect their content and uses. For this exercise, design organizations for one or more of the following data collections. Write a description of your overall approach and a declaration for each data structure. Draw a diagram for each connective data organization.

    (a) A saltwater marsh ecology, including permanent and migratory populations, vegetation, consumption and production of nitrates, fixed carbon, and minerals, feeding patterns, reproductive capacities, periodic census data, and surveys of acidity, dissolved oxygen, agricultural chemicals, and industrial wastes.

(b) A logic circuit design, including gates, interconnects, modular components, external connections and test points, loading rules, propagation delays and margins, thermal degradation, setup and hold times, stimulus patterns, and test output vectors and timing.

(c) A restaurant management program, supporting analysis of staff assignments and turnover, sales history, menu planning, food and equipment vendors, ordering quantities, inventory flow, overhead, labor productivity, spoilage and other loss, and margins.

9.2: Review the functions shown in the text for the manipulation of binary trees, using the CMP data structure. Write a CMP module, which includes cmp_create, as shown, and the additional functions described. For some of these, you may need to define recursive functions or utility workspaces. If you choose the latter approach, chain elements of the workspace in a linked list, and allocate them dynamically. Consider the alternative of rechaining the tree as a linked list.

(a) Write the function cmp_search, which will search the tree for a composer's name and, if found, return the birth year.

(b) Write the function cmp_delete, which will remove a specified composer from the tree.

(c) Write the function cmp_count, which will count the number of composers in the tree.

(d) Write the function cmp_print, which will print out all the composers in the tree.

(e) Write the function cmp_sort, which will re-sort the tree. This function is most easily built by decomposing and reconstructing the tree, using an approach similar to cmp_add. It should require only pointer manipulation.

(f) Write the functions cmp_name and cmp_year, to be used as comparison functions by cmp_sort, the first of which orders composers first by surname, and the second of which orders them first by birth year.

(g) Write the function **cmp_balance**, which will reorganize the tree structure so that at any node the number of composers reached via the left branch is as nearly as possible equal to the number reached via the right branch.

9.3: Create a program to deal a game of Bridge. For the hands, use an array of four structures, each of which has four arrays of **int** for the suits, each of which holds the values of cards dealt. For this purpose, as in many game programs, you will need a random number generator. A simple but effective way to make one is to keep multiplying an odd number by an odd prime and "pick some bits" out of the middle. As a pertinent example, to get a random number from 0 to 51:

```
int deal( )
{
    static int seed = 207 ;
    int pit ;
    while ( 1 )
    {
        seed = 263 * seed ;
        if ( seed < 0 )
            seed = -seed ;
        pit = ( seed / 16 ) % 64 ;
        if ( pit < 52 )
            return pit ;
    }
}
```

(a) Make sure that your dealer doesn't try to deal the same card twice.

(b) Using one of the several conventions for the game, bid the hands. Then see if you can work out a strategy to play the hands.

(c) Use the same data structures for a game that is played with a partially dealt deck, such as poker.

MASTERING

CHAPTER 10

DECLARING NAMES
AND DATA TYPES

A program written in C must declare the names and characteristics of its data. In addition to the capabilities previously described, the C language allows you to define symbols for data types. In this chapter, you will read about:

- declarations and definitions

- declarations involving functions

- interpreting data declarations

- sizes and ordering of data

- reach and scope of declarations

- symbolic data types

□ DECLARATIONS AND DEFINITIONS

In the C language, data must be declared before being used. Data declaration statements must always appear in a source file before any other statements referring to the data they declare. Declaration statements specify all characteristics of data except permanent values:

- identifiers for data items

- types of data items:
  —fundamental element types
  —modified element types
  —data arrays
  —data structures
  —pointers

- organization of composite data:
  —array sizes
  —structure members and types

- storage classes

Definition statements are similar to declaration statements. In addition to specifying identifiers and characteristics, they reserve main storage for data. Also, as explained in the next chapter, they may designate initial values for variables. The definition of a function includes the program statements that comprise the function.

The C language provides several classes of identifiers. The most common of these are names for the major program elements:

- names of functions
- names of variables
- names of structure members

C also allows programmer defined symbols, to describe quantities and data organizations. The types of symbols dealt with in this chapter and the preceding chapters are:

- structure tags
- #define constants
- symbolic data types

An *identifier* consists of one or more contiguous letters and numerals, starting with a letter. The underscore character (_) is also allowed in identifiers; it is treated as though it were a letter. Letters may be either upper- or lowercase; a letter in uppercase is treated as a different character from the same letter in lowercase. To make your programs easy to read, it has been recommended that you use all lowercase letters for names and all uppercase letters for symbols.

Certain identifiers, called keywords, are reserved for specific meanings in the C language. The 27 standard C language keywords are as follows:

auto	extern	short
break	float	sizeof
case	for	static
char	goto	struct
continue	if	switch
default	int	typedef
do	long	union
double	register	unsigned
else	return	while

Keywords are written entirely in lowercase. Some C compilers reserve a few other keywords. These include:

asm	entry	fortran
const	enum	void

A program must avoid using keywords for any purpose other than the meanings reserved for them.

A C compiler distinguishes between identifiers on the basis of a certain number of initial characters, called the *significance*. The significance length varies among compilers. The earliest C compilers provided a significance of eight characters. More recent compilers often allow up to 31 characters. A few provide unlimited significance. Names of functions and of global data elements that must be linked between separately compiled modules will also be limited by the significance of a linker. Some linkers provide significance of only six characters, others up to 31 characters. Linkers may fail to distinguish between upper- and lowercase.

Each C declaration concerns the characteristics of a single identifier. It does the following:

- gives the spelling of the identifier

- designates a storage class

- designates a fundamental data type or a structure organization

- designates data type modifiers

- shows how the identifier is used to yield a value or a structure of the specified type or organization

- if the identifier is for an array, gives the dimensions of the array

If a storage class is specified in a declaration, its keyword must come first;[1] the data type may then be determined by default. If a data type is specified, the storage class may be determined by default. Storage class defaults were discussed in Chapter 6. The default data type is **int**.

A declaration statement acts as a definition and causes storage to be allocated unless one of the following applies:

- A declaration contains the **extern** storage class specifier.

- A declaration concerns a function parameter.

- A declaration located within a function specifies the value returned by another function.

---

[1] Brian W. Kernighan and Dennis M. Ritchie, *The C Programming Language,* (Englewood Cliffs, N. J.: Prentice-Hall, 1978), p. 192. The wording of this reference is ambiguous, but the requirement is observed as stated by most compilers.

- A declaration designates only the organization associated with a structure tag.

Only two fundamental data types have been presented thus far, **int** and **char**. Two other fundamental types, **float** and **double**, will be discussed in Chapter 16. The C language has three data type modifiers, **long**, **short**, and **unsigned**, with the following standard combinations:

> **short int**
> **long int**
> **unsigned int**
> **long float**

Some C compilers allow additional combinations; usually only one modifier is allowed. When a data type modifier is used in a declaration, the data type's keyword can be omitted; by default, **int** will be assumed.

After the specification of a storage class and a data type or structure organization in a declaration statement come one or more identifiers, separated by commas, that are declared to have the specified storage class and data type or structure organization. It is good practice to write a separate declaration statement for each item declared, with a comment explaining its use or content.

In the place normally occupied by an identifier in a declaration statement there can also appear an expression involving a single identifier, together with function parentheses, array brackets and dimensions, indirection operators, and isolating parentheses, as required to describe the characteristics of an identifier. A later section of this chapter explains in detail how to compose and interpret such expressions.

The definition for an array must specify each dimension with a constant. The constant may be an expression. As an example, if DEGREES is a #define symbol, then an **int** array named minute could be defined thus:

> **int** minute[60 * DEGREES] ;

You can omit the first or only dimension constant when declaring an **extern** array or a function parameter, provided the brackets for the dimension are included, because such a declaration does not reserve storage. All dimension constants must be specified for arrays that are members of structures. An array of variable dimensions can be created in a C program only by explicit use of dynamic storage.

Declaration and definition statements for data structures were discussed in Chapter 9. The declaration of a structure can include the declaration of a structure tag, which describes its organization. A structure cannot include a copy of itself, via a structure tag, or a copy of any other structure whose organization has not yet been declared. But a structure may include a pointer to another structure of the same type or to a structure of a type that has not yet been declared, provided the organization of that structure is declared in a program before any statement that uses the pointer to it.

Subject to the conditions and limitations described above, a data declaration in C has the general form

   stclass datype iden-1, iden-2, . . . ;

In this format, **stclass** stands for a storage-class specifier, **datype** stands for a data type, including a structure organization, and **iden-1, iden-2,** and so on stand for expressions that each involve a single identifier which is being declared or defined. There is no comma after the last or only identifier in such a statement. All such statements must end with a semicolon.

□ DECLARATIONS INVOLVING FUNCTIONS

Declaring names of functions and the types of data that functions return can be a source of confusion, because the C language provides the same declaration format for this purpose as for declaring variable names and types. In C, an identifier is assumed to be a function name when it is followed immediately by an opening parenthesis.[2] Thus the first statement below declares **form** to be an **int** variable, but the second statement declares **form** to be a function that returns an **int** as its value:

```
int form ;
int form( ) ;
```

The declaration of a function's return value says nothing at all about any function arguments. It simply identifies a name as that of a function and tells what type of value will be returned. The C language requires a closing parenthesis for every opening parenthesis. A declaration for a function's return value will have both an opening and a closing parenthesis, with nothing between them.

---

[2] An exception to this rule is a macro definition, as discussed in Chapter 17, on the C preprocessor.

You've seen that an identifier immediately followed by an opening parenthesis denotes a function. When a statement outside any other function begins with this format, it is interpreted as a declaration or definition for a function that returns an **int**. When a statement including this format begins with a keyword for a data type or storage class, it is interpreted as either a declaration or a definition of the function. In all other circumstances, the appearance of this format in a statement is interpreted as invoking the function.

Unless a function has previously been declared, the first time a statement that invokes it appears, the function will be automatically declared in recognition of its use.[3] By default, it will be declared as a function returning an **int** value. The parameter names that appear between parentheses at the start of a function's definition are automatically declared to be **int** unless otherwise specified by declarations that follow immediately.[4]

The assumptions about the data types of function parameters and the values that functions return are the only automatic type declarations provided by the C language. Their use is hazardous; they leave a program internally undocumented and open to inconsistent usage. A robust program will always explicitly declare functions and their parameters; it will never rely on automatic declarations.

When one function is declared inside another function, the storage-class specifier **extern** is assumed. The C language does not allow a function definition to appear inside the definition for another function.[5] When a function is declared outside any other function, an opening brace following the parentheses marks the start of the function's defintion. The generally accepted conventions of the C language allow an **extern** declaration for a function in the same module that contains the function's definition.[6]

In most implementations of C, a function cannot receive as an argument or return as a value a data structure, an array, or another function. However, a pointer to a structure, an array, or a function may be used as a function argument or a return value. Some recent implementations of C allow structures to be used as function arguments and return values. This topic is further explored in Chapters 12, 13, and 16.

A definition for a function begins with the type of value that it returns. A function definition must be outside any data element and

[3] Kernighan and Ritchie, *The C Programming Language,* p. 68.
[4] Ibid., p. 205.
[5] Ibid., pp. 70–72.
[6] See the discussion in Chapter 6.

any other function. A function definition, unlike a declaration, names the function's parameters, if any, between the parentheses that follow the function's name. Declarations for the data types of these parameters follow the closing parenthesis. They are, in turn, followed by a block of program statements that constitute the function. This format is explained in more detail in Chapter 12, on functions and modules.

□ INTERPRETING DATA DECLARATIONS

When an identifier is a structure or an element of a fundamental data type, its declaration statement will contain, after the storage class and data type specifiers, only the identifier. This is known as a *simple* declaration. Examples of simple declarations follow:

```
int rise ;
struct LOW rise ;
```

If an identifier is an array of structures or fundamental data elements, a pointer to a structure or a fundamental data element, or a function that returns a fundamental data element, then it is written with brackets, an indirection operator, or function parentheses, respectively. These are *compound* declarations. Examples of all of them follow:

```
int cost[ ] ;
struct LOW cost[ ] ;
int *gain ;
struct LOW *gain ;
int loss( ) ;
```

A declaration for any other kind of identifier is known as a *complex* declaration. Complex declarations have more than one operator of the types just shown. They are subject to rules of interpretation and may need one or more pairs of isolating parentheses to achieve the necessary meaning. Some of the possible operator combinations are not allowed by the language. Ordinary implementations of C do not have functions returning arrays, functions returning functions, or arrays of functions, so the following declarations would all be invalid:

```
int weird( )[ ] ;
int weird( )( ) ;
int weird[ ]( ) ;
```

A *declaration expression* can be *unraveled* by a procedure that will first be shown in an example:

```
int ( *( *x[ ] )( ) )[ ] ;
```

In this declaration

(*(*x[ ])( ))[ ]	is	**int**
(*(*x[ ])( ))	is	array of **int**
*(*x[ ])( )	is	array of **int**
(*x[ ])( )	is	pointer to array of **int**
(*x[ ])	is	function returning pointer to array of **int**
*x[ ]	is	function returning pointer to array of **int**
x[ ]	is	pointer to function returning pointer to array of **int**
x	is	array of pointers to functions returning pointer to array of **int**

As explained in Chapter 13, the operations of array indexing and function invocation have priority over the indirection operator. Because of this, as you unravel a declaration, you interpret an indirection operator before you interpret array indexing or function invocation; they are more "tightly bound." If you reach a pair of isolating parentheses, you remove them. At no step should you have to deal with the invalid combinations shown above.

The *unraveling procedure* can be described by the following software outline:

Until the declaration expression is an identifier
    If there is an indirection operator
        Interpret it
        Remove it
    Else if there are array brackets
        Interpret them
        Remove them
    Else if there are function parentheses
        Interpret them
        Remove them
    Else (there are isolating parentheses)
        Remove the isolating parentheses

There is also a *raveling* procedure, the inverse of the procedure to interpret a declaration, that will construct a declaration expression from the desired interpretation. It is described by the following software outline:

Until the interpretation is a data type
    If the first operation is function formation

If there is an indirection operator
    Add isolating parentheses
Add function parentheses
Remove the function formation
Else if the first operation is array formation
    If there is an indirection operator
        Add isolating parentheses
    Add array brackets
    Remove the array formation
Else (the operation is pointer formation)
    Add an indirection operator
    Remove the pointer formation

Keep your programs easy to understand. Don't try to write a "book of ravelations." Declarations like the example that was unraveled should be avoided with the same determination as one avoids functions with excessive nesting of loops or conditions within loops or conditions. If more than one or two operations are necessary, the declaration of symbolic data types, as explained later in this chapter, can help to improve the understandability of your work.

□ SIZES AND ORDERING OF DATA

The data elements of a C program have certain sizes. Data *aggregates*— arrays and structures—have a certain order of data elements. Both of these data characteristics depend on the machine and the compiler. Most of the time, they do not concern a programmer. In order to allocate dynamic storage, however, a program must tell a storage management function the amount of storage needed. In order to use pointer arithmetic, a program may need to know the order of data elements within aggregates.

The C language provides a keyword, **sizeof**, to obtain the size of any data element, aggregate, or type. The **sizeof** operation is performed when a program is compiled. It cannot obtain the size of any aggregate whose size is variable. To obtain the amount of storage required to hold a data element or an aggregate, write **sizeof** before its identifier.

When **sizeof** operates on the name of an array or structure, it obtains the amount of storage occupied by the entire array or structure. It can also be applied to a substructure or a subarray, and it will

obtain their amounts of storage. The following examples show such
constructions:

```
int counts[ 10 ][ 20 ] ;
sizeof counts[ ]

struct TAG
{
    int number ;
    struct REG registration ;
}
    license[ 6 ] ;
sizeof license[ ].registration
```

In the first example, the size obtained is that of a subarray of 20 **int**
elements. In the second, the size obtained is that of a substructure of
type **REG**.

You can also apply **sizeof** to any expression. Be sure to place parentheses around the expression, so that **sizeof** does not operate only on
a part of it. Here are some examples of this sort:

```
sizeof ( number + 3 )
sizeof ( 7 * level[ j ] )
sizeof ( val_chk( top ) − 1 )
```

If you use an expression with **sizeof,** the expression is not evaluated when
the program runs. In the third example above, the val_chk function
would not be invoked. The only operation performed is to obtain the data
size of a value that would be provided by the expression.

Finally, **sizeof** can be applied to data types, including aggregates. A
data type is simply a declaration expression without an identifier.
Parentheses are required when you do this. The following examples
show such uses:

```
sizeof ( char * )

sizeof ( int [ 5 ] )

sizeof ( struct CON )
```

These examples provide the size of a pointer to **char,** of an array of
five **int,** and of an entire structure with the CON organization, respectively. Any data type, like those in the examples just shown, can be
used as the object of **sizeof.** Declaration expressions without identifiers have another use that will be explained in a later section.

The value of **sizeof** is stated in bytes, as explained in Chapter 5. The value of **sizeof (char)** will be equal to one.[7] The type of a **sizeof** value is not specified, except that it provides positive integers. Such a value must be able to express the difference between any two pointers that point to elements within the same array or structure. Most compilers give **unsigned int** values for **sizeof**, but certain implementations of C provide **sizeof** values of type **int**, **long int**, or **unsigned long int**.

The ordering of members of an array was discussed in Chapter 7. Briefly stated, as the value of an index increases, the value of a pointer to a member increases. For arrays with more than one dimension, the value of a pointer to a member increases fastest for the first dimension, less rapidly thereafter, and most slowly for the last dimension.

The C language does not guarantee that array members are packed. The difference in value between pointers to successive members will not necessarily equal the amount of storage occupied but will equal **sizeof**, applied to data elements or structures of the same types; this is how **sizeof** is defined. In most implementations, arrays of fundamental data elements will be packed. Arrays of structures are often not packed.

Structures are not guaranteed to be packed, and often they are not. The spacing between structure members need not follow any regular pattern. However, pointers to members of a structure will increase according to their order of appearance in a declaration of the structure's organization.[8] A pointer to the last member of an array contained in a structure will be less than a pointer to the next member of the containing structure.

□ REACH AND SCOPE OF DECLARATIONS

As explained in Chapter 6, data are potentially accessible only within a general area of a program known as the *span* of the data. Depending on how declarations are written, the span of data will be one of the following:

- *local* span, accessible only inside the block of statements within which it is declared
- *module* span, potentially accessible to functions within a single program module

---

[7] Kernighan and Ritchie, *The C Programming Language,* pp. 126, 188.
[8] Ibid., p. 196.

• *global* span, potentially accessible to all the modules in a program

Data that have global span will be inaccessible to program statements in a module unless defined or declared with the **extern** storage class specifier in that module.

The *reach* of a declaration is the portion of a program over which an identifier can be used. However, the fact that the declaration of an identifier is available to a part of a program does not mean that its declaration is actually in effect, as you will see. The parts of a program within which a particular declaration is active are known together as its *scope*. To understand the scope of a declaration, you need to know how identifiers in C are classified.

C permits the same identifier to be used for different purposes, a practice sometimes called *overloading* of identifiers. More than one use may be allowed at the same time, with a particular meaning determined by context in a program statement. When this is possible, the identifiers can be regarded as grouped into different *classes,* according to their types of use. The documentation for some compilers refers to these classes as "name spaces."

Early C compilers provided no *identifier classes;* each identifier could be used for only one purpose at any point in a program. By the mid-1970s, most compilers placed all the tags and member names of data structures in a separate class from all other identifiers. Most C compilers produced since the early 1980s maintain separate classes of identifiers for each type of structure and a separate class of identifiers for all structure tags. Some C compilers provide additional classes of identifiers.

The C language forbids redeclaration of an identifier for the same identifier class within the same level of a program. As explained in Chapter 6, data with global span must be defined exactly once, so that all **extern** declarations for an identifier will refer to the same definition. Within a module there can be only one declaration with module span. Once an identifier has been declared outside any function, it cannot be declared again for the same identifier class outside a function.

There are two minor exceptions to the injunction against redeclaration. First, the C language permits an **extern** declaration in addition to a definition for the same identifier, provided these statements are otherwise consistent.[9] Second, there can be multiple **extern** declarations for the same identifier, provided they are all consistent. Once an identifier with global span has been declared at any level, any subsequent declaration or definition in a module must be consistent.

---

[9] As noted in Chapter 6, a few C compilers violate this standard, causing portability problems.

The C language permits declarations at the start of any block of program statements, delimited by braces, including the block of statements that defines a function. Declarations of function parameters are treated as though located at the start of the main block of program statements for the function. You may place braces around one or more program statements for the sole purpose of inserting declarations at the start of a block so marked. These "internal" declarations, within a block, may include identifiers previously declared outside a block (or a function).

When an internal declaration uses fixed allocation, storage for its data is permanently reserved but is accessible only within the scope of the declaration. If an internal declaration uses automatic allocation, storage is reserved on entry to the block in which the declaration occurs.

Within a module, the reach of a declaration begins just after the statement in which the declaration appears.[10] It extends to end of the block within which it appears, including any blocks of statements that the declaring block contains. If a declaration occurs outside a function, its reach extends to the end of the module.

The scope of a declaration depends on whether an identifier is redeclared, in one of these ways:

- An identifier declared outside a function can be redeclared inside a function.

- An identifier declared within any block of statements can be redeclared inside another block of statements contained in the first.

As previously stated, once an identifier with global span has been declared, any subsequent declaration for the same identifier, using global span, must be consistent with the first. This declaration will in fact refer to the same identifier; it does not count as a redeclaration.

When an identifier is redeclared in one of these ways, the scope of the first declaration is interrupted for the reach of the second; this is called *superseding* a declaration. The scope of declaration for any identifier is its reach within a module, less those portions of the module in which it is superseded. An instance of supersession creates a "hole" in the scope of a declaration. The scope of an identifier with global span can be interrupted by an identifier with local span, and vice-versa.[11]

---

[10] In cases of doubt, most compilers interpret this reach to begin at the next semicolon at the same nesting level.

[11] Kernighan and Ritchie, *The C Programming Language*, p. 206. Unfortunately, a few C compilers incorrectly interpret the scope of an identifier with global span as extending from the point of declaration to the end of a module; these compilers will not permit redeclaration as described.

Overloading and superseding identifiers are among the riskiest adventures in any language, including that Maginot Line redoubt, Ada. Logical conundrums are easy to propound. Some of them involve the use of a previously declared identifier in declaring a new one; others revolve around the classes of identifiers provided by a particular compiler. The conventions of the C language in this area are imprecise. The results of overloading are unpredictable and will vary among compilers.

To write robust, reliable programs, then, avoid overloading and superseding identifiers. Inner declarations, at the start of a block within a function, rarely enhance the effectiveness of a program and sometimes slow it down. The naming conventions recommended in this book are aimed at minimizing confusion and maximizing the portability of your programs.

□ SYMBOLIC DATA TYPES

C provides a limited capability for programmer-defined data types. It is particularly useful for complex identifier expressions. To declare a symbol for a data type, write a statement beginning with the keyword **typedef**, followed by these components, in the order stated:

1. keywords for a fundamental data type, with data type modifiers if needed, or a declaration for a structure organization

2. a simple, compound, or complex declaration expression, as previously explained, that includes an identifier

It is possible to write more than one declaration expression for component 2, separating the expressions with commas. The identifiers they include then become **typedef** symbols.

To compose and interpret declaration expressions, use the raveling and unraveling procedures described earlier. The following are examples using **typedef**:

```
typedef char *VT_STR ;
typedef int VT_LIM[ 5 ] ;
typedef struct CON VT_DEF ;
```

The first of these declares VT_STR to be a symbol for a pointer to a **char**. The second one declares VT_LIM as a symbol for an array of five **int** members. The last declares VT_DEF as a symbol for a structure of the CON organization.

To declare data using a **typedef** symbol, begin a statement with the symbol and follow it with one or more identifiers, separated by commas. For example, the following declarations have the same effect:

```
int vt_limit[ 5 ] ;
```

```
typedef int VT_LIM[ 5 ] ;
VT_LIM vt_limit ;
```

The effect of such a declaration is to repeat the specifications found in the **typedef** statement, substituting for the **typedef** symbol the identifier being declared.

You cannot use a storage class specifier in a **typedef** statement. Like a structure tag, a symbolic data type does not carry information about storage classes. Where such a specifier is needed, it should precede a **typedef** symbol in a declaration. In the preceding example, if the **static** specifier were needed, the declaration using the **typedef** symbol would be written as

```
static VT_LIM vt_limit ;
```

The identifiers declared with **typedef** symbols can be contained in declaration expressions, as shown in the following example:

```
typedef struct
{
  int byc_tires ;
  int byc_tubes ;
  int byc_nuts ;
}
  BYC ;
BYC *bicycle[ 20 ]
```

This example declares bicycle to be an array of 20 pointers to structures. The effect of such a declaration will be the same as substituting the declaration expression in place of the **typedef** symbol, in the **typedef** definition.

Like other symbols, **typedef** symbols should be composed of all uppercase letters, to distinguish them from data and function names. As discussed in Chapter 8 and subsequent chapters, pointers must be used with special precautions. It is therefore recommended that **typedef** symbols be restricted to data organizations and that pointers to these organizations be explicitly specified within a declaration that uses a **typedef** symbol.

The scope of a **typedef** symbol is determined in the same way as the scope of other identifiers. Most C compilers place **typedef** symbols in the same identifier class as variable names. A few provide a special identifier class. It should be pointed out that the ability to create symbols for data types does not provide any new operations upon the data so declared. The **typedef** facility is simply a shorthand for data declarations that could be accomplished in other ways.

Occasionally, it is necessary for a statement to convert a value to a specific data type. This occurs most often when invoking functions. For example, if an **int** value is available, but the function to be invoked expects a **long int** argument, conversion is needed. One simple method is to assign the value to be converted to a variable of the type required. The C language also provides a general conversion operator, called a *cast*.

To create a cast operator, place in parentheses before the item to be converted a data type or structure organization, that is, a declaration expression without an identifier. This is the same form of type specification used with the **sizeof** operator. Perhaps the most common use of a cast is to specify a null pointer for a function argument, for example:

```
nx = vt_n( 3, ( char * ) 0 ) ;
```

The second argument is a null pointer to **char**, specified by using a cast operator.

Cast operators may be applied to constants in #**define** symbols. For example, it is common to find the symbol NULL defined by

```
#define NULL ( char * ) 0
```

Programmers sometimes assume this definition is provided by the stdio.h header file that is used with many C library functions. Some C implementations, however, provide this definition instead:

```
#define NULL 0
```

An error would occur on many computers if you used such a symbol for a null pointer, as in this statement:

```
nx = vt_n( 3, NULL ) ;
```

The availability of cast operators introduces an ambiguity into certain uses of **sizeof**. This occurs when you write an expression with **sizeof**, as applied to a data type, that has additional terms, for example:

```
nsx = sizeof ( long int ) -1 ;
```

Such a statement might be interpreted as the size of a **long int**, less 1, or as the size of the value -1 cast as a **long int**. A special convention of the C language provides that a parenthesized expression following **sizeof** denotes what is operated on by **sizeof**,[12] so that the first interpretation applies.

Cast operators are rarely necessary in C programs and should generally be avoided. They are sometimes used for "converting" a pointer to one type of data so that it will be a pointer to another type of data. This practice may be helpful as internal program documentation, but it does not make your program work any better. If the specific value of a pointer to one data type would be invalid for data of a different type, the "conversion" will take place without a problem, but an error will occur when the pointer value is used. The C language does not limit the machine representation of pointers, and it does not provide a general mechanism for pointer conversion.

The one generally acceptable use of a cast to "convert" pointers is with the **malloc** storage allocation function, available in most C implementations. This function returns a pointer to a storage area that is guaranteed to be usable for any type of data organization. It is nominally typed as returning a pointer to **char**. Often, a program will need dynamic storage for uses other than **char**. To avoid conflicting declarations for **malloc** but maintain consistency of types in pointer assignments, it is advisable to use a cast when assigning the value returned by **malloc**, as in the following example:

```
extern char *malloc( ) ;
int libsz ;
struct LIB
{
   char *lib_author ;
   char *lib_title ;
   char *lib_callno ;
   struct DT *lib_acq_date ;
}
   *newvol ;
libsz = sizeof ( struct LIB);
newvol = ( struct LIB * ) malloc( libsz ) ;
```

Here, **newvol** receives the pointer returned by **malloc**, regarded as a pointer to a structure of the **LIB** organization.

---

[12] Ibid., p. 188.

□ EXERCISES

10.1: Figure 10.1 shows three functions with a number of variables. Describe the class, declaration block, type, span, reach, and scope of each identifier.

```
extern int k[ KDIM ] ;                              /* 1*/
extern int scale( ) ;                               /* 2*/
int silver( i, j, m )                               /* 3*/
int i[ IDIM, JDIM ] ;                               /* 4*/
int j[ JDIM, KDIM ] ;                               /* 5*/
int m[ IDIM, KDIM ] ;                               /* 6*/
{                                                   /* 7*/
    int mupac( ), k, kk ;                           /* 8*/
    k = mupac( i, j, m ) ;                          /* 9*/
    {                                               /*10*/
        extern int k[ KDIM ] ;                      /*11*/
        kk = scale( m, k ) ;                        /*12*/
    }                                               /*13*/
    return k + kk ;                                 /*14*/
}                                                   /*15*/
int mupac( a, b, c )                                /*16*/
int a[ IDIM, JDIM ] ;                               /*17*/
int b[ JDIM, KDIM ] ;                               /*18*/
int c[ IDIM, KDIM ] ;                               /*19*/
{                                                   /*20*/
    int i, j, k ;                                   /*21*/
    for ( i = 0 ; i < IDIM ; i = i + 1 )            /*22*/
        for ( k = 0 ; k < KDIM ; k = k + 1 )        /*23*/
            for ( j = 0 ; j < JDIM ; j = j + 1 )/*24*/
                c[ i, k ] = c[ i, k ]               /*25*/
                    + a[ i, j ] * b[ j, k ] ;       /*26*/
    return i * k ;                                  /*27*/
}                                                   /*28*/
int scale( n, k )                                   /*29*/
int n[ IDIM, KDIM ] ;                               /*30*/
int k[ KDIM ] ;                                     /*31*/
{                                                   /*32*/
    int i, j ;                                      /*33*/
    for ( i = 0 ; i < IDIM ; i = i + 1 )            /*34*/
        for ( j = 0 ; j < KDIM ; j = j + 1 )        /*35*/
            n[ i, j ] = n[ i, j ] * k[ j ] ;        /*36*/
    return i * j ;                                  /*37*/
}                                                   /*38*/
```

Figure 10.1: *An example containing several identifiers.*

10.2: Declarations in each of the following short sets of statements won't work. Identify the problems.

(a)

```
int merry( a, go )
{
   int ho, hum ;
   hum = a * go( ho ) ;
```

(b)

```
char ( lady( ) )[ 8 ] ;
int **imate[ ] ;
```

(c)

```
struct
{ struct
   { int *a[ 8 ][ ] ;
      char **b ;
   } ; int c ;
} apple ;
```

(d)

```
int happy( hours, lost )
char hours[ lost ] ;
{
   int asa, lark( )
   {
      extern int asa ;
      asa = lark( ) ;
   }
```

(e)

```
int all( mixedup ) ;
char ( **mixedup )[ ] ;
{
```

(f)

```
char ( *long )( ) ;
int a, b ; char d ;
```

(g)

```
extern crystal( lake ) ;
static lake[ ][ ] ;
```

(h)

```
typedef struct RAG
{
    int loop ;
    struct RAG *purl[ ] ;
    RAG *knot ;
} ;
```

10.3: Use the raveling and unraveling procedures described in this chapter to compose and interpret the following declaration expressions:

(a) `int ( *g[ ] )( ) ;`

(b) g is a pointer to a function returning a pointer to **int**

(c) `int ( *( *g( ) )[ ] )( ) ;`

(d) g is a function returning a pointer to an array of functions returning **int**

(e) `int **( *g[ ] )[ ] ;`

(f) g is an array of arrays of pointers to functions returning pointers to **int**

10.4: Certain declarations permitted in C can be difficult to interpret. Investigate the meanings of each of the following examples:

(a)

```
struct TAG
{
    int *price ;
    char car ;
}

int confound( )
{
    struct TAG
    {
        struct TAG *tag ;
        char *dog ;
    } kennel ;
    . . .
}
```

In this example, within the **confound** function, is a reference to **kennel.tag –>dog** valid? Or, instead, is **kennel.tag –>price** valid?

(b)

```
extern char *preclude( ) ;

static char *require( )
{
   . . .
   lax = preclude( ) ;
   . . .
}

static char *preclude( )
{
   . . .
   vain = require( ) ;
   . . .

}
```

In this example, two functions invoke each other. They return values other than **int**, so at least one must be declared with **extern**. Yet both are to be **static**. Is this possible? If so, how can it be arranged?

(c)

```
static char *recurse( )
{
   . . .
   {
      extern int recurse( ) ;
      . . .
   }
   . . .
}
```

Within the **static recurse** function, there is a block that attempts to redeclare the identifier **recurse**, in order to use a different function, outside the module, with the same name but a different return value. Will this be allowed? If so, what will happen when **recurse** is invoked within the internal block?

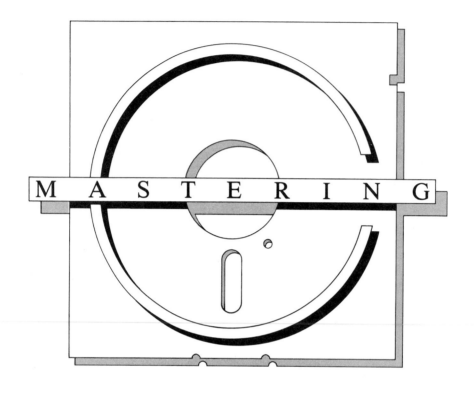

CHAPTER 11

DEFINING INITIAL VALUES

A program written in C can establish initial values for its data. These values are specified as part of definition statements for data elements, arrays, and structures. In this chapter, you will read about:

- forms of initial values

- requirements for initializers

- initializing arrays

- initializing data structures

- initializing automatic data

□ FORMS OF INITIAL VALUES

Statements that define data may also give them *initial values*. When a definition statement uses a simple declaration expression, an initial value specification looks like an assignment. Initial values are most useful for **static** data, as shown in the following examples:

```
static int number = 6 ;
```

```
static char virgule = '/' ;
```

To give an initial value to a data element in a definition statement, after the identifier name (or the declaration expression that contains an identifier name), write an equal sign followed by a value.

Initial values may be specified as expressions; these expressions can be formed using the same operations that can occur in expressions in assignment statements, for example:

```
#define MILS 20
static int value = 1728 / 3 + 27 ;
static int msize = ( MILS / 4 ) * sizeof ( int ) ;
```

The same values could be assigned to the variables by ordinary assignment statements in a program:

```
value = 1728 / 3 + 27 ;
msize = ( MILS / 4 ) * sizeof ( int ) ;
```

In a declaration statement that has a compound or complex declaration expression, the appearance of an identifier with its initializer will not match the equivalent assignment statement. For example, to define a pointer to **int** named fungus and assign as its value the location of member 21 of a previously declared array of **int** named mycotrope, you might write

static int *fungus = &mycotrope[21] ;

If the same form were used for an assignment statement in a program, the statement would assign the pointer value to an **int** whose location was given by fungus, rather than to the pointer fungus itself. An assignment statement equivalent to the above initialization would be written thus:

fungus = &mycotrope[21] ;

The indirection operator does not appear in this statement.

□ REQUIREMENTS FOR INITIALIZERS

The data types of a variable and its initial value should match. Otherwise, the initial value will be converted to the variable's data type. The matching must be carefully observed when assigning an initial value to a pointer. An initial value that is defined for a pointer with fixed allocation must be processed by a linker as well as a C compiler. Because of the limitations of linkers, you should not attempt to use any expression more complex than a location, plus or minus an integer constant.

You can construct pointer constants by applying the reference operator to the name of a data element or structure that has fixed allocation. The following examples both initialize pointers:

extern struct MAP xtp_route ;
extern int pla_locus[200] ;

static struct MAP *star = &xtp_route ;
static int *start = pla_locus + 32 ;

In the first example, a pointer to a **MAP** structure is initialized to the location of a structure of the same type. In the second, a pointer to an integer is initialized to the location of one member of an integer array, using an expression involving pointer arithmetic. In these examples, both the pointers and the data aggregates to which they point have fixed allocation.

As explained in Chapters 7 and 8, the name of a function or an array is a pointer constant. A name must always be declared before it can be used for a pointer constant. Consider this example:

extern int ref_locate( ) ;
static int (*finder)( ) = ref_locate ;

Here, the location of ref_locate becomes the initial value of finder, a **static** pointer to a function that returns an **int**. If ref_locate is to be used as a pointer constant, it must previously have been declared as the name of a function. Such a declaration could be provided either by an **extern** statement, as shown, or by previous definition of the function within the same module.

Initial values are assigned when storage for data is reserved. For data with fixed allocation, this step will occur before a program begins to run. By default, fixed data without specified initial values are initialized to the integer value zero. For data with automatic allocation, storage is reserved and initial values are set on entry to the function or block in which the data are defined. Automatic data without specified initial values have undefined values until a program assigns them.

In addition to the requirement for matching data types and initial values, C has several other rules for initial values. They specify when an initializer is permitted and what can be included in an initializing expression. These rules can be summarized as follows:

- An initial value may appear only in a statement that defines data. A declaration that includes the **extern** storage class specifier cannot also include an initializer.[1]

- An initial value may not be defined for a function or for a function parameter.[2]

- The elements of initializing expressions for data with fixed allocation may only be literal constants, previously specified #define symbols, **sizeof** applied to data types, or pointers to data with fixed allocation whose scope of declaration includes the statement with an initializing expression. They may not invoke functions or affect the values of data other than the datum being initialized.

- The elements of initializing expressions for data with automatic allocation may use, in addition, any identifier whose scope of declaration includes the statement with an initializing expression. They may invoke functions and affect the values of data other than the datum being initialized.

---

[1] Brian Kernighan and Dennis M. Ritchie, *The C Programming Language,* (Englewood Cliffs, N.J.: Prentice-Hall, 1978), p. 77.

[2] Ibid., p. 205, implies that initializers are allowed with function parameters, but such a use would defeat the purpose of a parameter.

- Structures and arrays may be initialized only when they have fixed allocation.

Just as you can write more than one identifier in a declaration, you can also initialize more than one identifier, as in these examples:

int abb = 2, bbc = 3, bcc = 6 ;

char period = '.', asterisk = '*' ;

To continue a declaration statement, place a comma after the initial value expression and write another declaration expression. This technique is not often useful. In a well documented program, each variable will have its own definition statement, with a comment explaining its content and use.

□ INITIALIZING ARRAYS

A one-dimensional array is initialized by a list of values, separated by commas and enclosed in braces. The following example uses integer constants to initialize all 12 members of the **holiday** array:

```
static int holiday[ 12 ] =
{
      1,   15,   43,   73,   97, 147,
    172, 185, 218, 268, 304, 332
} ;
```

You may supply fewer values than the number of members in an array. If you do, the values you specify are applied from the start of the array. The remaining, unspecified members of a **static** array have initial values of integer zero.

A dangling comma is permitted after the last value in an initializer list.[3] The braces that enclose the list do not delineate a block of program statements. There must be either a comma after the closing brace, to continue the declaration statement, or a semicolon, to indicate the end of the declaration statement. The format shown in the foregoing example is recommended, as it increases the visibility of punctuation and the readability of an initializer list.

An array of more than one dimension is initialized as an array of subarrays. This concept and the ordering of members in an array were

---

[3] Ibid., p. 198. However, some compilers reject this.

discussed in Chapter 7. Each subarray has a list of initializers, enclosed by inner braces; the sublists are separated by commas. In the following example, **season** is initialized as a four-member array of three-member arrays:

```
static int season[ 4 ][ 3 ] =
{
    {   1,  15,  43 },
    {  73,  97, 147 },
    { 172, 185, 218 },
    { 268, 304, 332 }
} ;
```

With higher-dimension arrays or more initializers, a fully indented format similar to that used with program statements helps to show the array structure.

As with one-dimensional arrays, you may specify fewer values within a sublist than there are members of the corresponding subarray. Also, fewer sublists may be specified than there are subarrays. All **static** array members that are left unspecified by short lists will have initial values of integer zero.

A list of initial values may be used to determine the first (or only) dimension of an array.[4] Normally, when defining an array, you must specify each dimension with a constant. If a definition includes initial values, however, you can simply write the array brackets for the first (or only) dimension and omit the dimension constant. A C compiler will count the number of initial values and create a first dimension just large enough to hold them all. The linear and two-dimensional arrays used as earlier examples can be defined in this way:

```
static int holiday[ ] =
{
     1,  15,  43,  73,  97, 147,
   172, 185, 218, 268, 304, 332
} ;
static int season[ ][ 3 ] =
{
    {   1,  15,  43 },
    {  73,  97, 147 },
```

---

[4] Ibid., p. 84., is imprecise as to arrays with more than one dimension; most compilers behave as stated.

```
    { 172, 185, 218 },
    { 268, 304, 332 }
} ;
```

When you use an indeterminate first dimension, you can retrieve the value of the dimension length by using an expression involving **sizeof**. As noted in Chapter 10, when **sizeof** is applied to an array or an array data type, its value is the amount of storage required for the entire array or array type. Dividing this value by **sizeof** applied to an array member or major subarray gives the dimension length. For the previous examples, you could write

```
n_holidays = sizeof holiday / sizeof ( int ) ;
n_seasons = sizeof season / sizeof ( int [ 3 ] ) ;
```

The value of n_holidays will be equal to 12, and the value of n_seasons will be equal to 4.

The value obtained by **sizeof** is defined so that such expressions will always be correct.[5] Thus, whether or not an array is packed, when using dynamic storage you can always determine the amount of storage needed for an array by multiplying the number of members by **sizeof**, applied to the data type of an array member.

When initializing an array of more than one dimension, you may omit part or all of the inner braces. If you omit all of them, the array members are initialized in the order in which they appear in the array, as discussed in Chapter 7. With this approach, the season array from previous examples could be initialized thus:

```
static int season[ 4 ][ 3 ] =
{
      1,  15,  43,  73,  97, 147,
    172, 185, 218, 268, 304, 332
} ;
```

If you choose to omit some but not all of the inner braces when listing initial values for a multidimensional array, a C compiler will keep track of the nesting depth of your braces. Each open brace will be taken to mark the start of values for the next subarray of the corresponding depth. A partially subdivided list of initalizers may be handy for initializing a small fraction of a large array, but it is generally difficult to write and interpret.

---

[5] Ibid., p. 126.

At any level of an array, it is an error to specify too many initial values. The sole exception to this rule is made for the first (or only) dimension, when the dimension constant is omitted and the compiler is determining the array size. You may place braces around an initializer for a single data element or a single array member. It is an error, however, to provide a nesting depth of braces that exceeds the number of array dimensions by more than one.

As discussed in Chapters 7 and 8, a quoted string is equivalent to a character array. Its value is a pointer giving the location of an array containing the characters specified between quotation marks, plus a terminating null character. Both the pointer value and the characters are constants. You can initialize an array of pointers to **char** with quoted strings, as in Figure 11.1. Here, the array dimension is indeterminate. The value of **sizeof** droll / **sizeof (char *)** would be 8. The value of *(droll[2] + 1) == 'f' would be 1.

```
static char *droll[ ] =
{
    "'It seems a shame,' the Walrus said,",
    "  'To play them such a trick.",
    "After we've brought them out so far,",
    "  And made them trot so quick!'",
    "The Carpenter said nothing but",
    "  'The butter's spread too thick!'",
    "          -- Lewis Carroll",
    "          The Walrus and the Carpenter"
} ;
```

Figure 11.1: *Initializing an array of pointers to* **char** *with quoted strings.*

Initializing an array of pointers to **char** is sometimes called creating a "ragged array," as though one had made a two-dimensional **char** array in which the dimension of each subarray varied with the length of data. Keep in mind, however, that the data in the initialized array are pointers, not characters. The characters in the strings are constants, not values of variables. You can use their values, but you must not try to change them. On some machines, an error will occur if your program tries to do so.

As first mentioned in Chapter 7, a **char** array can be assigned initial values using a string, for example:

static char lemma[50] = "Eye of the Pig" ;

C provides a special interpretation for such a statement.[6] The string characters go into the **char** array, starting with its first member. At least one null character is supplied as a string terminator. Any remaining characters in the array will also have values of integer zero.

When an array of **char** (not **char ∗**) is initialized by a string, no pointers are created, and the string characters are not constants but values of the specified array. This form of initialization is a convenience. The last example could also have been specified in this way:

static char lemma[50] =
{
  'E', 'y', 'e', ' ', 'o', 'f', ' ',
  't', 'h', 'e', ' ', 'P', 'i', 'g', 0
} ;

An indeterminate dimension can be used with string initialization. For the example just shown (in either form), if the dimension constant of the array were omitted, the dimension would be 15. One byte with the integer value zero is always placed at the end of specified string characters.

You cannot use indeterminate dimensions for subarrays that are initialized by strings. Consider Figure 11.2. It is not a "ragged array"; exactly 40 characters are reserved for each subarray. Unspecified characters have binary zero for an initial value. The second dimension must be specified, and it must be at least 40, because each subarray must be large enough to hold the longest string. The first dimension can be indeterminate; for this example it is eight. If the inner braces had been

```
static char drawl[ ] [ 40 ] =
{
    { "'It seems a shame,' the Walrus said," } ,
    { "  'To play them such a trick."        } ,
    { "After we've brought them out so far,"  } ,
    { "  And made them trot so quick!'"       } ,
    { "The Carpenter said nothing but"        } ,
    { "  'The butter's spread too thick!'"    } ,
    { "          -- Lewis Carroll"            } ,
    { "            The Walrus and the Carpenter" }
} ;
```

Figure 11.2: *An array whose subarrays are initialized by strings.*

[6] Ibid., p. 84.

omitted, the result would be the same. When a string constant appears as an initializer, it is treated as the equivalent of a list, in braces, of single character values, ending with a null character.[7]

□ INITIALIZING DATA STRUCTURES

A data structure may be initialized by a list of values matching the order and types of its members. As an example, the members of the following structure are initialized as shown:

```
extern char *chk_citation( ) ;

static struct TOP
{
    int top_count ;
    char *top_title ;
    char *( *top_lookup )( ) ;
}
    topic =
{
    NEM_NER,
    "Nerves of Nematodes",
    chk_citation
} ;
```

When you need to initialize a structure that contains another structure, you should write sublists for each inner structure. Such sublists look like those for arrays of more than one dimension, except that a structure may have values of different types. Use a fully indented format, similar to that of program statements, to keep the organization of your list clear.

Uninitialized members of a structure with fixed allocation have integer zero as an initial value. It is an error to specify more values than there are structure members. When an array is a structure member, a sublist should be used to specify the array members. To initialize an array of structures, you should write an outer list for the array and inner lists for the structures that are members of it.

As with arrays, you may omit some or all of the inner braces when initializing a complex structure or a combination of structures and arrays; a C compiler will keep track of the nesting depth of your

---

[7] Ibid., pp. 84, 199. Some compilers do not accept braces around string constants.

braces. Each open brace will be interpreted as the start of the next sub-array or substructure. Except for very small structures, however, this facility makes a program particularly hazardous to write and painful to read. It should usually be avoided.

□ INITIALIZING AUTOMATIC DATA

The generally accepted specifications of the C language do not allow initial values in declarations for arrays or structures with automatic allocation.[8] Initial values for variables with automatic allocation are more general in form than those for variables with fixed allocation. While initial values for fixed data may include only constants, those for automatic data may also use variables and functions. In fact, initial values for automatic data can include any expression that would be valid in an assignment statement.

One problem with the intialization of automatic data is that the scope of a variable used to obtain an initial value must include the initializing declaration. Consider the following example:

```
int tempus = 4 ;

char *fugit( locus, thermis )
int locus ;
char *( *thermis )( ) ;
{
   int tempus = 2 ;
   char *sol = ( *thermis )( tempus ) ;
   . . .
```

In this example, sol obtains an initial value by invoking the thermis function, using tempus as an argument. As shown, tempus has just been set to an initial value of 2. However, tempus is also a global variable, with an initial value of 4. If declarations of sol and tempus are interchanged, an initial value of sol will be obtained with the global tempus, rather than the tempus that is local to the fugit function.

As this example shows, the initialization of automatic data is fragile, because it is performed before all the data declarations on which it may depend have become stable. Initializing automatic data adds nothing to program efficiency, because exactly the same work is performed for initialization as for assignment statements. The initializations of the

---

[8] Ibid., p. 198. A few compilers permit one or both types of automatic aggregates to be initialized.

previous example are equivalent to the following:

```
int tempus = 4 ;

char *fugit( locus, thermis )
int locus ;
char *( *thermis )( ) ;
{
    int tempus ;
    char *sol ;

    . . .

    tempus = 2 ;
    sol = ( *thermis )( tempus ) ;

    . . .
```

Here, the manipulation of the variables is an obvious part of the function, rather than a partly concealed feature of its declarations. Since all variables have been declared, no ambiguity can result from supersession.

Because of the potential for misinterpretation, you will generally write more reliable programs by avoiding the use of initialization for automatic data. If you initialize automatic data at all, constant values are much safer than those involving variables or functions.

□ EXERCISES

11.1: Sometimes it's necessary to make a "ragged array" in which character strings are assigned to variables, instead of being constants that cannot be changed.

(a) Find a way to accomplish this. You will find it necessary to use pointers.

(b) Discover how to extend the method so that you can initialize data organizations that represent, for example, groups of paragraphs of lines of text.

11.2: Review Figure 9.8, the diagram using names of composers that appeared as an illustration of a binary tree structure.

(a) Write data definitions that initialize data structures for this organization, using pointers.

(b) What constraints on writing initializations are imposed by the binary tree data organization?

(c) Write a program to read in the organization contents from a text file, using the **cmp_add** function shown in Chapter 9 and adding a **cmp_compare** function to perform an alphabetic comparison.

(d) When is initialization practical for a connective data organization? What are its implications for testing, documentation, and maintenance?

11.3: Sometimes initialization statements can be difficult to write or confusing to interpret. Consider the following short sets of statements and find the problems.

(a)

```
extern struct STP *stp_locate( ) ;
struct STP *search( ) = stp_locate ;
```

(b)

```
static char *loqua[ ][ 12 ] =
{
    { "salamander", },
    { "muskellunge", ),
    { "verbena", },
    { "archiannelid" }
} ;
```

(c)

```
char *seraglio = "\"Xanadu\" ;
```

(d)

```
char *ha[ ] =
{
    "prawns",
    "potatoes",
    "parsnips",
} ;
char *has[ ] =
{ ha, ha + 1, ha + 2, ha + 3 } ;
char ***hash = &has ;
```

(e)
```
int *( carob[ ] )( ) ;
int *( pod )( )
   = &carob
```

(f)
```
struct
{
    int x, y, z ;
    char a, *b ;
} *wyr =
{
  1, 5, 7,
  "v", "34"
} ;
```

PART 3

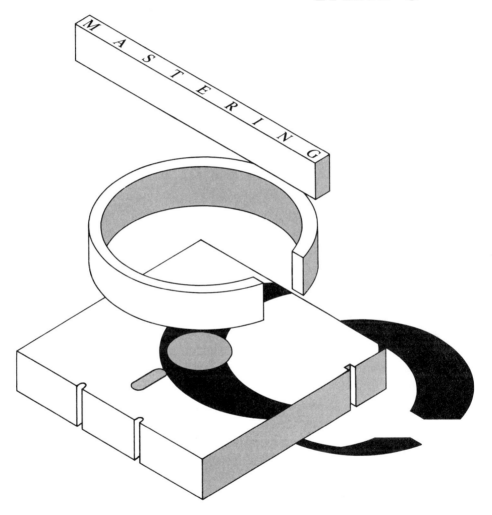

PROGRAM STRUCTURE

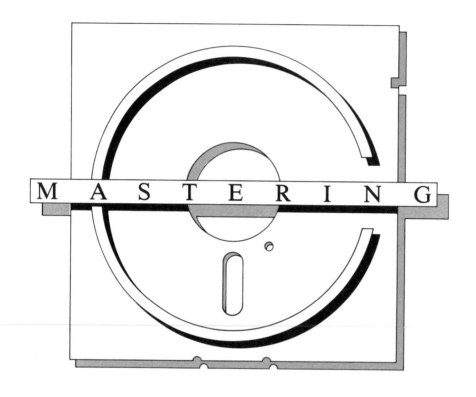

MASTERING

CHAPTER 12

FUNCTIONS AND MODULES

Functions are the individual actors of a C program. Normally performing together in modules and larger assemblies, they are the smallest complete entities of a program. In this chapter, you will read about:

- functions as program procedures

- declaring and defining functions

- parameters and return values

- invoking functions

- pointers to functions

- storage allocation and recursion

- designing program modules

- C library functions

☐ FUNCTIONS AS PROGRAM PROCEDURES

Like most other procedural languages, C applies the concept of a single control path. Languages of this type generate programs that are structured as linked *procedures*. A procedure has these characteristics:

- It must be invoked by an explicit action of another procedure.

- It may receive information from and return information to the procedure that invoked it.

- It may invoke other procedures.

- All actions of a program are performed under the control of a procedure.

- Only one procedure controls a program's actions at any time.

- A procedure's actions are performed under the direction of *executable statements,* which operate in a specific sequence.

- Only one executable statement is active at any time.

- A procedure maintains a record of the procedure that invoked it and can return control to that procedure.

Some languages, such as Pascal, FORTRAN, and PL/I, have more than one type of procedure. Distinctions between types of procedures are generally based on whether they can modify information received when invoked and whether they are able to return a single value of information. The C language has only one type of procedure, known as a *function*. C functions have the following characteristics, described in detail in later sections of this chapter:

- A C function can have one or more information-transfer variables, with local span, known as *parameters*.

- A statement that invokes a function specifies values for parameters, if any, by means of *arguments*. Parameters of a function will receive copies of these arguments.

- A function can provide one value to the invoking function when it exits, known as its *return value*.

- Invocations of functions, or *function references*, can appear as components of expressions in C statements. They have the value that is returned by the function invoked.

- Functions may declare other variables with restricted scope, in addition to parameters, that become available when they are invoked.

- A function in C has only one point of entry, but it may have more than one exit. The invoking function receives no special indication about the point of exit.

- A function in C may invoke itself, or it may be invoked by a function it has invoked, a process known as *recursion*.

Outside a function, the C language permits only declarations of identifiers, data, and data organizations. All program operations and all executable statements must be contained inside functions. Any C program begins execution at the start of one of its functions. In most C environments, this function is identified by the name **main**. Other functions in a program are executed as they are invoked.

The form of a C function and the form of a statement that invokes a function are illustrated by Figure 12.1. Here, the **evaluate** function is invoked because of its appearance in a statement of the invoking function. It has one parameter, named **parm**. When **evaluate** receives control, the value of **parm** will be equal to the current value of the argument—that is, to the most recent contents of **arg**—in the invoking function. Upon return, **value**, in the invoking function, will receive the most recent contents of **datum**, in the **evaluate** function.

```
    int value ;      /* result of evaluate     */
    int arg ;        /* argument for evaluate  */
                     /* declaration of evaluate */
    int evaluate( ) ;

    . . .
                     /* invoke evaluate function */
    value = evaluate( arg ) ;

    . . .

                     /* define evaluate function */
int evaluate( parm )
int parm ;
{
    int datum ;      /* variable in evaluate   */

    . . .

    return datum ;   /* return value of evaluate */
}
```

Figure 12.1: *A function and the statement that invokes it.*

□ DECLARING AND DEFINING FUNCTIONS

Declarations of C functions closely resemble declarations of variables, but the names of functions are subject to several restrictions that do not apply to the names of data. In a C statement, a name is recognized as a function name when it is immediately followed by an opening parenthesis. A function name can be used in only four ways:

1. in its declaration or definition

2. to invoke the function

3. for the value of a pointer to a function

4. as an argument when invoking a function

Uses 3 and 4 are possible only within the scope of a previous function definition or declaration.

A function is declared by specifying the type of value it returns and by adding a pair of parentheses after the identifier. In most implementations of C, both the parameters and the return values of functions are limited to data elements and pointers. A declaration resembles the following example:

extern int evaluate( ) ;

Here, **evaluate** is declared to be the name of a function, defined elsewhere, that returns an **int** value.

A function definition begins like a declaration but has these additional characteristics:

- A function definition must occur outside any other function.

- A function definition must stand alone; it cannot be combined with any other declaration or definition in any way.

- Between the parentheses following the function name appears a list of parameter names, separated by commas, in an order that must be used when the function is invoked.

- After the closing parentheses appear declaration statements for parameters, each ended by a semicolon.

- After the declaration statements, if any, is the function body, consisting of a block of declaration statements and executable statements. The block must be enclosed in braces, even if it consists of only a single statement.

The definition of a C function resembles the following example:

```
int evaluate( parm )
int parm ;
{
    int datum

    . . .

    return datum ;
}
```

Here, **evaluate** is declared to be the name of a function that returns an **int** value. This function has a parameter, **parm**, of type **int**. The function definition has an additional **int** variable, **datum**, that is used to hold the value returned by a **return** statement. A block of statements constituting a function is written like any other statement block; it is not followed by a semicolon.

The definition of a function will sometimes have a more complicated appearance, when the declaration expression for the return value is complex, as in the following example:

```
int ( *( *vector( prm ) )[ ] )( )
int *prm ;
{
    . . .
}
```

This example shows a function, named vector, that has one parameter, prm, which is a pointer to an **int**. The vector function returns a pointer to an array of pointers to functions that return **int** values.

The only storage class specifiers that may be used in function declarations and definitions are **static** and **extern**. These affect only span and not allocation; all functions have fixed allocation. When **static** is specified, a function name has module span.[1] When **extern** is specified, it has global span. When neither is specified, but the function name was previously declared or defined, it has the span established earlier. Otherwise, a function name has global span by default. It is an error to specify **static** after a function name has acquired global span, and it is an error to specify **extern** after a function name has acquired module span.

In a function definition, neither a storage class specifier nor a data type is required. If a data type for a return value is omitted from a function definition, the function is assumed to return an **int** value. A function declaration cannot omit both a storage class specifier and a data type; one or the other must be present. Otherwise, outside a function, the appearance of a name followed by an opening parenthesis may be interpreted as the start of a function definition, while inside a function such a construction will invoke the named function.

Whenever a statement invokes a function that has not previously been declared or defined, the function is implicitly declared to have global span and return an **int**. Suppose myzlplk is previously undeclared and the following statement appears:

```
coccyx = myzlplk( gluteus, maximus ) ;
```

The effect of this statement, aside from invoking myzlplk, is the same

---

[1] Brian W. Kernighan and Dennis M. Ritchie, *The C Programming Language,* (Englewood Cliffs, N.J.: Prentice-Hall, 1978), pp. 193, 204, and 206. This reference does not say whether a declaration using **static** is permitted if there is a subsequent declaration or definition of the **static** function, but such a construction is the only format of forward declaration consistent with the design of the language. Unfortunately, not all compilers accept it. Some that do not will accept an **extern** declaration but treat it as **static** if a **static** definition appears in the same module.

as if the following statement appeared just before the first executable
statement of the current block:

extern int myzlplk( ) ;

Any declaration of the span of a function name and the type of its
return value, including an implicit declaration, must be consistent with
any subsequent declaration and with the function's definition.

In the generally available implementations of C, identifiers for data
and functions belong to the same class. A name can be used only for a
function or an item of data, not both. It is an error to declare an identifier for data or a data type and then use it as though invoking a
function. It is also an error to declare an identifier as the name of
a function and then use it in other ways.

The reach of a function name begins after the statement in which it
is declared or defined. The reach of a definition always extends to the
end of the module in which it occurs. If a declaration occurs outside a
function, its reach extends to the end of its module. When a declaration is implicit, its reach is restricted to the block within which it
occurred, although consistency is required with any other declaration
or definition for the same function in the same module.

A function need not have any parameters. In a declaration, definition, or invocation, the parentheses that follow its name are always
required, whether or not it has parameters. Declarations of parameters
are not required as part of a function definition. If omitted, the
parameters are assumed to be **int**. When present, parameter declarations may occur in any order. They may not include identifiers other
than those in the list of parameters between parentheses. The only storage class specifier allowed in a parameter declaration is **register**.

A function is not required to return a value. A statement that
invokes a function need not use any value that is returned. Some
implementations of C provide a pseudo data type named **void**, whose
sole use is to indicate, in a declaration or definition, that a function
does not return a value. These implementations will reject any attempt
in a **void** function to return a value and any attempt to use a value
from a **void** function.

Although function definitions in C resemble data definitions to some
degree, functions are not data. As discussed later in this chapter, a
pointer mechanism is available to pass the identity of one function to
another, but function pointers do not necessarily have the same format
or content as data pointers. On some machines, particularly signal processors using the "Harvard architecture," instruction memory is logically distinct from data memory; its contents cannot be written or read

by a program. Some machines with common memory store program instructions in protected areas; attempts to address them as data will cause errors.

The resemblance of function name declarations to data name declarations in C can lead to misuse of function names. Following are some invalid uses of function names:

- applying the reference or indirection operator to the name of a function

- assigning to a function pointer anything other than the name of a function or a zero value

- exchanging a function pointer with any other type of pointer

- performing arithmetic with a function pointer

- applying the indirection operator to any pointer that has been assigned a function name as its value, for any purpose other than to invoke the function

- applying the **sizeof** operator to the name of a function

- assigning an initial value to a function in its definition

- declaring an array of functions or a structure that includes a function as a member

A few C compilers will accept some of these constructions, but their meaning is nonstandard and their use nonportable.

□ PARAMETERS AND RETURN VALUES

The parameters of a C function are variables that are given initial values when the function is invoked. These initial values are the arguments specified by the statement that invoked the function. The parameters of a function have automatic allocation and local span. A function may use parameter values or change them, without affecting anything in the invoking function.

Some languages, including FORTRAN and Pascal, distinguish between parameters that communicate values of data and those that communicate locations of data. In C, all parameters communicate values, but a parameter might be a pointer; its value, of course, would be a location. A pointer parameter can have a value that gives the location of data being used by the invoking function.

By means of the indirection operator, a function can inspect and make changes to data whose locations are provided by pointer parameters. In this way, a function can exchange, with an invoking function, data other than those communicated directly by its parameters and its return value. As an example, repeated from Chapter 8, the following statement invokes a function with two pointer arguments:

```
zeroct = val_check( spot, len, &smin, &smax ) ;
```

A portion of the corresponding function definition, using the pointer parameters, is shown below:

```
int val_check( value, length, minimum, maximum )
int value[ ] ;
int length ;
int *minimum ;
int *maximum ;
{
    int datum ;
    . . .
    if ( datum < *minimum )
        *minimum = datum ;
    if ( datum > *maximum )
        *maximum = datum ;
    . . .
}
```

Here, minimum and maximum are declared as pointer parameters of the val_check function. Using the indirection operator, val_check inspects and changes smin and smax, maintained by the invoking function.

The C language does not allow the declaration of parameters in the declaration of a function. It does not check to see that the number, order, and types of arguments correspond to those of function parameters. It does not convert arguments to the data types of parameters. When parameter information is available from a function definition in the same module, some C compilers may detect and report mismatches, but any such information is purely advisory. Correct use of C function parameters is entirely the responsibility of the programmer. Data types of return values are declared, and they will be converted in the same ways that any other values are converted in an executable statement.

As discussed in Chapters 7 and 8, pointers are often used to give functions access to the data contained in arrays. To manipulate a linear array, a parameter can be declared as either a pointer or an array type. For example, the following statements set up equivalent definitions for the **inspect** function:

```
char *inspect( van )          char *inspect( van )
char *van ;                   char van[ ] ;
{                             {
```

The function declaring an array can manipulate data with pointers, and the function declaring a pointer can manipulate data with array indexing. The following statements are valid for both examples:

```
char t ;                      char t ;
t = van[ 3 ] ;                t = *( van + 3 ) ;
```

Because the value of an array name is a pointer to its first member, it should not be surprising that when a parameter is declared as an array, it can be manipulated using pointer arithmetic. Nonetheless, it may be surprising that when a parameter is declared to be a pointer it can be indexed like an array. However, this construction is specifically permitted in C.[2] Its most common use is to manipulate pointer parameters in functions. For any pointer value **pval** and **int** value **index,** the following expressions are equivalent:

pval[index]

*(pval + index)

To use pointer parameters for multidimensional arrays in such a way that a function correctly accounts for all the dimensions, a parameter declaration must include all dimension lengths except the first. Suppose you are working with this two-dimensional array:

int rivet[3][5] ;

Following the concepts explained in Chapter 7, **rivet** is a three-member array of five-member arrays of **int**. Because an array name is a pointer to its first member, when you use **rivet** alone as a function argument, you are specifying a pointer to the first five-member array. This information can be given in the declaration for a corresponding function parameter, **privet**, in either of the following ways:

int privet[ ][5] ;

---

[2] Ibid., p. 210.

```
int ( *privet )[ 5 ] ;
```

Having done this, you could use any of the following expressions to address the array members, where i and j are **int**:

```
privet[ i ][ j ]

( *( privet + i ) )[ j ]

*( *( privet + i ) + j )
```

Sometimes it is undesirable to have a C compiler handle array dimensions. When a dynamically allocated array has variable dimensions, this will be impossible, because C accepts only constants for dimension lengths in declarations. As shown in Chapter 8, there is an alternative: declare a function parameter as a pointer to the data type of array members, and perform pointer arithmetic instead of indexing. In the example just shown, the correct pointer argument with which to invoke a function would be

```
&rivet[ 0 ][ 0 ]
```

This expression is literally a pointer to the first member of the **rivet** array. The corresponding function parameter could then be declared as

```
int *privet ;
```

You may also simply use the array name, **rivet**, as a function argument, instead of **&rivet[0][0]**. This practice is formally incorrect, because **rivet**, written alone, is a pointer to a five-member array of **int**, while **&rivet[0][0]** is a pointer to **int**. However, this form of pointer punning can work reliably, for the following reasons:

- Because C permits free exchange of indexing and pointer arithmetic, the value of a pointer to an array must be the location of data for its first member. It cannot be a pointer to some kind of information about the array, such as a descriptor structure, because there would be no such structure for an ordinary pointer.

- C does not check to see whether the types of function arguments match those of corresponding parameters, does not convert data types of arguments to those of parameters, and does not, in fact, perform any conversions for pointer values. For these reasons, a pointer argument derived from an array name is passed to a function unchanged.

- Because C performs no bounds checking on pointer arithmetic, a function can use such a value without producing an error, as long as the actual locations addressed are valid.

In most implementations of C, neither function parameters nor function return values may be arrays, data structures, or functions, although they can be pointers to any of these. The exclusion of functions is simplest to understand. Functions are not data; there is no way to access them as data. While it might be possible to transmit an entire array, there is no way to specify such a quantity in an executable C statement. An array name has the value of a pointer. There is no construction that specifies the entire contents of an array.

Structure names do not have pointer values; they designate the data contained in the entire named structure. To create a pointer to a structure, you must use the reference operator. It is therefore possible to use a structure's name to designate its contents. As mentioned in Chapter 9, some C compilers produced since the early 1980s permit the use of structures as function parameters, arguments, and return values; they also allow the assignment of contents from one structure to another.

In C implementations that support structure assignment, a function with a structure parameter has an automatically allocated structure, initialized with a complete copy of its corresponding argument. It can change anything in such a structure without affecting the structure maintained by the invoking function. To transmit structure contents back to the invoking function, you could use either an assignment, via a structure pointer, or a return value that is a structure with the same organization:

```
int empty( bin )                struct BIN empty( )
struct BIN *bin                 {
{                                   struct BIN bin ;
    . . .                           . . .
    *bin = . . .                    return bin ;
```

As previously mentioned, a function need not return a value, and the invocation of a function need not use any value that is returned. A function invocation that does not use a return value most often stands as a separate statement. The following statement uses the function **printf** to write "next choice" to standard output:

```
printf( "next choice" ) ;
```

In this example, no use is made of any value that may be returned by **printf**.

A **return** statement without an expression returns no value. A function that ends without a **return** statement has the same effect.[3] After the last statement in its function body, control is returned to the invoking function. You should not attempt to use a return value when no value has been returned. An indeterminate value will be obtained, just as when the value of an automatically allocated variable is used before one has been assigned.

□ INVOKING FUNCTIONS

When a function is invoked, several program actions occur in succession:

1. Space is reserved for function parameters.

2. Values of arguments are calculated, and they are assigned as initial values of parameters.

3. Space is reserved for other automatic data of the function; any initial values for automatic variables are assigned.

4. Control of program operation passes to the first executable statement of the function.

5. The function operates. It may invoke additional functions.

6. When a **return** statement with an expression is encountered, the value of the expression is calculated.

7. After a **return** statement, if present, otherwise after the last statement in a function body, program control returns to the invoking function.

8. Space for function parameters and other automatic function data is released.

9. The return value is used, if required, by the statement in the invoking function that contained the function reference.

Any expressions that would be valid in assignment statements can be used as function arguments and return values. As previously explained, although arguments should correspond in number, order, and data type with function parameters, C does not check for such correspondence.

---

[3] Ibid, p. 203.

However, function arguments and return values must use only constants or variables. They cannot be structure tags or **typedef** symbols. In most implementations of C, function parameters and return values cannot be declared to be functions, arrays, or structures. As previously explained, however, some recent C compilers do handle structures and treat structure names as designating whole collections of data.

The C language does not specify any particular order in which function arguments will be evaluated. Usually the order is of no consequence. However, you should not write arguments whose evaluations can affect one another in any way. For example, you might write the following function reference:

    least_value = minimum(next(aa), next(bb)) ;

Here, both arguments for **minimum** are obtained through use of a function named **next**. For this statement to work reliably, it is essential that **next(aa)** not affect the value from **next(bb)**, and vice-versa, because you cannot be certain of the order in which they will be evaluated.

A function can never be used as the target of an assignment, because a function itself is not data, the return value of a function is not a variable (it has no name), and the value of a function name is a constant (a pointer constant). Thus, if **place** has been declared as a function of any kind, it is invalid to write statements such as either of the following:

    place = aa + bb ;

    place(cc) = d ;

For the same reasons, it is invalid to apply the reference operator to a function name in any context.

As explained in Chapters 10 and 14, the C language will treat **char** values as **int**, and **float** values as **double**, whenever they are used in a program statement—as function arguments, parameters, and return values, as well as other uses. Whenever a parameter is declared as **char**, a function will expect to receive its value as **int** and should convert it from **int** to **char** before using it. If a return value is declared **char**, an invoking function should behave likewise. A parallel consideration applies to **float** declarations and **double** values.

Occasionally, this interpretation can prove troublesome. Suppose, for example, that you are working in an environment in which **char** values are unsigned and have eight bits, while **int** values use a twos complement representation and have sixteen bits. Consider the effects of the following statements:

```
int k ;
char read_chr( ) ;
    . . .
k = read_chr( ) ;
char read_chr( )
{
    . . .
    return  − 1 ;
}
```

These statements should cause the value − 1 to be converted to **char** and then back to **int**. Because of the representation of data, − 1 has the hexadecimal value 0xFFFF. The data conversions would truncate the high-order eight bits, assigning to k a hexadecimal value of 0x00FF. You should be able to defeat this truncation, however, by using a cast:

```
k = ( int ) read_chr( ) ;
```

Problems can arise if you try to suppress or force the conversion of an argument, a parameter, or a return value by using a cast, as in the following statements:

```
char w ;
    . . .
write_chr( ( char ) − 1 ) ;
int write_chr( x )
char x ;
{
    int k ;
    . . .
    k = ( int ) x ;
```

Unfortunately, the specifications of the C language in this area have been interpreted differently, and the behavior of C compilers is not very reliable. To write portable programs, avoid **char** and **float** as data types for function parameters and return values, and avoid applying casts to function arguments, parameters, and return values. Anticipate that a **char** argument will be converted to **int**, and a **float** argument to **double**.

A few C compilers allow declarations of function parameters and return values to specify functions and arrays. However, these compilers treat parameters and return values so declared as though pointers to functions and arrays had been specified instead. When the name of such a parameter appears in an executable statement, an indirection operator is implicitly applied. The invocation of such a function generally uses array or function names as arguments; their values are pointer constants. These features do not add anything to the capabilities of a program and should be avoided because they are not portable.

□ POINTERS TO FUNCTIONS

The C language provides an anonymous form of function usage, through pointers. When it is not followed by an opening parenthesis, an identifier that has been defined or declared a function name has the value of a pointer constant, providing the location of that function. You can use such a value in only the following ways:

- to assign a value to a variable, provided the variable is a pointer to a function with the same type of return value, without pointer arithmetic or any other modification

- to provide an initial value for a pointer to a function returning the same type of value, without modification

- as an unmodified argument when invoking a function, corresponding to a parameter that is a pointer to a function with the same type of return value

A variable that is a pointer to a function can be used only for the following purposes:

- to invoke the function whose location is given by its current value

- to assign an unmodified value to another variable that is a pointer to a function with the same type of return value

- to provide an unmodified initial value for a pointer to a function returning the same type of value

- as an unmodified argument when invoking a function, corresponding to a parameter that is a pointer to a function with the same type of return value

Figure 12.2 shows statements using a pointer to invoke a function and using function names as pointer values for function arguments.

```
    int gallonage( ), footage( ) ;
    int size, measured, volume_units ;
    int excess( ) ;
    . . .
    if ( volume_units )
        size = excess( measured, gallonage ) ;
    else
        size = excess( measured, footage ) ;
int excess( allocation, units )
int allocation ;
int ( *units )( ) ;
{
    int fraction ;
    . . .
    return allocation + ( *units )( fraction ) ;
```

Figure 12.2: *Using a pointer to invoke a function and function names as pointer values.*

Here, the **excess** function receives a pointer, via parameter units, to either the **footage** or the **gallonage** function. In its **return** statement, it invokes the function to which it has received a pointer. Because function invocation would otherwise have priority over an indirection operator, the statements using a function pointer enclose it in parentheses. The **if** and **else** statements of Figure 12.2 might instead have assigned a value to a function pointer, which could then be used as a function argument, as shown in the following statements:

```
int ( *wastage )( ) ;
. . .
if ( volume_units )
    wastage = gallonage ;
else
    wastage = footage ;
size = excess( measured, wastage ) ;
```

Notice that function pointers are not followed by parentheses when used as arguments or in assignments. Parentheses are used in declarations and when functions are invoked.

One particularly useful application of function pointers is to make a decision table. When a program will take distinctly different actions depending on the data it receives, a structure that represents a decision table can include function pointers, designating functions that will handle different cases. The following example shows an array of structures initialized with such function pointers:

```
int full( ), upper( ), diagonal( ) ;
struct
{
    int offset ;
    int spacing ;
    int ( *variance )( ) ;
}
    mat_evaluate[ 3 ] =
{
    {  0,  1, full },
    { 10, 11, upper },
    {  0, 21, diagonal }
} ;
```

In this example, three functions returning **int** values are first declared. Their names are then used as pointer values to initalize the function pointers in the **mat_evaluate** data structure, along with integer constants.

A number of special considerations should be observed when you use function pointers:

- It is dangerous to use function pointers for purposes other than those previously listed; particularly risky are attempts to store data into locations to which they point.

- Function pointers must be declared before they are used, and functions must be declared before their names are used as pointer values.

- When you invoke a function by using a function pointer, parentheses are required, as shown in the examples.

- Parentheses are otherwise not used with function pointers.

- Pointer arithmetic is invalid with function pointers.

- Although you cannot apply **sizeof** to a function name, you can apply it to a function pointer; the result is the pointer size.

□ STORAGE ALLOCATION AND RECURSION

The outline of the steps that occur when a function is invoked shows how a C function uses storage. Each time a function is invoked, it gets a new set of parameter variables and other automatic variables and a record of the function that invoked it. Each time it returns, the invoking function gets a return value. Mechanisms provided by a C compiler, a C library, an operating system, or a computer itself provide the necessary storage. Each invocation of a function requires overhead in both main storage and processing.

Each invocation of a function operates in a new environment of parameters and other automatic data. The only possible connections between separate invocations are through **static** variables or data that reside outside the function. A function that uses no such data is said to be *reentrant*. You can apply these characteristics when using C functions recursively. Unless you deliberately use data with fixed allocation, each time a function is invoked, it responds only to the parameters it receives. The number of times a function can be invoked consecutively without returning is limited only by the storage and processing resources available.

An effective use of recursion is to count the number of items in a binary tree. Suppose that a node structure for a tree is defined as follows:

```
struct NODE                     /* node structure */
{
    struct NODE *left ;         /* left branch */
    struct NODE *right ;        /* right branch */
        . . .                   /* node data */
} ;
```

The following function will operate recursively until all the nodes of this type in a tree have been counted:

```
int node_count( node )
struct NODE *node ;
{
    if ( !node )                /* if no node, */
        return 0 ;             /* count is zero */
    return 1                    /* else return sum */
    + node_count( node->left )
    + node_count( node->right ) ;
}
```

When the node_count function is invoked with a NODE pointer, its responsibility is to return the total number of nodes including and beyond that node. If invoked with a null pointer, it returns a zero count. Otherwise, it invokes itself with pointers to branch nodes. It returns the sum of left and right nodes, plus one. The total number of nodes in the tree is obtained by calling this function with a pointer to the first node. The function is reentrant, since it uses only parameters.

When you declare a parameter or an automatic variable with the **register** storage class specifier, the compiler will attempt to assign the variable to a high-speed register, if the computer provides registers. Machines have a limited complement of such registers, when they have them at all. Such declarations should be limited to variables used frequently. Most compilers do not accept **register** applied to an array or a structure. It is an error to apply a reference operator to the name of a variable with this specifier. Some compilers simply redesignate any such variable for normal automatic allocation.

It is an error to invoke a function in order to initialize one of its own automatic variables. Compilers will not always detect such an error. If not, an indefinite loop will begin when the function is invoked, eventually terminated by exhaustion of space for automatic variables.

□ DESIGNING PROGRAM MODULES

Functions are the foundation of modular design. A good procedural design and a good data design are often linked by modules of closely related functions. Many complex, sophisticated programs are based on data abstraction, discussed in Chapter 9. Modules to manage user interactions, perform input and output, control processes, interpret commands, compute statistics, respond to exception conditions, and provide utility functions have also been introduced.

Data abstraction modules perform characteristic operations on data structures. Data in such structures is accessed through the functions of a data abstraction module rather than through the structure itself. Such modules are particularly useful for connective data organizations and for the management of complex databases.

While it is a powerful concept, data abstraction will not solve all software design problems. Some applications focus on control actions, others on computation or interactive response. As Chapter 9 emphasizes, the most critical task in software design is to develop an organizing principle for a program. This principle will dominate the design of its modules.

The concept of producer and consumer modules, introduced in Chapter 4, and reviewed in Chapter 6, is an important consideration for module design. Most modules are designed to provide services to other modules. Each module has a set of conventions that must be observed by its users. Most modules are the producers of some conventions and the consumers of others. Such conventions include #define constants, data organizations, format of function arguments and return values, order of function usage, methods of exception handling, and requirements for program conditions precedent to use.

In the C language, a module can export some of the conventions it produces through a header file, first introduced in Chapter 6. This book refers to exportable conventions as *control information*. A header file usually contains the following forms of control information:

- **#define** constants

- structure organizations and tags

- **typedef** symbols

- **extern** data declarations

- **extern** function declarations

It is a conventional C programming practice to place all the control information produced by a module in a single header file. If the name of a module file is **XXX.C**, the name **XXX.H** is usually given to the corresponding header file. A module that will make direct use of the functions in another module will also incorporate the other module's control information by means of a statement of this form:

    #include "XXX.H"

Good module design is characterized by internal cohesion and external independence. Cohesion means, more than anything else, that a module addresses a single purpose and observes a reasonable set of conventions; the module is as uniform in its approach and as easy to understand as possible. Independence means that it can be exercised with a minimum of mechanics, and that changes to other modules are unlikely to affect it. Modules with these properties make a program easy to test and maintain. The C language has many features that help make modules cohesive and independent, but it also has some that may invite abuse.

The key to designing testable, maintainable modules is a single path of access. Everything comes in the "front door" and leaves the same way. In a soundly designed module, data and control flow side by side. There is a minimum of *conditioning,* special circumstances that must be set up before a module can do its work; preferably there is none at all. The parameters and return values of C functions and the flexibility of C data structures are powerful aids in module design. Judicious use of fixed data, particularly data with module span, is also helpful.

Use of global data undermines a single path of access. Global data are subject to "change without notice." They can radically affect module behavior without so much as knocking on the door. To test a module that uses global data, you must not only test the functions in the module, you must also set up and check out the global data. To ensure reliability in a program that uses global data, you will need carefully documented and observed procedures for what the data contain, which functions change them, which functions use them, when data can be changed, and when data will be used. These procedures must be tested not merely within a single module but across an entire set of program modules under all circumstances of operation.

Many modules require some conditioning, such as allocating dynamic storage or opening access to files. Often this can be performed internally. When it can be, it should be, to make the module independently testable. The usual approach is to create a "startup" and a "shutdown" function. The startup function does whatever is necessary for normal operation of the module's other functions and makes sure it can't be operated more than once. The shutdown function reverses these actions and prepares a program for orderly termination.

A program constructed with internally conditioned modules will need an "executive" module, which coordinates the startup and shutdown procedures and makes sure the functions involved have access to necessary data and are invoked in the proper sequence. Judicious use of data with module span, as mentioned earlier, is often needed to manage these internal conditioning procedures and to communicate their effects to all the functions in a procedure that must be aware of them.

An **int** return value from a C function is often used to provide the status of its operation. Some sound programming environments use return values for this purpose exclusively and communicate all other information via arguments and parameters. In simple circumstances, you can return the value 1 to indicate success and 0 to indicate failure. When more complicated status conditions are involved, **#define** constants in header files serve the purpose.

Header files are another potential source of tangled threads in a C program. It is essential to keep them independent. Sometimes a whole group of modules is affected by some convention—for example, a decision to use **unsigned** integers to represent status codes. When such a need develops, a convention can be observed by explicitly including a special header file in each affected module. However, the C language allows you to embed **#include** statements in files brought in by other **#include** statements. Doing so is extremely poor programming practice. It conceals dependencies and makes a program difficult to understand, test, and maintain. Good programming practice also limits the variety of control information in a header file to those items listed earlier in this section.

Pointers are among the most powerful, but also among the most hazardous, features of C. Design conventions can minimize most of the hazards. Programs that must perform with high reliability will embed pointers in *descriptor structures,* which provide information about data types and about valid sizes and offsets. In these programs, a function that sets up a pointer value will also set up its control information. Functions that use pointers will check their validity. The same approach can be used to communicate and check the dimensions of arrays.

As previously mentioned, C provides string constants that create both pointers and characters. Many programs use these constants as function arguments, but a function cannot detect through any mechanism provided by C whether it is receiving a pointer to a variable array or a pointer to constant data. Programs designed for reliability must avoid the use of strings as function arguments in any circumstance where values might be stored into them.

A uniform module format will enhance the reliability of your programs. Module-wide declarations should always be placed at the start of a module. All automatic data with local span should be declared at the beginning of a function. For the reasons discussed earlier, a well-structured function will not declare data at the start of internal blocks, even though the C language allows it. A simple, well-documented naming convention should eliminate most of the needs for overloading and supersession of identifiers.

As described in Chapter 4, good module design includes attention to documentation. The following recommended module organization attaches most design details as closely as possible to the code:

```
Module documentation (comments)
    module organization (comments)
    summary of functions (comments)

Module header
    #include statements
    #define statements
    structure-tag declarations
    typedef declarations
    global data definitions
    extern data declarations
    static data definitions
```

Function 1
    function documentation (comments)
    function definition

Function 2
    function documentation (comments)
    function definition

Function 3
    function documentation (comments)
    function definition

    . . .

A substantial part of designing good modules and good functions is perhaps best described as "common sense." This includes a healthy respect for human frailty and a willingness to leave well enough alone. For example, C is designed to implement the **int** data type efficiently. If you don't have a particular need for **long int** or **unsigned int**, don't use them. Don't use an isolated **char** simply to save an atom of space. Avoid fiddling with data types just for some aesthetic pleasure or sense of orderliness. Don't use **typedef** symbols when keywords will do. Don't **#define** constants when what you mean is zero or nonzero; just use zero and one. Resist casts; they're for broken bones. Don't create data structures if there's nothing inherently structured about your data. Use short names when they say what you mean.

Eliminate the ornaments of programs and instead focus on the clarity of your code and the ingenuity of your methods. You will program rings around Fancy Dan, who never learned to leave well enough alone. While Fancy Dan is becoming an expert on the faults of compilers, because his programs stress their limitations, you are getting your work done.

□ C LIBRARY FUNCTIONS

Many users of C work in a programming environment that includes a function library. The function library provides an interface to commonly needed operating system services, including input, output, and memory allocation. Sometimes it also provides utilities, such as string manipulation and mathematical functions. The following explains how to use a few of the most common functions for input, output, and memory allocation. Additional details about these and other library functions are covered in Chapters 18 and 19.

In most environments that include a function library, one function that you write has a special role in starting a program. This function is ordinarily named **main**. A function with this name receives control when a program begins. It invokes other functions to carry out a program. In most environments, you run a program by typing a command; the **main** function receives arguments taken from the command line that started the program. To make use of these arguments, define a **main** function as follows:

```
int main( argc, argv )
int argc ;
char *argv[ ] ;
{
```

When **main** is defined as shown, each member of the **argv** array holds a pointer to a null-terminated character string. These strings come from the command line, and they are contiguous strings of characters that were separated by blanks or tabs. The first member of **argv** is supposed to point to a string containing the name of the command that started the program. The value of **argc** tells how many members **argv** has; there will always be at least one.

On some systems, the command name is not made available; the first position in **argv** is reserved anyway. It will point to a null string. Both the pointers and the string characters must be treated as constants. On some systems, an error will occur if **main** tries to store anything into them. Command lines are frequently used for file name arguments.

Some systems can parse command lines in a way that makes possible strings which include embedded blanks, but others cannot. Some systems impose restrictions on characters that can occur in a command. The total length of a command line is restricted by operating system conventions. Sophisticated uses of command line arguments are likely to prove nonportable. In some environments, **main** can return a value that is used by the operating system as a status code. The availability and use of such a feature varies widely among environments.

In most environments, library functions for input, output, and memory allocation are modeled on those originally developed for the Unix operating system. The following paragraphs discuss the most needed of these functions and the conventions and definitions for them that are most commonly encountered.

The C library functions for input and output export control information in a header file. The name **stdio.h** is usually given to this file. A module that is to use these functions should contain, in its module header, this statement:

#include "stdio.h"

In some environments, header files for C library functions are kept in a special place, known to the compiler. For such systems, the file name is enclosed in angle brackets:

#include <stdio.h>

A header file **stdio.h** will sometimes contain many more definitions than are needed to use the C library input and output functions. To prevent conflicts between this information and the control information that your program has defined, it is a good idea to make a copy of **stdio.h** and weed out extraneous matter. You may need to understand the C preprocessor, explained in Chapter 17, before you can do this correctly.

There are four symbols usually found in **stdio.h** that are likely to be needed by your programs:

FILE	a **typedef** symbol for control data describing a data file in use
EOF	a **#define** constant (an **int** value) for a status value indicating an end of file
stdin	a **#define** constant (a pointer value) describing a standard input file, generally your interactive terminal
stdout	a **#define** constant (a pointer value) describing a standard output file, generally your interactive terminal

The most generally useful C library input/output functions are defined as follows:

Open access to a file:

FILE *fopen(filename, access)

Close access to a file:

int fclose(stream)

Read one character:

int fgetc(stream)

Write one character:

int fputc(value, stream)

Read formatted input:

int fscanf(stream, format, . . .)

Write formatted output:

int fprintf(stream, format, . . .)

Check for file error:

int ferror(stream)

The parameters of these input and output functions have the following declarations and general content:

Declaration	Contents
char *filename	name of data file
char *access	type of file access
FILE *stream	file control pointer
int value	character value
char *format	formatting string

Access to files is opened and closed by **fopen** and **fclose**. The **fopen** function returns a FILE pointer, which can be used when invoking all the other functions. The symbols **stdin** and **stdout** can be substituted wherever **stream** appears, to use a standard input source and a standard output destination, ordinarily your interactive terminal. The files associated with these symbols are automatically opened before a program begins and closed after it terminates. An error will occur if any function but **fopen** is called without a **stream** argument that corresponds to a file open for access.

The **fopen** function requires a string argument, named **access** above. The value of **access** should be "w" if a file is to be written and "r" if it is to be read. On some systems, options denoted by "wb" and "rb" are available for "binary mode" access. Some systems provide additional access modes. The character string whose location is given by **filename** must be null-terminated. On most but not all systems, upper- and lowercase letters in this string are treated as equivalent. The **fopen** function will return a null pointer if a file cannot be opened. The **fclose** function will return EOF if an error occurs, otherwise zero.

These functions manipulate *text* files, consisting of characters and line terminators. A line terminator is designated by the newline special character value (\n). The line terminator may occur in this form in a file, or it may be translated to some other form. Where a binary mode is available, a file can be read and written without this type of translation. Although text files are often referred to as *stream* files, implying that they can consist of an unbroken stream of characters, many systems impose a maximum length on the number of characters between line terminators. Such a maximum, when imposed, may be as little as 72 characters.

The fgetc and fputc functions provide sequential file operations by single characters. If an error or an end of file condition occurs, either function returns EOF. Otherwise, fgetc returns the character that was read and fputc returns the character, provided by value, that was written. In order to detect the value of EOF, the return value of these and any other functions must be either tested as they are invoked or assigned to an **int**. On many systems, the value EOF cannot be assigned to a **char** variable.

The ferror function can be used to distinguish between an end of file and a file error condition. If no error has occurred, it will return zero. Otherwise, it will return a nonzero status code, whose meaning depends on the operating system and C library implementation. Once an error or end of file condition has occurred, any subsequent operation will report the same status until the file is closed.

The fscanf and fprintf functions perform *formatted* input and output, that is, they translate between characters, appearing in some well-defined format in a data file, and the internal forms of data, under the control of a *formatting string*. Both functions return EOF if an error or an end of file condition occurs. Otherwise, they return some other value. In some implementations, this value is the number of data file characters processed. In others, it is the number of arguments after the format string being processed. In a few, it is the value zero.

The functions fscanf and fprintf accept a variable number of arguments. The first argument is always a FILE pointer and the second a formatting string. The remainder are data arguments, whose meanings are determined by interpreting the formatting string. For fprintf, these other arguments are values of data to be written. For fscanf, they are pointers to variables for data to be read. Since there is no portable mechanism for writing a function with a variable number of arguments in C, these functions cannot be written in a standard form of C.

A formatting string consists of text characters and format control sequences. Each control sequence begins with a percent sign (%). The

printf function writes text characters as they occur in a formatting
string, interspersed with formatted output data, governed by control
sequences. The **scanf** function matches any text characters against
input characters and interprets formatted input data, governed by control sequences.

This chapter will explain only a few format control sequences. Others
are detailed in Chapter 19. The following control sequences produce output and interpret input for the data types and the types of fields in a data
file, as shown:

Control Sequence	Data Type	Type of field
%d	**int**	decimal integer
%x	**int**	hexadecimal integer
%c	**char**	single character
%s	**char ***	character string

Figure 12.3 shows a **main** function that gets two file names from a
command line and copies the contents of the first file to the second.

The storage allocation functions **malloc** and **free** were introduced in
Chapters 9 and 10. The **malloc** function requires one argument, an **int**
or **unsigned int** value giving the amount of storage required. A correct value should be obtained by applying **sizeof** to the identifier or
data type for which an allocation is needed, multiplied by the number
of members of an array. A null pointer will be returned if the function
is not able to allocate a block of the requested size. Otherwise, a
pointer value will be returned that can be used for a data element
of any type.

As explained in Chapter 10, the return value of **malloc** is usually
declared a pointer to **char**, and a cast is used to signify that the
pointer returned can be assigned to a pointer for a different data type.
The storage obtained from **malloc** has indefinite contents. Its contents
should not be used by a program until values have been assigned.

A block of storage allocated by **malloc** can be released by invoking
free, using the pointer value from **malloc** as an argument. The **free**
function is sometimes typed as returning an **int**, but in fact no value is
returned. After storage has been released, it must not be referred to
again for any purpose. Storage released to **free** is eligible for realloca-
tion by **malloc**. When using dynamic storage, you must be careful not

```
#include "stdio.h"              /* I/O header file     */
int main( argc, argv )
int argc ;
char *argv[ ] ;
{
    FILE *fin ;                 /* input file pointer  */
    FILE *fout ;                /* output file pointer */
    int value ;                 /* character copied    */

    if ( argc < 3 )             /* check argument count */
    {
        fprintf( stdout, "Missing file name(s)\n" ) ;
        return ;
    }                           /* open input file      */
    fin = fopen( argv[ 1 ], "r" ) ;
    if ( !fin )
    {
                                /* report opening error */
        fprintf( stdout,
          "Unable to open %s\n", argv[ 1 ] ) ;
        return ;
    }                           /* open output file     */
    fout = fopen( argv[ 2 ], "w" ) ;
    if ( !fout )
    {
                                /* report opening error */
        fprintf( stdout,
          "Unable to open %s\n", argv[ 2 ] ) ;
        fclose( fin ) ;         /* close input file     */
        return ;
    }
    while ( 1 )                 /* copying loop         */
    {
        value = fgetc( fin ) ;  /* read input char      */
        if ( value == EOF )     /* check for input      */
            break ;             /*  exception           */
                                /* write output char    */
        value = fputc( value, fout ) ;
        if ( value == EOF )     /* check for output     */
            break ;             /*  exception           */
    }
    if ( value = ferror( fin ) )
        fprintf( stdout,        /* report input error   */
          "Input error, code = %x\n", value ) ;
    if ( value = ferror( fout ) )
        fprintf( stdout,        /* report output error  */
          "Output error, code = %x\n", value ) ;
    fclose( fin ) ;             /* close input file     */
    fclose( fout ) ;            /* close output file    */
}
```

Figure 12.3: *An example using the input/output functions.*

to store anything outside an allocated area. Otherwise, errors can result that may be extremely difficult to trace and correct.

Unfortunately, there are small but significant differences among the functions provided by different environments, including the several versions of Unix and systems that emulate it. To write portable C programs, you must isolate your use of library functions in small areas of your programs. Usually it is practical to set up a few modules that perform all input, output, and memory allocation. Then, when moving a program to a new environment, you need adapt only these modules.

☐ EXERCISES

12.1: For this problem, review the binary tree organization presented in Chapter 9 and the counting function that was shown in one of this chapter's examples.

(a) Compared to the order in which nodes are ordered by the tree connections, in what order does the counting function visit the nodes? In what order does it count them?

(b) Write a recursive function that prints data from nodes in the sorting order provided by the tree connections.

(c) Write a nonrecursive function to print data from the nodes in the sorted order. What additional data does such a function require?

(d) What affects the relative speed and storage use of a recursive versus a nonrecursive approach?

(e) How could you make a connective data organization provide easy access for both random searching and linear processing? When would a hybrid organization of this sort be effective?

12.2: One of the most interesting connective data structures, a ternary tree, is developed from a binary tree by adding a third branch to each node. A key use of a ternary tree is to represent concatenated information. For this use, the "left" and "right" branches maintain a sorting order and provide rapid random searches. A "center" branch at each node gives the location of the first node in a new tree, whose information is to be concatenated with information through the current node. This exercise involves organizing a data abstraction module for a ternary tree.

As an example, consider the ternary tree shown in Figure 12.4, set up to represent words in a vocabulary by syllables. Each node of this tree has left and right branches, pointing to alternative syllables and a center branch, pointing to syllables that may be concatenated.

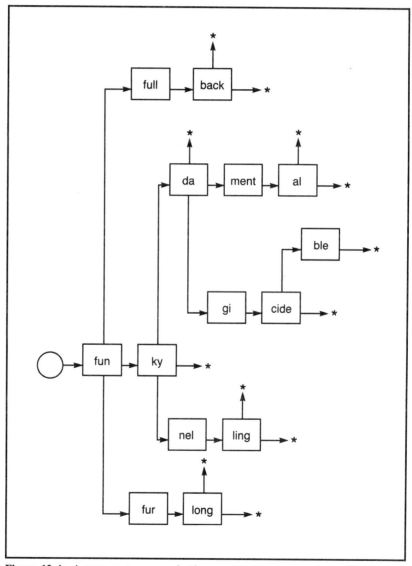

Figure 12.4: *A ternary tree organization.*

This tree represents the following list of words:

full
fullback
fun
fundament
fundamental
fungible
fungicide
funky
funnel
funnelling
fur
furlong

The ternary tree requires a special node, represented in the diagram by an asterisk, that is sometimes called a "terminus." When a terminus node occurs in the tree attached to a center branch, a word can stop at that point. The terminus node has been assigned a higher collating position than any syllable, as shown.

(a) Define data structures to represent a ternary tree for a vocabulary, analyzed by syllables, where the data for each node consist of a character string of arbitrary length and a character count.

(b) Plan the elementary functions to be provided by a data abstraction module. Your planning should start with the way in which concatenated information is to be communicated. If you choose a simple string, there will have to be a method for parsing a word into syllables. You should also specify a method for representing a terminus, which must be distinguished from a null branch.

(c) Write functions to add a word to the tree and to search the tree for a given word. Include any support functions internal to the module that may be required. Construct a header file of control information required by users of your functions.

(d) Write a function to print the vocabulary that is contained in the tree.

(e) Write a function to delete a word from the tree and remove any nodes that become extraneous.

12.3: A procedure generally known as "quicksort," invented by Anthony Hoare,[4] is the fastest known algorithm for sorting randomly ordered data. A description of it is based on data "items" that include "keys," on which the sorting comparisons are performed. Data items must be arranged into a list that can be explored forward from the start or backward from the end. The list can be an array, a linked list, or any other organization that provides the required access.

Regardless of how data are actually configured, a quicksort procedure can be implemented, provided the operations of moving from one item to the next item and to the previous item are efficient. Like the bubble sort and Shell's sort, quicksort operates in place. Keys of the items are compared, and two items may be interchanged.

Quicksort is an intrinsically recursive algorithm. It works by rearranging a list into "left" and "right" lists, on the basis of the key of a pivot item, so that items with keys "less than" the pivot are in the left list and the remainder are in the right list. Then the quicksort procedure is applied separately to the left list and the right list. This process continues until all lists are either sorted or consist of one item. The reason for quicksort's speed is that it rapidly reduces the size of lists being sorted.

A software outline for quicksort follows. In this version of quicksort, the pivot item is the first item found for which the next item is out of place. Notice that the pivot item will often be interchanged.

```
Procedure: quicksort
Parameters: starting item in list
            ending item in list
Outline:
    Set left position at starting item
    Set pivot value from key at left position
    While left position not at ending item
        Move left position forward
        If left key less than pivot value
            Break
        Set pivot value from left key
    If pivot value equal to key of ending item
```

---

[4] C. A. R. Hoare, "Quicksort," *Computer Journal* 5, no.1(1962):10–15.

Return (sort is complete)
Set left position at starting item
Set right position at ending item
Until left position same as right
    If left key not less than pivot value
        Until right position same as left
            If right key less than left key
                Interchange left and right items
                Move right position backward
                Break
            Move right position backward
        If left position not same as right
            Move left position forward
    If right key less than pivot
        Move right position forward
    Else move left position backward
Quicksort, from starting to left position
Quicksort, from right to ending position

(a) Write a C function to perform quicksort on a linear array of integers.

(b) Write a C function to perform quicksort on a bidirectionally linked list of structures with integer keys.

(c) Modify the function in (b) to keep track of the lengths of lists and use a bubble sort when the length of a list is less than ten items.

(d) Modify the function in (c) to perform quicksort with the following parameters:

- a pointer to a starting structure

- a pointer to an ending structure

- a pointer to a function receiving a structure pointer and returning a pointer to the next structure

- a pointer to a function receiving a structure pointer and returning a pointer to the previous structure

- a pointer to a function receiving two structure pointers and returning either 0 if the first can go before the second or 1 if they should be interchanged

- a pointer to a function receiving two structure pointers and interchanging their positions in a list

(e) Design a structure to represent a list of sales contacts, including the name of the person, company name, street address, location, and telephone number. Write a data abstraction module for this list, including the functions described in (d) that are needed to sort the list by name of contact person, company name, and location.

12.4: Write a C program to read input one character at a time, up to a line terminator, and then calculate and print out the value of an integer expression. An integer expression should be able to use the operators of the C language:

+ − * / %

Addition and subtraction should be performed before multiplication and division; operations should otherwise be performed from left to right. An expression may include any number of parentheses to rearrange the order of calculation. All forms of integer constants used in C should be accepted, including those that begin with a minus sign.

(a) Make your program independent of any spacing that may be embedded in the expression.

(b) Make your program check for syntax errors, including unbalanced parentheses and more than one operator in a row (allow a minus sign on a number).

(c) Make your program check for numbers, at any stage of calculation, that exceed the range of an **int**.

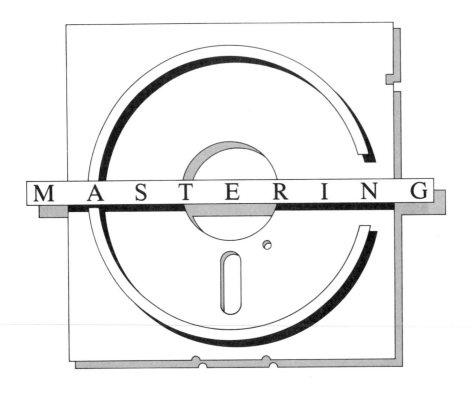

CHAPTER 13

OPERATORS

Operators direct a C program's data manipulations, such as addition, assignment of a value, and selection of a structure member. The C language offers a large variety of data manipulations. In this chapter, you will read about:

- data evaluation expressions

- operator formations and operands

- precedence and function reference

- selection and location operations

- arithmetic operations

- logical and comparison operations

- bitwise operations

- assignment operations

- data type and sequence operations

- categories of operations

□ DATA EVALUATION EXPRESSIONS

C is not only a procedural language, it is also a stepwise, operational language. A program written in C is carried out one statement at a time. Each statement creates or manipulates data. There are three types of statements:

- declaration statements

- control statements

- evaluation statements

Declaration statements designate data that a program will work with, as explained in Chapter 10, and begin its functions, as explained in Chapter 12. Control statements are described in Chapter 15. The most important control statements, **if, while**, and **for**, were introduced informally in Chapters 2 and 5; they have been used in many examples. All other C statements evaluate data.

A C program causes data to be evaluated by stating names of variables and values of constants, together with instructions about the operations to be performed on them. Data evaluations are used in certain parts of declaration and control statements. Evaluation statements are exclusively devoted to data evaluation.

A single data evaluation is controlled by a combination of data values, identifiers, and operators, called an *expression*. Details about the interpretation of expressions are explained in the next chapter; this chapter describes components from which evaluation expressions are composed.

☐ OPERATOR FORMATIONS AND OPERANDS

In C, instructions for data manipulations are provided by operators. An *operator* is a character or a group of characters that will cause a specific data manipulation to be carried out when it occurs, within a program statement, in a well-defined relation to data values or identifiers.

Most operators in C are designated by symbol characters, such as *
and &. Several operators have more than one character. Of those,
some use characters that are written together, such as -> and ==.
Others use characters that enclose data values or identifiers with which
they operate, such as the brackets for array indexing. One operator,
sizeof, is a keyword.

Because different operators use many of the same characters, because they differ in their usage restrictions, and because they acquire meaning from the context of data designations and other operators, this book will describe them in terms of *operator formations* or *operations*. An operator formation is a combination of operators with data values and identifiers that specifies a particular data manipulation; an operation is the manipulation that is performed.

Operator formations may involve one, two, three, or more data values or identifiers, known as the *operands*. According to the number of operands, operators can be classified as *unary, binary, ternary,* and *plurative*. Each operator formation yields a single result, known as its *value*. The value of one operator formation may be used as an operand of another. The process of combining operator formations, discussed in Chapter 14, creates expressions.

Operator formations with two operands may have the same value if the operands are reversed, or they may have a different value. Those that give the same value are called *commutative* operations. This chapter will identify the commutative operations, and Chapter 14 will discuss some consequences of using commutative operations in expressions.

Operator formations are governed by rules that prescribe data types for operands and resulting values. Some operations can be performed with different data types. For these operations, the data type of the result is determined by the data type of the operands. Sometimes when an operand has an incorrect data type, it will be automatically converted to another data type before it is used. In other circumstances no conversion is possible, and a compiler should indicate that a statement is in error. Rules for type conversion are discussed in Chapter 14.

Many operands must satisfy restrictions. Some must have one of the fundamental data types (**char, int, float, double,** or a modified version of one of these). Others must have an integer data type (**char, int,** or a modified version of one of these). For the rest of this chapter, certain types of operands will be designated by the following symbols:

element	a data element, or a structure or array member that is a data element, with one of the fundamental data types
value	a data element or an expression that has one of the fundamental data types
intelem	a data element, or a structure or array member that is a data element, with one of the integer data types
intvalue	a data element or an expression that has one of the integer data types
pointer	a pointer element or a member of structure or an array that is a pointer
pointval	a pointer element or an expression that has a pointer value

In general, you should assume that no operand is valid unless specifically stated. In particular, only a few operator formations will accept structure, array, or function names as operands.

□ PRECEDENCE AND FUNCTION REFERENCE

When an expression is evaluated, high-priority operations are performed before low-priority ones. Chapter 14 explains this process in detail. This chapter is concerned with only one aspect of priority, which is provided by the *precedence* operation. Any part of an expression that is enclosed in parentheses is evaluated before it is combined with operations outside the parentheses. Parentheses used in this way designate a precedence operation.

The characters used for operators are overloaded, in the sense that C language identifiers may be overloaded, as discussed in Chapter 10. The same characters may be used for different purposes; the purpose in a given instance is determined by context. Parentheses are the most heavily overloaded operator characters. Depending on context, they can indicate any of the following:

- precedence, grouping parts of an expression that otherwise could have lower priority

- function reference, enclosing arguments of a function, if any

- a cast, enclosing a declaration expression without an identifier

- boundaries of a control statement expression, as discussed in Chapter 15

- macro expansion, a feature of the C preprocessor, explained in Chapter 17

The last two uses of parentheses are not part of the ways in which expressions are evaluated. In these uses, parentheses are not considered operator characters.

Precedence has, by definition, the highest priority of all operator formations. Its purpose is to combine whatever is operated on and to override priorities that might apply because of other operators. The single operand of precedence is whatever occurs between the parentheses. The precedence operator formation is

(**gen_exp**)

where **gen_exp** is an identifier, an expression equivalent to an identifier, a constant, a data type (with or without an identifier), or a value resulting from an expression.

Parentheses in C statements must always be balanced. When a C compiler encounters the opening parenthesis of a precedence operation, it will look forward for a closing parenthesis, counting up by subsequent opening parentheses and down by subsequent closing parentheses. The first closing parenthesis at a count of zero is taken as the end of a precedence formation.

Precedence causes whatever is inside the parentheses to be evaluated before being combined with whatever is outside. The resulting type of expression is unchanged. For example, when invoking a function whose location is specified by a function pointer, one may write

```
result = ( *function_pointer )( argument ) ;
```

The parentheses around *function_pointer cause the indirection operator to be applied to function_pointer before the function given by its location value is invoked.

In this chapter, precedence will be used frequently, even where it is not necessary. Discussion of the priorities of operations, when precedence is not indicated, has been left to the next chapter. Here, precedence is used to make the order of operations unambiguous.

There are two forms of function reference. One uses only a pair of parentheses, the other uses a pair of parentheses and one or more commas between them. Function reference is the only plurative operation in C. It has one or more operands. The first form of function reference is

fun_loc(ref_exp)

where **fun_loc** gives the location of a function and an optional **ref_exp** is an argument for that function. The second form of function reference is

fun_loc(ref_exp, ref_exp, . . .)

where there is more than one argument for the function and the arguments are separated by commas.

The value of the first function reference operand must be the location of a function. This location is usually given by writing a function name, but it can also be given by applying the indirection operator to a function pointer. The function location operand must appear immediately before the opening parenthesis of a function reference.

All other operands of function reference, shown above as **ref_exp**, are function arguments. If there is more than one, they are separated by commas. An argument can be any expression that designates a data element, a data aggregate, a value, or a function location. Expressions defining data types and identifiers providing only organizing information, such as structure tags or **typedef** symbols, cannot be arguments. Also excluded as arguments are references to whole arrays or functions, which C statements cannot handle as data. Function arguments should correspond in number, order, and type to the parameters of a function definition.

The value of a function reference can be of any type that is allowed as an argument. If it has not been declared, the value returned by a function is assumed to be **int**. Chapter 12 discusses these matters in detail. As explained there, the data types allowed by most C compilers for function arguments and values exclude structures, but some recent compilers allow them.

Function arguments and a function location are evaluated completely before a function is invoked, but they may be evaluated in any order. No function reference operation should depend on the order of evaluation for the function location and the function arguments. An argument of a function may not involve a sequence operation, as explained in a later section, unless that operation is enclosed in the parentheses of a precedence operation.

A statement with a function reference should not use the values of any data that may be changed, directly or indirectly, by the function. A statement with a function reference should not be able to change the value of any data on which the function depends, directly or indirectly, before the function is invoked. If a function always invokes another function whose location is supplied as an argument, the location of the function being invoked should not be used for that argument.

☐ SELECTION AND LOCATION OPERATIONS

Selection operations designate a member of a data aggregate. The selection operation for arrays, called indexing, was discussed in detail in Chapter 7. The selection operations for structures were presented in Chapter 9. All of these are binary operations, in which the first operand designates a data aggregate; the second, a member of it. The forms of selection operations are as follows:

struc.strmem

strpt->strmem

array[intvalue]

In these forms, **struc** is a structure name, **strpt** is a pointer to a structure, **strmem** is a member of a structure, **array** is an array name, and **intvalue** is an integer value. The member named by **strmem** must belong to the type of structure named by **struc** or pointed to by **strpt.** Each operand may be an expression of equivalent type. The values of selection operations are those of the members selected. Like parentheses, brackets must be balanced. When a C compiler finds the opening bracket of an indexing operation, it will search forward for a closing bracket.

Location operators were discussed in Chapter 8. The indirection operator designates the value at a location given by the current value of a pointer. The reference operator designates the location of data. The operator formations for indirection and reference are as follows:

*pointval

&locatable

The value of an indirection operation is that of the type of data to which **pointval** points. This can be a data element, an array, a structure, a function, or another pointer.

In a reference operation, the operand **locatable** must designate generally accessible data to which a C statement might assign a value. It must be one of the following:

- the name of a data element
- an array member that is a data element or a data structure
- the name of a data structure
- a structure member that is not an array
- the name of a pointer
- a pointer value to which an indirection operator has just previously been applied in the same statement

A **locatable** operand cannot be the name of an array or a function. It cannot be a value resulting from any operation other than indirection or member selection. It cannot be a constant of any type.

The reference operator constructs a pointer value. The reason for the restrictions on its operand is that one must be able to use such a value to obtain and assign values. The reference operator will not provide pointers to arrays or functions. The only ways to obtain such a pointer are to assign an array or function name to a pointer and to use an array or function name as a function argument.

□ ARITHMETIC OPERATIONS

C statements can perform the four standard functions of arithmetic, using operators that were introduced in Chapter 2. The arithmetic operations with two operands have the following forms:

value + value

value − value

value * value

value / value

Of these, addition and multiplication are commutative. If both operands are **int**, **long int**, **unsigned int**, or **double**, the result has the same data type as that of an operand. Otherwise, type conversion is performed, as described in Chapter 14.

Subtraction can also be expressed as a unary operation, sometimes called *arithmetic negation,* in the form

− value

This expression produces the negative of the operand **value,** the same result as if **value** were subtracted from integer zero. If the operand is **int**, **long int**, **unsigned int**, or **double**, the result has the same data type as the operand. Otherwise, type conversion is performed, as described in Chapter 14.

There is an arithmetic operation to obtain the remainder of one integer divided by another. It has the form

intvalue % intvalue

If both operands are **int, long int,** or **unsigned int**, the result has the same data type as that of an operand. Otherwise, type conversion is performed, as described in Chapter 14. If the second operand is zero or one of the operands is negative, the result of this operation is machine-dependent.

There are four convenient operators for numeric data to add or subtract one. The forms of these operations are

++ element

element ++

- - element

element - -

If an operand is **int, long int, unsigned int,** or **double,** the result has the same data type as the operand. Otherwise, the data type is converted as described in Chapter 14.

In an incrementing or decrementing operation, the value of the operand is always changed. When the operator occurs after the operand, however, the result of the operation is the value before incrementing or decrementing. When the operator occurs before the operand, the result is the value after incrementing or decrementing. For example, ++ number means "Increment number and get the result after incrementing," while number ++ means "Get the value of number as a result, then increment number."

Changes to operands resulting from incrementing and decrementing operations will occur after the location of the operand is evaluated. They are not otherwise guaranteed to occur at any particular time during execution of a program statement.[1] A change to an incrementing or decrementing operand will be in effect before the next statement is executed.

Nothing that depends on the value of an incrementing or decrementing operand should be used for any other purpose, directly or indirectly, by the same program statement. Nothing that affects the location of an incrementing or decrementing operand should be changed, directly or indirectly, by the same program statement. Suppose number is an **int** with a value of 3 and mystery is an array of **int:**

(mystery[number]) = ((++number) + (number ++)) ;

Such a statement is allowed in a C program, but its effect is implementation dependent. Any one of three members of mystery may be assigned a value of 7, 8 or 9.

Values of arithmetic operations that exceed ranges of the result data types are implementation dependent. Ranges can be exceeded under many different circumstances. Among the most common are division by zero and multiplication of two large numbers. It is the programmer's responsibility to write a program so that such operations either cannot occur or are detected before being performed.

Operations on unsigned integers other than division by zero have predictable results, based on the number of bits in a binary representation,

---

[1] Brian W. Kernighan and Dennis M. Ritchie, *The C Programming Language,* (Englewood Cliffs, N. J.: Prentice-Hall, 1978), p. 50.

as shown in Chapter 5, and on modular arithmetic.[2] If an unsigned result has a binary representation with n bits, it will have the correct value, modulo 2^n. Taking the negative of an unsigned value will always yield a positive value. Whether x is signed or unsigned, the value of (x + (−x)) is always zero.

As stated in Chapter 8, three forms of arithmetic that use pointers and integers are allowed, subject to several conditions and restrictions. The operations of pointer arithmetic have the following forms:

>**pointval + intvalue**
>
>**pointval − intvalue**
>
>**pointval − pointval**

The results of these operations are machine dependent if a **pointval** operand is a null pointer value.

The first two forms of pointer arithmetic produce values of the same type as the operand **pointval.** The first form is commutative. The value of the last form is of type **int.**[3] These forms using pointers are not considered to represent special types of operations, only special types of allowed operands. Notice that taking the negative of a pointer is not allowed, because a pointer value cannot be subtracted from an integer value.

The incrementing and decrementing operations are also allowed to use pointers as operands. The forms are as follows:

>**++pointer**
>
>**pointer++**
>
>**−−pointer**
>
>**pointer−−**

The results of these operations are machine dependent if the value of an operand is a null pointer.

The values obtained from incrementing and decrementing pointers are determined in the same ways as values from incrementing and decrementing numerical quantities. Changes to a **pointer** operand are the same as would be obtained in pointer arithmetic by adding or sub-

---

[2] Ibid., p. 183.
[3] Ibid., p. 189. Some compilers will use **unsigned int** or **long int**, when the range of **int** is insufficient to hold all possible values.

tracting 1. All conditions and restrictions discussed in Chapter 8, for pointer arithmetic, apply to such operations.

□ LOGICAL AND COMPARISON OPERATIONS

Operations to compare numeric values were introduced in Chapter 2. Comparisons can be for equality or for relative value. The latter are algebraic; any positive value will be found greater than any negative value. The operator formations are as follows:

> **value** < **value**
> **value** > **value**
>
> **value** <= **value**
> **value** >= **value**
>
> **value** == **value**
> **value** != **value**

The last two forms are commutative.

Results of comparisons are determined by subtracting operands and inspecting a signed result. If both operands are **int**, **long int**, or **double**, the result of subtraction has the same type as that of an operand. Otherwise, the data type is converted as described in Chapter 14.

The result of a comparison is logically TRUE or FALSE, depending on whether the relation being tested is found to hold or not. Unlike some other languages, however, C has no special data type for logically valued quantities. Instead, the result of a comparison is of type **int**. The value is 1 if the relation holds and 0 otherwise.

One conditional operator uses a logical value as an operand. It is the only ternary operator, and its operator formation is the following:

> **value ? value : value**

If the first operand is nonzero, interpreted as TRUE, the second operand is evaluated as the result of the operation; the third operand is not evaluated. Otherwise, the third operand is evaluated as the result, and the second operand is not evaluated. If both the second and third operands are **int**, **long int**, **unsigned int**, or **double**, then the result has the same type. Otherwise, type conversion is performed, as described in Chapter 14.

Logically valued quantities can be combined in logical operations. Two operands are used by the following forms:

value && value

value || value

An operand of a logical operation is evaluated by determining whether it is zero. It is considered TRUE if nonzero, otherwise FALSE. The values of these operations are **int** and are either 1 or 0, according to the logical combination of the operands. The operands need not be of the same type, and no type conversions are performed.

For logical AND (**&&**), the first operand is evaluated. If it is FALSE, the value of the operation is 0, and the second operand is not evaluated. Otherwise, the second operand is evaluated. If it is TRUE, the value of the operation is 1; if false, the value of the operation is 0.

For logical OR (**||**), the first operand is evaluated. If it is TRUE, the value of the operation is 1, and the second operand is not evaluated. Otherwise, the second operand is evaluated. If it is TRUE, the value of the operation is 1; if FALSE, the value of the operation is 0.

There is also a logical NOT operator, which tests and inverts the logical value of an operand. It has the following operator formation:

!value

This results in an **int** value of the opposite logical sense, namely, 0 if the operand is nonzero and 1 if it is 0. Conversion to logical values and their inverses can also be obtained from these forms:

value != 0

value == 0

As stated in Chapter 8, comparisons of pointer values are permitted, subject to several conditions and restrictions. Pointer comparisons have the following forms:

pointval < pointval
pointval > pointval

pointval <= pointval
pointval >= pointval

```
pointval == pointval
pointval != pointval
```

All forms of pointer comparison produce **int** values of 0 or 1. The last two forms are commutative. The results of the first four operations are machine dependent if the operands are of different pointer types or if one of the operands is a null pointer value.

Valid results will always be obtained when testing whether two pointers are equal, provided they are pointers of the same type. Also, you can always test whether a pointer is equal to a null pointer value. The integer constant 0 can be used in such a comparison. It will automatically be converted to a null pointer value.

The conditional operation can be performed with pointer operands. The forms allowed are the following:

pointval ? value : value

value ? pointval : pointval

pointval ? pointval : pointval

In the first and third forms, the first operand **pointval** is tested to see whether it is a null pointer or not, corresponding to a logical value of 0 or 1. The value of the second and third forms is a pointer. You may supply the integer constant 0 as the second or the third operand of these forms. It will be converted to a null pointer.

Pointers can also be used as operands in logical operations. The following forms are permitted:

pointval && value
value && pointval
pointval && pointval

pointval || value
value || pointval
pointval || pointval

!pointval

When a **pointval** operand in one of these forms is evaluated, it is tested to see whether it is a null pointer or not, corresponding to a logical value of 0 or 1. Logical and comparison operations using pointers are not considered to represent special types of operations, only special types of allowed operands.

Some recent C compilers permit structures to be used in assignments and function references. Many of these compilers also allow a conditional operator formation in which the second and third operands are structure names or structure values of the same type:

value ? strucval : strucval

pointval ? strucval : strucval

The results of these operations are structure values: entire contents of structures. They can be used to select a member or provide a function argument or return value. Values cannot be assigned to results of these operations.

□ BITWISE OPERATIONS

Several operations in C affect individual bits of a binary representation of integer values, as discussed in Chapter 5. Three of the bitwise operations perform logic. Sometimes called the bitwise AND, OR, and XOR operations, they have the following operator formations:

intvalue & intvalue

intvalue | intvalue

intvalue ^ intvalue

If both operands are **int, long int**, or **unsigned int**, the result has the same type as an operand. Otherwise, the data type is converted, as described in Chapter 14.

Bitwise logic operations produce result bits by logical operations on corresponding operand bits. Both inclusive OR and exclusive OR (XOR) are available. The results are most easily described in a *logic table,* giving the bit value resulting from each operation, for all possible pairs of operand bits, as shown in Figure 13.1.

As Figure 13.1 shows, all the bitwise logic operations are commutative. Bitwise AND will clear bits, using an operand with zeros in bits to be cleared and ones in bits to be left unchanged. Bitwise OR will set bits, using an operand with ones in bits to be set and zeros in bits to be left unchanged. Bitwise XOR will invert bits, using an operand with ones in bits to be inverted and zeros in bits to be left unchanged.

First Operand	Second Operand	AND· &	OR │	XOR ^
0	0	0	0	0
0	1	0	1	1
1	0	0	1	1
1	1	1	1	0

Figure 13.1: *Bitwise logic table.*

There is also an operation, called bitwise NOT, that will invert all the bits in an operand. It has this form:

~ intvalue

If the operand is **int, long int,** or **unsigned int**, the result has the same type. Otherwise, type conversion occurs, as described in Chapter 14. The effect is the same as performing a bitwise XOR with an operand that has ones in all bits.

Two operations are available to shift the bits in an integer value. Called *left shift* and *right shift,* they have the following operator formations:

intvalue ≪ intvalue

intvalue ≫ intvalue

If the first operand is **int, long int,** or **unsigned int**, the result has the same type. Otherwise, type conversion occurs for this operand, as described in Chapter 14.

The second operand of a shift operation, called the *shift count,* states the number of bit positions to shift the bit values of the first operand. In a left shift (≪), bit values are shifted toward high-order positions, and zero bits enter the low-order positions. In a right shift, bit values are shifted toward low-order positions. In a right shift of an unsigned integer, zero bits enter the high-order positions. Otherwise, the bits entering high-order positions for a right shift are implementation dependent.[4]

A left shift will multiply a value by a power of two, until overflow occurs. A right shift will divide a positive value by a power of two, but the effect for a negative value is implementation dependent.[5] Shifting is useless when the shift count exceeds the number of bits in a value. A negative shift count has an implementation dependent effect. It does not generally reverse the shift direction.

Bitwise operations can increase the efficiency of many programs. For example, shifting is sometimes faster than multiplying or dividing, and bitwise logic is often faster than the logical operations that test for zero or nonzero quantities. Once logical values have been obtained, the bitwise operations can be used instead of logical AND and OR, because logical values contain all their information in the low-order bit. Note that bitwise NOT will generally fail to have the same effect as logical NOT. If **x** has a value of 0 or 1, to get the effect of logical NOT from bitwise operations, use (**x ^ 1**).

Bitwise operations must be used with caution. They can easily make a program nonportable, because their use may require knowledge about sizes and formats of data elements. To write programs that are both portable and efficient, you should assume, when using bitwise operations, that a **char** has no more than 7 bits and that no integer data type may be available with more than 16 bits. It is easiest to restrict the use of bitwise operations to unsigned quantities. Otherwise, you should not use bitwise operations to test or change the sign bits of signed values.

□ ASSIGNMENT OPERATIONS

So far in this book, only one assignment operation has been used, with an equal sign. A value produced by such an operation has been ignored. In C, assignment is considered to be an operator, and it has a value. The operator formation for simple assignment is

element = value

If both operands are **int**, **long int**, **unsigned int**, or **double**, assignment involves no conversion. Otherwise, type conversion is performed, as described in Chapter 14. The location of the first operand

---

[4] Ibid., p. 45.
[5] Ibid., p. 189.

is evaluated. The value of the second operand, converted if necessary, is assigned to the first operand. That value, which has the type of the first operand, becomes the value of the operation.

Besides simple assignment, the C language also has several compound assignment operators. Each of these uses a combination of an arithmetic or bitwise operator followed by an equal sign. If @ = is a compound operator, then the following forms are equivalent, except that the location of **element** is evaluated only once:

> **element @ = value**
>
> **element = (element @ value)**

Requirements for operands of compound assignment differ with the types of operation combined with assignment. These operators have the following operator formations:

> **element += value**
>
> **element −= value**
>
> **element ∗ = value**
>
> **element / = value**
>
> **intelem % = intvalue**
>
> **intelem & = intvalue**
>
> **intelem | = intvalue**
>
> **intelem ^ = intvalue**
>
> **intelem >>= intvalue**
>
> **intelem <<= intvalue**

The conversion and processing of all these operators is the same as would be required for an expression written with an arithmetic or bitwise operator and a simple assignment, except that the location of the first operand is evaluated only once. The arithmetic or bitwise operation is carried out before assignment. The value resulting from the operation is always assigned to the first operand and has the type of the first operand.

Changes to operands resulting from assignment operations will occur after evaluation of the location of the first operand and the value of operation's result, but they are not otherwise guaranteed to occur at any particular time during execution of a program statement.[6] The location of the first operand may be evaluated before or after the value of the operation's result has been determined. Assignments to operands will be in effect before the next statement is executed.

Except within the same assignment, nothing that depends on the value of the first operand of an assignment should be used for any other purpose, directly or indirectly, by the same program statement. Nothing that affects the location of the first operand of an assignment should be changed, directly or indirectly, by the same program statement. Suppose **number** is an **int** with a value of 3 and **mystery** is an array of **int**:

(mystery[number]) = ((number = 4) + (number ++)) ;

Such a statement is allowed in a C program, but its effect is implementation dependent. Any one of three members of **mystery** may be assigned a value of 7 or 8.

Certain assignment operations can also be performed with pointers. The following forms are allowed:

pointer = pointval

pointer += intvalue

pointer -= intvalue

The results of the last two operations are machine dependent if the first operand has a null pointer value.

In the first form of pointer assignment, you can supply the integer constant 0 as the second operand. It will be converted to a null pointer. Otherwise, pointer assignments are subject to the conditions and restrictions stated in Chapter 8, taking into account pointer arithmetic implied by the compound forms of assignment.

Some recent C compilers permit structures to be used in assignments and function references. Only simple assignment can involve structures. The operator formation for this use is

struc = strucval

The first operand must be a structure name. The second can be either the name of a structure of the same type or a structure value of the

---

[6] Ibid., p. 50.

same type returned by a function or obtained from a conditional operation or another assignment. The value of such an assignment is a structure value.

□ DATA TYPE AND SEQUENCE OPERATIONS

Two operations in C are related to properties of data types. They are casts and **sizeof**, both introduced in Chapter 10. A cast operator can cause data type conversion. The **sizeof** operator obtains the amount of storage occupied by a data type or by actual data, on the basis of operations and declared data types.

A cast causes a data value to be converted to a value of a different data type. It has the following operator formation:

(**typ_exp**) **value**

In this formation, **typ_exp** is a data type expression without an identifier. Data type conversions that may be required by casts are explained in Chapter 14. As explained there, no actual changes to data occur when converting between pointer types or when converting between signed and unsigned integers of the same size.

Casts are operations that produce a result. They do not determine how their results will be used in subsequent operations.[7] As Chapter 14 explains, the automatic data conversions of the C language require numerical operations for only four data types: **int, long int, unsigned int**, and **double**. In addition to these, the arguments and return values of functions can be pointers and, for some recent compilers, structures. Casts do not override these limitations. They affect only data values, not operations with values. Casts cannot change an aggregation status or type of usage. They do not convert between any of these categories: array, structure, function, and data or pointer element.

If **moe** and **joe** are **int**, you can "characterize" them in a cast. However, the expression

((**char**) moe) + ((**char**) joe)

will not produce "character addition." Instead, **moe** and **joe** are first converted to characters. Some high-order bits will be lost. The resulting

---

[7] Ibid., p. 42.

values are operands for addition. The rules governing the automatic conversion of data type for addition specify that **char** values will be converted to **int** before being added. The **char** values are reconverted to **int** values. They are added as **int**, and the result is **int**. If you want such an expression to produce a value of type **char**, apply a cast to the result, or simply assign the result to a **char**.

The same considerations apply to the arguments and return values of functions. Any expression you specify for an argument is evaluated, even if it consists of only the name of a data element. If an argument is **char**, the rules of automatic data type conversion cause it to be converted to **int**. If you apply the cast (**char**) to a value, it will first be converted to **char** but will then be reconverted to **int**, as the result of an expression.

Because of the automatic data type conversion rules, you cannot actually transmit a numerical quantity in a function argument or return value except as one of the data types **int**, **long int**, **unsigned int**, or **double**. If you declare a numerical function parameter or return value as a different type, a C compiler will recognize that a quantity has been evaluated and transmitted as one of these four data types, and it will apply a cast of the declared type before using the value.

As explained in Chapter 10, the **sizeof** operator obtains the amount of storage, in bytes, required to hold a data value, element, or aggregate. It has the following set of operator formations:

> **sizeof** element
> **sizeof** pointer
> **sizeof** array
> **sizeof** struc
>
> **sizeof** (gen_exp)

The **sizeof** operator is evaluated when a program is compiled. Any of the above operations behaves like an integer constant. The last form of the operation accepts as an operand an identifier, an expression equivalent to an identifier, a constant, a data type (with or without an identifier), or a value resulting from an expression.

Ordinarily, the **sizeof** operator returns the amount of storage that would be occupied by its operand, appearing as an expression. An exception is made for arrays, when all of the dimensions have been declared. While an array name will ordinarily be interpreted as a pointer, **sizeof**, applied to such an array name, returns not the size of a pointer to an array but the total size of the named array.

When not all array dimensions have been declared, **sizeof** applied to an array identifier obtains the size of a pointer to an array element. Similarly, the name of a function has the value of a pointer to the function; **sizeof** obtains the size of a pointer to a function. Any expression that attempts to treat a function as data, such as applying an indirection operator to a function pointer, is invalid; **sizeof** cannot be used to obtain the size of a function.

The integer data type generated by the **sizeof** operator is implementation dependent. It may be **int, unsigned int, long int,** or **unsigned long int**. Usually, it will be the same as the data type generated by subtracting pointers. The operand of **sizeof** may include operators that can ordinarily change data values: assignment, incrementing, decrementing, and function reference. However, such an operand is not evaluated when a program runs and produces no effect.

The C language includes a sequence operator, which is indicated by placing a comma between expressions. It has the following operator formation:

val_exp, val_exp

The operands of the sequence operator can be any expressions whose values are of a fundamental or modified data type, a pointer type, or, for recent compilers, a structure type.

A sequence operation proceeds by evaluating the first operand, then evaluating the second operand. Any data elements affected by the first operand are changed before the second operand is evaluated. Thus the evaluation proceeds in sequence, like a sequence of statements. The result of a sequence operation is the value of the second operand, and it has the same type.

Sequence operations are commonly found in the control expressions of repetitions, particularly **for** loops. As an example, look at the short function listed in Figure 13.2, written to find an occurrence of one string in another string.

If the **index** function finds **pattern** in **string**, it returns the index in **string** of the starting character of the first occurrence. Otherwise, it returns − 1. Both strings must be null-terminated for this function. Notice that the inner **for** loop uses sequence operators for both the clause that sets up initial conditions and the one that is executed after each repetition. The last clause increments two pointer values. In this example, the sequence of the incrementing happens to be immaterial. Besides sequence operations, this example also uses pointer arithmetic, pointer incrementing, integer incrementing, and logical operations, one

```
int index( string, pattern )
char *string ;              /* string to search      */
char *pattern ;             /* pattern searched for */
{
    int i ;                 /* position in string    */
    char *s, *p ;           /* positions compared    */
    int c, d ;              /* characters compared   */

    for ( i = 0 ; 1 ; ++i )
    {
        for ( ( s = string + i ), ( p = pattern )
        ; ( c = *s ) && ( d = *p ) ; ++p, ++s )
            if ( c != d )
                break ;
        if ( !c )               /* end of string     */
            if ( *p )           /* no match          */
                return -1 ;
            else                /* matched pattern   */
                return i ;
        else if ( !d )          /* matched pattern   */
            return i ;

    }
}
```

Figure 13.2: *A function that illustrates sequence operations.*

of which depends on values of assignment operations. The **if (*p)** statement is used because when **c** is zero the second expression in the logical AND, involving **d**, will not be evaluated.

As previously noted, if sequence operations are used in arguments, they must be parenthesized, so that they are not confused with the commas that separate arguments. Sequence operations are rarely useful in function arguments and are best avoided, to minimize confusion. One of their occasional appearances in this context is to set a null pointer value, for example:

```
char **list, *first ;
search( list, ( first = 0, &first ) ) ;
```

This example relies on the fact that **first** will receive an assigned value before its location is passed as the second function argument. Keep in mind that, unlike the commas of sequence operations, commas between function arguments do not guarantee a particular order of evaluation.

□ CATEGORIES OF OPERATIONS

The following series of tables summarizes the operator formations of the C language. Figure 13.3 shows all the operator formations that involve operands other than pointer and structure values. The operations are grouped by the categories under which they were explained in the text of this chapter. Each entry shows a particular combination of operator, operands, and result. The selection and location operator formations may have different types of results; each potential type is shown. The type of operation is also listed for each operator formation. In this column, U means unary, B means binary, T means ternary, P means plurative, and C means commutative.

Category	Operator Formation	Result	Type
Precedence	(gen_exp)	gen_exp	U
Function	fun_loc(ref_exp)	ref_exp	P
	fun_loc(ref_exp, ref_exp)	ref_exp	P
Selection	struc.strmem	element	B
	struc.strmem	pointer	B
	struc.strmem	array	B
	struc.strmem	struc	B
	strpt −>strmem	element	B
	strpt −>strmem	pointer	B
	strpt −>strmem	array	B
	strpt −>strmem	struc	B
	array[intvalue]	element	B
	array[intvalue]	pointer	B
	array[intvalue]	array	B
	array[intvalue]	struc	B
Location	*pointval	element	U
	*pointval	pointer	U
	*pointval	array	U
	*pointval	struc	U
	*pointval	fun_loc	U
	&locatable	pointval	U

Figure 13.3: *General operator formations.*

Arithmetic	value + value	value	BC
	value − value	value	B
	value * value	value	BC
	value / value	value	B
	intvalue % intvalue	intvalue	B
	− value	value	U
	++element	value	U
	element ++	value	U
	−−element	value	U
	element −−	value	U
Comparison	value < value	intvalue	B
	value > value	intvalue	B
	value <= value	intvalue	B
	value >= value	intvalue	B
	value == value	intvalue	BC
	value != value	intvalue	BC
Conditional	value ? value : value	value	T
Logical	value && value	intvalue	B
	value || value	intvalue	B
	!value	intvalue	U
Bitwise	intvalue & intvalue	intvalue	BC
	intvalue | intvalue	intvalue	BC
	intvalue ^ intvalue	intvalue	BC
	~ intvalue	intvalue	U
	intvalue >> intvalue	intvalue	B
	intvalue << intvalue	intvalue	B
Assignment	element = value	value	B
	element += value	value	B
	element −= value	value	B
	element *= value	value	B
	element /= value	value	B
	intelement %= intvalue	intvalue	B
	intelement &= intvalue	intvalue	B

Figure 13.3: *General operator formations (continued).*

	intelement | = intvalue	intvalue	B
	intelement ^= intvalue	intvalue	B
	intelement >>= intvalue	intvalue	B
	intelement <<= intvalue	intvalue	B
Data type	(typ_exp) value	value	B
	sizeof element	intvalue	U
	sizeof pointer	intvalue	U
	sizeof array	intvalue	U
	sizeof struc	intvalue	U
	sizeof (gen_exp)	intvalue	U
Sequence	val_exp, val_exp	val_exp	B

Figure 13.3: *General operator formations (continued).*

Figure 13.4 summarizes the operator formations that involve pointer values as operands. As in Figure 13.3, the operations are grouped according to the categories of this chapter. The types of operators use the same abbreviations in this table as in Figure 13.3.

Figure 13.5 summarizes the operator formations involving structure values that are provided by some of the more recent compilers. As in Figures 13.3 and 13.4, these formations are grouped according to categories of this chapter, and they use the same abbreviations for operator types.

The classes of operands used in Figures 13.3 through 13.5 and in the text of this chapter are summarized in Figure 13.6. There is a major distinction between declared data, for which storage is explicitly reserved, and derived quantities, obtained from constants and from the application of operators to data in expressions. The C language provides no way to determine the locations of derived values. As the tables show, derived values cannot be the subject of incrementing and decrementing or the object of an assignment.

Two restricted subclasses of declared data are shown. One of these concerns elements that take on integer values. The other is pointers to structures. The first of these classes has a counterpart among derived values: those that are of an integer type. One class is described as *abstracted*: the data organizations expressed by data types, **typedef** symbols, and structure tags. Finally, there are *composites,* made up of more than one of the other classes.

Category	Operator Formation	Result	Type
Arithmetic	pointval + intvalue	pointval	BC
	pointval − intvalue	pointval	B
	pointval − pointval	intvalue	B
	++pointer	pointval	U
	pointer++	pointval	U
	−−pointer	pointval	U
	pointer−−	pointval	U
Comparison	pointval < pointval	intvalue	B
	pointval > pointval	intvalue	B
	pointval <= pointval	intvalue	B
	pointval >= pointval	intvalue	B
	pointval == pointval	intvalue	BC
	pointval != pointval	intvalue	BC
Conditional	pointval ? value : value	value	T
	value ? pointval : pointval	pointval	T
	pointval ? pointval : pointval	pointval	T
Logical	pointval && value	intvalue	B
	value && pointval	intvalue	B
	pointval && pointval	intvalue	B
	pointval || value	intvalue	B
	value || pointval	intvalue	B
	pointval || pointval	intvalue	B
	!pointval	intvalue	U
Assignment	pointer = pointval	pointval	B
	pointer += intvalue	pointval	B
	pointer −= intvalue	pointval	B

Figure 13.4: *Pointer value operator formations.*

Figure 13.6 shows classes of C operands that are used to create data-evaluation expressions. It does not break down details of data organization operands, described in Chapter 10, because they have few uses in data expressions.

C compilers may accept operands of types other than those indicated. One common example is integer values other than zero in place of pointer values. While such additional operator formations are helpful in some

Category	Operator Formation	Result	Type
Conditional	**value ? strucval : strucval**	**strucval**	T
	pointval ? strucval : strucval	**strucval**	T
Assignment	**struc = strucval**	**strucval**	B

Figure 13.5: *Structure value operator formations.*

Category	Class	Characteristics
Declared	**element**	any fundamental or modified type
	pointer	pointer to any data type
	struc	structure of any organization
	array	array of any data type
	fun_loc	name or location of function
Restricted	**intelement**	**element** of an integer type
	strpt	**pointer** to **struc**
Abstracted	**typ_exp**	data type or organization
Derived	**value**	any fundamental or modified type
	pointval	any pointer type
	strucval	any structure organization
Ordinal	**intvalue**	**value** of an integer type
Composite	**locatable**	**element, pointer, struc**
	val_exp	**value, pointval**
		strucval (recent compilers)
	ref_exp	**element, pointer, fun_loc, val_exp**
		struc (recent compilers)
	gen_exp	**ref_exp** (including **struc, strucval**)
		array, typ_exp

Figure 13.6: *Classification of operands and results.*

circumstances, their meanings are implementation dependent, and their use will render a program nonportable. C provides only a few fundamental data types but allows great flexibility in combining them, through arrays, structures, and pointers. There are, in contrast, at least 48 distinct C operators. The next chapter shows how to use the powerful expression forming capabilities of C, to assemble combinations of operations with any degree of complexity.

□ EXERCISES

13.1: Functions constructed for the following exercises should use the bitwise operators to set, test, or shift the bits of data elements.

(a) Write a function with a **long int** as one argument and a bit length as another, which specifies a number of low-order bits of the **long int** to be printed out in binary. For example, the low-order five bits of the value 105 (decimal) should print as 11001.

(b) Write a function that will determine the number of bits in data elements of types **char**, **short int**, **int**, and **long int**.

(c) Write a function that will reverse the order of bits in a **char**.

(d) Write a function that will determine whether the parity of an **int** value (the number of one bits) is even or odd, by shifting and counting bits.

(e) Write a program that will determine whether a computer uses ones complement, twos complement, or sign-magnitude representation for negative integers.

13.2: A good random number generator is hard to find. The most common method on computers is to multiply integers and extract some of the high-order bits, to produce pseudorandom integers with a uniform distribution. Other distributions are created by manipulating the numbers from a uniform distribution. However, as Birger Jansson's book on pseudorandom numbers shows, the predictability of the bits from a multiplicative generator increases toward the low-order end of the numbers.

(a) Make a random-number generator for **int** values that multiplies an odd seed by an odd prime, somewhat larger than $2^{n/2}$, where n is the number of bits in an **int**, then extracts the $n/2$ bits below the sign bit. If the sign bit is set by a multiplication, it should be cleared before the next multiplication. What is the range of values that this method can generate?

(b) Make a random-number generator that maintains two different seeds, using one for high-order bits and the other for low-order bits of a generated number. What range of values can it generate?

(c) Make a random-number generator, based on (b), that will generate random numbers that lie between two limits specified as function arguments, by relating each integer between the specified limits to a number that will be produced by the multiplicative procedure, rejecting a generated number that does not relate to a value in the required range, and otherwise converting a generated number to an output value.

13.3: The following exercises should be addressed by making use of the conditional operator.

(a) Write an expression whose value is the minimum of three **int** variables.

(b) Write an expression whose value is the middle of three **int** variables.

(c) Write an expression, using a function, whose value is 1 if the parity of an **unsigned int** value is odd, − 1 if the parity is even, but 0 if the number is equal to zero.

(d) Write an expression that compares high-order and low-order halves of an **unsigned int**, producing a value of 1 if the high-order half is greater, − 1 if the low-order half is greater, and 0 if they are equal.

(e) Write an expression that will shift the bits of an **unsigned int** variable the number of places given by an **int** variable, producing an **unsigned int** value, such that a positive number of bit positions means a left shift and a negative number of bit positions means a right shift.

13.4: Use pointer incrementing and decrementing to work out the following exercises.

(a) Write a statement that counts the number of blanks in a **char** string.

(b) Write a function with a **char*** argument that returns as a **char*** value a pointer to the start of the next parameter in the string, where parameters can be separated by commas and by any number of blanks or tabs.

(c) Write a function with a **char*** argument that returns as a **char*** value a pointer to the start of the data in the next parameter, where parameters may be either character strings without embedded blanks, tabs, double quotes, or commas, or strings with any character between double quotes.

(d) Write a function with a **char*** argument that returns as a **char*** value a pointer to the end of the data in the next parameter, where parameters are defined as in (c) and may contain double quote characters specified by two such characters in a row.

(e) Write a function that accepts as arguments the pointers returned by (c) and (d) and returns as an **int** value the number of characters in a parameter, correcting for the representation of double quotes.

13.5: The following exercises create functions to print histograms. Use array and pointer manipulations for this work.

(a) Write a function that will print a horizontal bar graph for an argument to be specified as an array of **int**, automatically scaling values so that the largest and the smallest values will be represented by the numbers of characters specified in other arguments.

(b) Modify the function in (a) so that it will present a histogram for data with error estimates, using two **int** array arguments, one of which gives an estimate of the error width, generating printed lines of the following form:

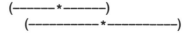

(c) Write a function that will print a vertical bar graph for an array of **int**, making columns of specified minimum and maximum height, in characters, each a specified number of characters wide.

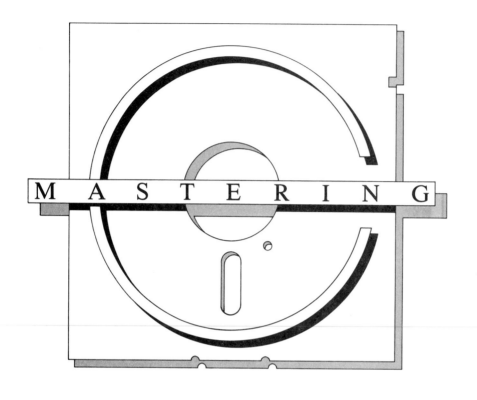

CHAPTER 14

EVALUATING EXPRESSIONS

Data manipulations in C statements often involve more than a single operation. A data evaluation, controlled by a combination of data identifiers, values, and operators, is known as a *data evaluation expression* or, more commonly, as simply an *expression*. The C language offers a flexible and powerful capability for creating expressions. In this chapter, you will read about:

- automatic conversions of data type
- controlled conversions of data type
- operator priorities and grouping
- writing and interpreting expressions
- using expressions in statements

□ AUTOMATIC CONVERSIONS OF DATA TYPE

The C language applies a set of data conversions, sometimes called the *automatic unary conversions,* to all data appearing in any context. They are as follows:

- Any item of type **char** is converted to **int**.
- Any **short int** is converted to **int**.
- Any **float** is converted to **double**.

These rules mean that C, in its conventional implementations, performs all operations with just four data types:

> **int**
> **unsigned int**
> **long int**
> **double**

When a **char** value is converted to **int**, the **int** value is numerically the same. This is possible because all ordinary implementations of C provide an **int** with a larger size than a **char**. As mentioned in Chapter 5, **char** data may be signed or unsigned, depending on the implementation. When **char** is unsigned, it is converted to **int** by adding high-order zero bits. When a signed **char** or a **short int** is converted to **int**, high-order bits of the appropriate form are added to preserve the sign and magnitude of a value. Conversions between **float** and **double** are explained in Chapter 16, on implementation features. Basically, **float** has less precision. Any float value can be expressed exactly as **double**.

An additional set of conversions is performed for the operands of certain binary and ternary operators, shown in Figure 14.1. These are sometimes called the *automatic binary conversions.*

Automatic binary conversions apply to both operands of the binary operator formations and to the second and third operands of the conditional operator formations shown in Figure 14.1. They are carried out after automatic unary conversions and behave as follows:

- If one operand is **double** and the other is not, the latter is converted to **double**.

- Otherwise, if one operand is **long int** and the other is not, the latter is converted to **long int**.

- Otherwise, if one operand is **unsigned int** and the other is not, the latter is converted to **unsigned int**.

If none of these conditions apply, the operands have the same type.

When **int** is converted to **unsigned int**, the result follows the rules of modular arithmetic, as explained in Chapter 13. If the **int** value is negative, the value obtained is the same as that produced by subtracting an **unsigned int** value of the same magnitude from zero. For a twos complement binary representation, no bits change.

When an **int** value is converted to **long**, the numerical value is unchanged. The **long int** always has a size equal to or larger than **int**. When an **unsigned int** is converted to **long int**, if the size of **long int** is greater, the unsigned value is converted by adding high-order zero bits. If the sizes are the same, there is a possibility of overflow. The result will usually be to leave the bits unchanged. When an **unsigned int** value is too large to be represented as **long int**, however, the result of conversion is implementation dependent.

Conversions of integer values to **double** are explained in Chapter 16, on implementation features. Basically, these conversions preserve the sign and approximate magnitude. If the precision of **double** is at least as great as the number of significant bits in an integer value, then the magnitude of the value will be preserved exactly by a conversion.

A special automatic conversion from any integer type to a pointer type occurs for the operator formations listed in Figure 14.2. When **intvalue** is zero, it is converted to a null pointer of the **pointval** type. Conversion of any other integer value is implementation dependent.

The data types **int, unsigned int, long int,** and **double** can be regarded as *operating* types of C data, since all the operations are performed with them. These are also the data types used to pass arguments to functions and to return values from them. The other C data types can be regarded as *storage* data types. Data can be stored in these forms; choosing the minimum necessary size of data element can help to conserve storage.

Some C compilers offer additional data types. Such a data type may be supported by data operations; otherwise, it should have a rule for automatic data conversion. Ordinarily, for example, **unsigned short int** will be converted to **unsigned int**. However, the use of such data types makes a program nonportable; this book describes only applications and conversions for conventional data types.

Category	Operator Formation
Arithmetic	**value + value**
	value − value
	value * value
	value / value
	intvalue % intvalue
Comparison	**value < value**
	value > value
	value <= value
	value >= value
	value == value
	value != value
Bitwise	**intvalue & intvalue**
	**intvalue	intvalue**
	intvalue ^ intvalue
Conditional	**value ? value : value**
	pointval ? value : value

Figure 14.1: *Automatic binary conversion operations.*

□ CONTROLLED CONVERSIONS OF DATA TYPE

Data type conversions may be controlled by C statements and operations. Controlled conversions can occur to data that appear in the following circumstances:

- as the second operand of an assignment

- as the return value of a function

- as the operand of a cast

Under the following conditions, controlled conversion must occur:

- if the data type of the second operand in an assignment differs from that of the first operand

Category	Operator Formation
Comparison	pointval < intvalue
	pointval > intvalue
	pointval <= intvalue
	pointval >= intvalue
	pointval == intvalue
	pointval != intvalue
	intvalue < pointval
	intvalue > pointval
	intvalue <= pointval
	intvalue >= pointval
	intvalue == pointval
	intvalue != pointval
Conditional	value ? pointval : intvalue
	pointval ? pointval : intvalue
	value ? intvalue : pointval
	pointval ? intvalue : pointval

Figure 14.2: *Operator formations for which integer-to-pointer conversion is performed.*

- if a value in a **return** statement does not have the type declared for the function's return value

- if a data value does not have the data type of a cast applied to it

Controlled data conversions that are the same as automatic data conversions are performed in the same ways. In general, automatic data conversions widen the size of a data type, maintain unsigned data values, or promote integer types to a more flexible floating type. Controlled data conversions may also narrow the size of a data type, abandon unsigned values, or demote floating types to less flexible integer types.

When a value of an integer type is converted to another integer type of smaller size, high-order bits that do not fit into the binary representation of the smaller type are discarded. This type of conversion can occur for **long int** to **unsigned int, int, short int,** or **char,** for **unsigned int** or **int** to **short int** or **char,** and for **short int** to **char.** Unless the value being converted is within the range of the smaller data type, the result of such a conversion will be implementation dependent.

When an **unsigned int** value is converted to **int,** the resulting value is unchanged, provided it is within the range of **int.** Otherwise, the conversion will usually leave the bits unchanged, but the result is implementation-dependent.

When a **double** is converted to **float,** the result is to reduce the precision, unless the two types are implemented as identical. When a **double** is converted to an integer type, unless it has an integer value, an integer part is first extracted. The technique is implementation dependent; it may give the next higher integer, the next lower integer, or the closest integer. Then the value is converted to the format of the result, provided it is within the range of that data type. If it is not, the result obtained will be implementation dependent.

Pointer conversion occurs in any of the circumstances for controlled data conversion when the value to be converted is integer and the result of conversion is a pointer. If the integer value is zero, it is converted to a null pointer of the required type. The result of converting any other integer value is implementation dependent.

The C language does not specify when conversion occurs for the return value of a function. It guarantees only that if the data type declared in a function invocation matches the data type declared in the function definition, a correct result will be obtained. Conversion controlled by a function's declaration or definition may occur in the function itself, after the function has returned, or in both places. To make robust, portable programs, you must make sure function declarations match function definitions.

Some compilers support additional controlled data type conversions, such as from a pointer type to some integer type. Both the availability and the result of any such conversion are implementation dependent. A number of compilers fail to implement casts correctly when a narrowing or demoting cast would immediately be reversed by the widening or promoting effect of another operation. A few compilers ignore casts except for function arguments. To make readily portable programs, you should avoid casts when possible and use assignments instead.

□ OPERATOR PRIORITIES AND GROUPING

When expressions are written without parentheses, their interpretation is governed by the priority and grouping of operators. Each operator in C belongs to a priority level and has a grouping rule. With a knowledge of these priorities and groupings, you can construct and understand C expressions. Figure 14.3 shows the priority levels and grouping of all the C operators.

The interpretation of an expression consists of recognizing operators and their operands and of describing the order in which operations must be performed. This is known as *parsing* an expression. An expression can be parsed by placing parentheses, where they do not already occur, in the places assumed by a C compiler as a result of priorities and grouping of operators. Once an expression has been parsed, it can be evaluated by beginning within the innermost pairs of parentheses and working outward until all results and changes to data have been determined and a value is obtained for the expression as a whole.

The basic rule for parsing expressions is that operations of higher priority are carried out before those of lower priority. For example, consider the expression

```
a + b * c
```

Because multiplication has higher priority than addition, parentheses reflecting the priorities of C operators belong in the following places:

```
( a + ( b * c ) )
```

When adjacent operations have equal priority, grouping rules must be examined. In Figure 14.3, you can see that all operators with the same priority have the same grouping rule. For example, consider this expression:

```
x / y * z
```

Priority	Operators	Type	Category	Grouping
16	( )	U	Precedence	forms groups
15	( )	P	Function	left to right
15	(,)	P	Function	left to right
15	[ ]	B	Indexing	left to right
15	. ->	B	Selection	left to right
14	++ -- -	U	Arithmetic	right to left
14	~	U	Bitwise NOT	right to left
14	!	U	Logical NOT	right to left
14	*	U	Indirection	right to left
14	&	U	Reference	right to left
14	**sizeof**	U	Size	right to left
14	( )	B	Cast	right to left
13	* / %	B	Arithmetic	left to right
12	+ -	B	Arithmetic	left to right
11	>> <<	B	Bitwise shift	left to right
10	< > <= >=	B	Comparison	left to right
9	== !=	B	Comparison	left to right
8	&	B	Bitwise AND	left to right
7	^	B	Bitwise XOR	left to right
6	|	B	Bitwise OR	left to right
5	&&	B	Logical AND	left to right
4	||	B	Logical OR	left to right
3	? :	T	Conditional	right to left
2	=	B	Assignment	right to left
2	*= /= %=	B	Assignment	right to left
2	+= -=	B	Assignment	right to left
2	>>= <<=	B	Assignment	right to left
2	&= ^= |=	B	Assignment	right to left
1	,	B	Sequence	left to right

Figure 14.3: *Priorities and grouping of operators.*

The multiplication and division operations group from left to right. This means that parentheses reflecting grouping belong in the following places:

((x / y) * z)

The priority and grouping of indexing and selection are particularly important to understand, because these operations usually appear in data manipulations without parentheses. Consider an array of structures, each of which contains an array, another structure, and an array of structures. Such an array is listed in Figure 14.4.

Selection and indexing have the same priority of operation, the highest except for precedence parentheses. They group from left to right. This means that the following combination of indexing and selection is parsed as shown:

plot[first] . area

((plot[first]) . area)

Indexing is performed first, selecting a particular structure from the **plot** array, as determined by the value of **first**. Then member selection occurs, selecting the **area** member of that structure. To obtain one of the members of **reference** from that structure, the combination

```
struct VEC
{
    int heading ;
    int extent ;
} ;

struct SEC
{
    int origin[ 2 ] ;
    struct VEC vector[ 2 ] ;
} ;

struct PLT
{
    int area ;
    int reference[ 2 ] ;
    struct VEC centroid ;
    int sector_count ;
    struct SEC sector[ PLT_SEC ] ;
} plot[ PLT_COUNT ] ;
```

Figure 14.4: *An array of structures.*

of indexing and selection is parsed as follows:

> plot[first] . reference[i]
>
> (((plot[first]) . reference)[i])

Continuing with the plot example of Figure 14.4, to select a member of the centroid substructure, the combination of indexing and selection would be parsed as follows:

> plot[first] . centroid . extent
>
> (((plot[first]) . centroid) . extent)

Finally, a vector from one of the sector members is parsed:

> plot[first] . sector[2] . vector[1] . heading
>
> ((((((plot[first]) . sector)[2]) . vector)[1]) . heading)

Although such an expression can appear long and messy, its interpretation is quite regular; the indexing and selection operations occur as read, from left to right.

A function reference cannot be combined with indexing, since an array cannot be returned, but it might be combined with selection of a structure member. Using the declarations of the previous example, suppose the search function returns a pointer to an SEC structure. A member of a vector might be designated and parsed as follows:

> struct SEC *search( ) ;
>
> search(last)–>vector[0] . extent
>
> ((((search(last))–>vector)[0]) . extent)

In this example, vector member zero is obtained indirectly from the pointer returned by search, and then the extent member of that structure is selected. Again, the expression reads regularly, from left to right. A function reference can occur only at the start of such an expression.

The unary operators at priority 14 are also important to understand clearly, since they often occur in combinations and are usually written without parentheses. These operators all group from right to left. The incrementing and decrementing operators can occur either before or after an operand that designates a data element. Because they must have a locatable operand, only one such operator can appear in a sequence. Once it has acted, the result is a nonlocatable value, which is not eligible for another such operation.

As an example of these unary operators, consider the following expression, where **p** is a pointer to **char**, which will be parsed as shown:

```
!*p++

( ! ( *( p++ ) ) )
```

Grouping from the right, first the postincrementing operator is applied to **p**, obtaining the current value of this pointer but scheduling it for subsequent incrementing. Then the character pointed to is obtained (and immediately converted to **int**). Finally the logical value of this character is tested and inverted. The result of the expression is an **int** value, 0 or 1.

Because function reference, indexing, and selection have higher priority than these unary operators, you will need to write parentheses if one of the unary operators is to be applied first. For example, if **sect** points to one of the **SEC** structures in a **sector** array, shown in Figure 14.4, and you want to use an **origin** member from the next structure in the **sector** array, then you might write the following expression:

```
struct SEC *sect ;

( ++sect )->origin[ nvis ]
```

If there were no parentheses around ++**sect**, the incrementing operator would apply to **origin** member **nvis**, instead of to pointer **sect**.

There is a peculiar form of expression involving an incrementing or decrementing operator and either indexing or selection, in which parentheses might not seem necessary:

```
( sect++ )->origin[ nvis ]
```

Here, because of the positions of identifiers and operators, the ++ could "logically" operate only on **sect**. Your C compiler may or may not agree; use parentheses.

□ WRITING AND INTERPRETING EXPRESSIONS

Expressions are evaluated by regular application of the operator priorities and the grouping rules. The grouping of binary operations at priorities 4 through 13 is straightforward, although the number of operator categories is large. All of these operators group from left to right. Some expressions and their parsings are shown in the following examples:

```
x == y && c < d
( ( x == y ) && ( c < d ) )

3 * n >> 8 & 0x20
( ( ( 3 * n ) >> 8 ) & 0x20 )

x – y – 5 > z ^ p == q != e
( ( ( ( x – y ) – 5 ) > z ) ^ ( ( p == q ) != e ) )
```

Some expressions that require parentheses for correct interpretation are shown in the following examples:

```
( u || v ) && ( x || f > g )

( n & 0x300 ) == 0x100

( a + b ) / ( c – d )

( w | 020 ) << 3

j << ( k & 3 )

r – ( s + t )
```

The first and third operands of a conditional operator group from right to left, but this grouping is seldom of use. More than one conditional operator in an expression looks confusing and should generally be avoided. A rare exception might be the following expression, which has a value of – 1, 0, or 1 as the value of nn is less than zero, zero, or greater than zero:

```
nn < 0 ? – 1 : nn == 0 ? 0 : 1

nn < 0 ? – 1 : ( nn == 0 ? 0 : 1 )
```

A step in parsing this expression is to form a group on the right, as shown. Because a question mark is used for no other purpose, the conditional operator characters, like array brackets, can enclose a middle operand of lower priority. This operand can be only assignment or sequence, as shown in the following example:

```
ee ? vv = 1 : ( vv = 2 )
```

Here, if ee is nonzero, vv is set to 1, and that is the value of the expression. Otherwise, vv is set to 2, and that becomes the value of the expression. Parentheses are required for the second assignment. For clarity, it is probably advisable to use them around the first one as well.

The assignment operators also group from right to left, making possible a form of statement often found in C programs, shown in the following example:

ii = jj = kk = nn = 0 ;

The right to left grouping of assignment operators causes such a statement to be parsed as thus:

ii = (jj = (kk = (nn = 0))) ;

The value of every variable in the statement is set to zero. Assignments can be used for incrementing and decrementing, and they often are, as in these expressions:

(pp += PINC)

(mm −= MDEC)

If **PINC** and **MDEC** have values of one, the effects of these expressions are the same as those of the incrementing and decrementing operators. However, expressions of this kind can increment or decrement by any amount, not just one. Compound assignments using binary logic are sometimes used to keep track of status variables:

error_status |= new_errors ;

success &= current_success ;

Although Figure 14.3 describes the sequence operator as grouping from left to right, this description simply confirms the meaning of the operator: to evaluate the expressions that are separated by sequence commas from left to right, producing the last one as a value. Unlike all other operators, the sequence operator guarantees that changes resulting from incrementing, decrementing, and assignments will be in effect before successive operands are evaluated. For that reason, you might write a **for** statement such as

for (ii = nn, kk = 3 * ii ; ii < 52 ; ++ii)

In this statement, ii will be set to the current value of nn before a value for kk is computed. Therefore, kk must receive a value three times the current value of nn rather than three times the previous value of ii.

At first, the operator priorities and groupings may look complex, but with a little use their patterns will come to seem natural. It may be useful to think of the operators as falling into fewer categories, as listed in Figure 14.5. In the categories of this table, it is fairly easy to remember that primaries are highest and unaries just below and that sequence is lowest and assignment just above. With that in mind, you can focus on the inner six categories. Of these, conditionals are at the bottom, perhaps because they are rarely used. Arithmetic operations are at the top; they are found throughout most programs.

The ranking of the center four categories is probably the hardest to remember:

Shift
Comparison
Bit
Logic

Category	Operators
Primary	( ) **fun_loc( ) fun_loc(,) [ ] . ->**
Unary	++ -- - ~ ! * & **sizeof** (typ_exp)
Arithmetic	* / % + -
Shift	>> <<
Comparison	< > <= >= == !=
Bit	& ^ |
Logic	&& ||
Conditional	? :
Assignment	= *= /= %/ += -= >>= <<= &= ^= |=
Sequence	,

Figure 14.5: *The operators grouped into a few categories.*

The priorities of the bit operators can be unhandy. Often, one wants to clear or set some bits, then compare the result with something else. To do that, you must use parentheses:

if ((value & mask) == check)

Without parentheses, a C compiler would parse the control expression incorrectly:

(value & (mask == check))

When you start to use C, it is probably best to parenthesize all expressions involving shift, comparison, logic, and bit operators. As you grow more familiar with such expressions, you will probably find yourself dropping the parentheses first around logical AND and OR, then around comparisons. However, even experienced C programmers usually parenthesize the shift and bit operators in all but the simplest cases.

The overloading of operator characters in C and the possibility of multiple unary operators can lead to ambiguities in expressions. The most common sources of difficulty are expressions similar to the following:

```
int *x, *y ;
int k, m, n ;
char *p, *q ;
```

Ambiguities can arise in the following cases:

Case 1.   n = *x/*y ;

    Does this mean   n = (*x) / (*y) ;

           or   n = *x   /*y ; . . . comment

Case 2.   p = q+++n ;

    Does this mean   p = (q++) + n ;

           or   p = q + (++n) ;

Case 3.   k = m----n ;

    Does this mean   k = (m--) - (-n) ;

           or   k = m - (-(--n)) ;

           or   k = m - (-(-(-n))) ;

C has a rule of interpretation that resolves these ambiguities. If spacing separates operator characters, the operator characters are interpreted as they are divided by spacing. If you write (--n), n is negated twice. If spacing does not separate operator characters, a compiler, starting from the left and proceeding to the right, will make the longest possible combination that constitutes an element of the language.[1]

Following this rule, for Case 1 above, the second interpretation is correct. The characters /* mark the start of a comment. For Case 2, the first interpretation is the one in effect. A postincrementing operation is performed on q. Case 3 is troublesome. The interpretation is none of those suggested. Instead, it is this:

$$k = ((m--)--) n ;$$

The statement originally shown, without parentheses or spacing, has no valid interpretation. To make your programs portable and easy to read, avoid ambiguous use of operator characters. Never use spacing between the characters of multicharacter operators. Always use spacing, parentheses, or both to separate adjacent operators whenever the characters might have more than one interpretation.

When the parsing of an expression does not require a particular order of evaluation, the C language does not guarantee one. Consider, for example, the expression,

$$(a - b) + (x - y)$$

The subexpressions (a − b) and (x − y) have to be computed before these values can be added, but either of them may be computed first. Ordinarily, this type of rearrangement should matter only if, during evaluation, functions are invoked that change the value of some quantity which is used more than once. For example, if the next function returns the "next" integer in an array, the value of the following expression is unreliable:

$$a * next( ) + b * next( )$$

A robust program will not contain an expression whose value depends on its order of evaluation.

The C language has a peculiar *rearrangement rule* for expressions, found in no other language. Even though precedence parentheses have the highest priority of all operators, for certain commutative operators they may be disregarded.[2] This can happen when the same operator occurs more than once in sequence. The operators involved are:

---

[1] Brian W. Kernighan and Dennis M. Ritchie, *The C Programming Language,* (Englewood Cliffs, N. J.:, Prentice-Hall, 1978), p. 179. A few C compilers cause portability problems by allowing characters of multicharacter operators to be separated by spacing, ignoring the spacing, and applying the interpretation rule.

[2] Ibid., pp. 49 and 188–190.

*	(multiplication)
+	(addition)
&	(bitwise AND)
^	(bitwise XOR)
|	(bitwise OR)

The rearrangement rule states that when an operator from this set occurs more than once in sequence, the operations can be performed in any order, regardless of parentheses.

According to the rearrangement rule, the expression (a + b + c), for example, can be evaluated as indicated by any of the following:

```
( ( a + b ) + c )
( ( a + c ) + b )
( ( b + c ) + a )
```

Although you may have parenthesized the expression in one of these ways, a C compiler is allowed to disregard your parentheses and evaluate it in any order. An order of evaluation will matter only if there is a possibility of overflow that you can anticipate. If, for example, you are adding large positive value a to large negative value b and you want that done before the other addition, use a separate assignment:

```
partial_sum = a + b ;
complete_sum = partial_sum + c ;
```

Parentheses will not be rearranged when a different operator appears inside them. Consider this expression:

```
( a – b ) + ( c – d ) + ( e – f )
```

The rearrangement rule does not allow a compiler to peek inside the subexpressions and make an evaluation such as this:

```
( a + c + e ) – ( b + d + f )
```

□ USING EXPRESSIONS IN STATEMENTS

Certain forms of C expressions occur so frequently in the work of experienced programmers that they can be regarded as characteristic of the language. This section demonstrates several of these "idioms" of the language.

The conditional operator makes a handy "floor" and "ceiling," limiting the value of a variable:

```
floor = a < MIN ? MIN : a ;

ceiling = a > MAX ? MAX : a ;

bounded = a < MIN ? MIN : a > MAX ? MAX : a ;
```

The incrementing operators in a **for** statement make a string length measurement. As shown, length is **int** and p is a pointer to **char**:

```
for ( length = 0, p = string ; *p++ ; ++length ) ;
```

Here, nothing is controlled by **for**. All the work is done by the control expressions. The loop terminates when a null character is found. A similar statement copies characters from one place to another:

```
for ( p = origin, q = destination ; *q++ = *p++ ; ) ;
```

As shown, both p and q are pointers to **char**. The loop is ended by a null character, which is copied. Adding an **int**, as in the counting loop, can be used to limit a string copy to some maximum string LENGTH:

```
for ( p = origin, q = destination, i = 0 ;
i++ < LENGTH && ( *q++ = *p++ ) ; ) ;
```

Parentheses are required around the assignment. After this loop ends, if i equals LENGTH a string copy may be incomplete.

The use of **for** statements in counting takes a number of characteristic forms:

```
for ( i = COUNT ; i-- ; )
```

Here, i is **int**, and COUNT, which must be greater than zero, controls the number of repetitions. When indexing an array, it is often desirable to have i count up from zero:

```
for ( i = 0 ; i < COUNT ; ++i )
```

A loop may occur within a loop, for example, in bubble sort. Here, i and j are both **int**:

```
for ( i = 0 ; i < MAX − 1 ; ++i )
   for ( j = i + 1 ; j < MAX ; ++j )
```

Sometimes one index runs up while another runs down. They can both be included in the same **for** statement:

```
for ( i = 0, j = MAX ; i < j ; i += INC, j -= DEC )
```

Patterns sometimes require detection every **k** repetitions:

if (!(i % k))

When the first repetition should not be included:

if (!(i % k) && i)

Expressions sometimes depend on the fact that the second operand of logical AND is not evaluated when the first one is FALSE. This example suppresses division by zero:

if (d && f / d > LIMIT)

This example suppresses an invalid function reference:

if (s >= 0 && square_root(s) <= BOUND)

The following statement tests to see that a pointer does not have a null value before testing to see that the character it points to is not a null character:

if (p && *p)

The last example of this type invokes a function to read in a character, assigns the character value obtained to an **int**, tests to see that it is not a null character, and, provided it is not, checks the end of file indication:

```
#include "stdio.h"
int c ;

if ( ( c = fgetc( stdin ) ) && c != EOF )
```

When bitwise operators are required, some programmers make a fetish of using **unsigned int**. This has the virtue of guaranteeing that zero bits will always be entered by a shift in either direction, but it has the liability of requiring conversions for many operations. In all the binary operations with an **unsigned int** and an **int**, the **int** must be converted to **unsigned int**. Depending on details of an implementation, this conversion may or may not actually change data.

Unfortunately, the C language does not provide a way to define a constant that has data type **unsigned int**, so conversions will occur for all integer constants and all default integer values. Rather than fret over which conversions will occur or have an actual effect, it is simpler to use signed integers for all data, except when an operation clearly requires an unsigned value. If this policy is followed, most bitwise operations will involve two **int** values, and no type conversions will be needed.

Many programs that work with text use either pointer arithmetic or array indexing to reach members of a string of **char**. The effectiveness of these methods varies with the instructions available on different computers. The incrementing and decrementing operators can be particularly effective on computers that provide instructions with automatic address incrementing. They are likely to be ineffective on computers that do not provide address incrementing instructions. Computers that split an address into two parts, such as base and offset, will be relatively slow at any form of member selection.

□ EXERCISES

14.1: *Diophantine* equations are equations for which the allowed solutions must have integer values. Components of the following problems can be expressed this way.

(a) What is the sum of all the numbers less than 500 that, when repeatedly divided by three, produce a remainder of one at least four times?

(b) How many different boxes whose sides are an integral number of units in length have a diagonal that is also an integral number of units long (but not more than 100)?

(c) A proposition by the mathematician Fermat states that no positive integers a, b, and c will satisfy the equation $a^n + b^n = c^n$, when n is greater than 2. Are there integers all less than 10,000 that satisfy $a^3 + b^3 = c^2$?

14.2: Managers of advertising campaigns have grown fond of programs to generate "personalized" mail. In this exercise you will construct such a program. The program will use three files, one containing a prototype text, one containing a mailing list, divided into entries, and one for output copies of the text. The last of these might be directed to a printer.

Your program will need a convention for marking substitutions in the prototype text, such as "%%01" to indicate the first substitution field, "%%02" to indicate the second, and so on. You will also need a convention for indicating substitution fields in a list entry, such as using lines of text as fields and treating a blank line as the end of an entry.

(a) Outline a program consisting of a main control procedure and these operating procedures:

- Read prototype text. This procedure accepts lines of text and stores them in an internal buffer.

- Read list entry. This procedure reads substitutions for one copy of the text and stores them in an internal buffer.

- Write substituted text. This procedure merges substitutions with prototype text and generates an output copy.

Consider whether to use dynamic storage, how you will treat the division of text into lines, how much text and how many substitution fields you will allow, and how you will handle errors.

(b) Write functions for the control procedure and the procedure to read prototype text. Test them by counting the number of substitution fields and finding the highest numbered one.

(c) Write a function to read in a list entry. Test it by writing out the fields separately.

(d) Write a function to write an output copy. Allow individual fields to be substituted as many times as necessary.

(e) Add formatting capabilities to the output function, recognizing words in the text and starting a new line if the next word would extend beyond the end of the current line.

(f) Add hyphenation capabilities, using a character that will normally not be printed, such as ~ , to mark a "discretionary hyphen." When the formatting for a word starts a new line, place as much as possible of the word on the current line, up to a discretionary hyphen, and add a real hyphen.

14.3: All computers are limited in the sizes of numbers—that is, the number of decimal places—that their basic instructions will process. Sometimes it is necessary to handle numbers of much greater precision. If extensive work with large numbers must be performed, it will probably be necessary to write efficient data manipulations in an assembler language. If only occasional uses are required, it is not difficult to write functions in C.

Numerical processing requires a convention for the number of significant figures to be calculated. If the purpose of the processing is analysis of measurements, the number of significant figures will be smaller than if the purpose is mathematical investigations.

(a) Design a decimal number representation based on characters. Allow numbers to have signs and decimal points. Specify your conventions for the precision of calculations. Write functions that will allocate and release space to hold a number string with a specified number of digits in the integer part and fraction.

(b) Write a function to accept input and place it in a number string. Write a function to print a number string.

(c) Write a function that will add two numbers, considering signs and decimal points. Allocate space for the result before adding.

(d) Write a function that will multiply numbers by repeated addition. Allocate space for the result before multiplying.

(e) Write a function that will divide numbers by repeated multiplication, subtraction, and testing.

(f) Expand your number representation and processing to include a signed exponent, as used in scientific notation.

14.4: The most challenging part of a calculator program is usually not the arithmetic but the process of interpreting an expression. In this exercise you will construct a simple expression interpreter.

(a) Write a function that will read in text and store it in a string. The input function should be able to cope with some form of line continuation, such as placing the character \ at the end of a text line that will be continued by the next line.

(b) Design a representation of an expression as a string of *tokens,* each indicating an element of information. For this interpreter, tokens will consist of integer numbers, open and close parentheses (forming subexpressions), and the four operator characters of C for addition, subtraction, multiplication, and division. A number is a contiguous set of numerals, delimited by spacing or another token. Spacing is allowed anywhere except within a number. The token representation should include a marker to represent data, which can be stored outside a token string.

(c) Write functions that will allocate and release dynamic storage holding strings of tokens. Also, set aside a reasonably large working buffer to hold a token string of unknown length as it is being built.

(d) Write a function to parse an expression read as text into tokens. As a text string is parsed, check for invalid characters and convert numbers from their representation as numeral characters into one of the internal forms used in C.

(e) Write a function to check a parsed token string for validity. Parentheses should be balanced. Two numbers should not occur in sequence. There should be a number or a close parenthesis before each operator. There should be a number or an open parenthesis after each operator.

(f) Write a function that will assign priorities within a validated token string. This constructs a token string with parentheses around each operator formation. Use the priorities and groupings of C. Do not consider the "revaluation rule." Place outer parentheses around the entire expression.

(g) Write a function that will evaluate a prioritized token string. First extract the operator and the operands. If the operands are numbers, perform the operation. Otherwise, at least one of the operands is a subexpression. The function should invoke itself to evaluate a subexpression. Subexpressions can be evaluated in place, if the function evaluates from an open parenthesis to a matching close parenthesis.

14.5: This exercise constructs and interprets a printer control table, which you can use to convert a text file so that it will be printed correctly on printers that use different control codes.

(a) Design a main program that will provide overall control for the program. It should obtain parameters from the command line or the user for a control table file, an input text file, and an output text file. It should check for file availability and should open and close these files, passing file pointers to two operating functions.

(b) Design the translation capabilities. Invent a series of codes that can be placed in text to mark such printer control actions as the following: bold weight, normal weight, 10 pitch, 12 pitch, italic characters, standard characters, condensed width, expanded width, normal width, superscript, subscript, normal placement, underline, no underline, clear tabs, set tab, advance to next tab, backspace, set form length, and formfeed.

(c) Design the operating functions. One will read a control file and assemble a code translation table. The other will read the input file, translate codes, and write the output file. Design a control file format using only printable characters.

(d) Write and test the operating functions. Try out the program using a printer. Printers offer different features and combine control actions in different ways. Investigate ways in which your program organization could adapt to these variations.

CHAPTER 15

CONTROL STATEMENTS

A program's actions are regulated by control statements. Control statements determine either whether or not other parts of a program are executed or how many times they are repeated. The C language has a small but flexible repertoire of such statements. In this chapter, you will read about:

- structured and nonstructured control
- repetitions: **while, for,** and **do**
- interruptions: **break** and **continue**
- conditionals: **if . . . else** and **switch**
- statement labels and **goto**
- using controls in program statements

☐ STRUCTURED AND NONSTRUCTURED CONTROL

In Chapter 2, this book introduced the basic organization of C programs:

- statements
- blocks of statements
- the **if . . . else** conditional
- the **while** repetition

Any programmed process can be performed with just these elements of organization. All other forms of control can be regarded as conveniences. Chapter 3 introduced the **break** statement, a convenient way of interrupting a repetition. Chapter 5 introduced the **for** repetition, which is helpful in counting and other sequential processes. These are forms of *structured* program control.

In addition to the structured controls previously introduced, this chapter presents the **switch** conditional, the **continue** statement, and the **do . . . while** repetition. These are more rarely used than **if, else, while, for,** and **break,** but they can be convenient for some types of processing.

Structured program controls have well defined relationships to the parts of a program they control. In C, the scope of control exercised by **if, else, while,** and **for** is a single statement or block of statements, located immediately adjacent to the control. A **break** will interrupt the innermost repetition in which it is located, passing control to the next statement. There is no ambiguity or conditioning attached to structured forms of control. Their behaviors in a program are always visible, local, and explicit.

The C language was created at a time when this type of program control was still struggling for acceptance. Most older computer languages, such as BASIC and FORTRAN, allowed a program to jump around without restriction. Many 1950s and 1960s programmers could not imagine writing programs without this unlimited flexibility. Unfortunately, nonstructured controls make testing and maintenance much more difficult, and they diminish reliability. C retains a vestige of nonstructured control in the **goto** statement.

The controls of the C language have been loosely referred to as "statements." In terms of program syntax, however, only **break**, **continue**, and **goto** behave like independent statements. The main controls—**if, else, while, for, do,** and **switch**—are attached as clauses to other statements or blocks of statements. Each clause has an expression, the *control expression,* that is interpreted at a well defined point in a program, regulating actions in the statement or block being controlled. As the last section of this chapter will show, control clauses can be combined in a syntax that resembles unary operators.

The **if, while, for,** and **switch** controls each have one or more expressions, enclosed in required parentheses, that are evaluated at well defined points of processing. When one of these expressions is evaluated, any changes to data resulting from incrementing, decrementing, assignment, or function reference will be completed before any subsequent processing step is begun.

□ REPETITIONS: **while, for,** AND **do**

A repetition causes the statement it controls to be executed a predictable number of times, as determined by a control expression that is evaluated each iteration. The **while** repetition, introduced in Chapter 2, is the simplest repetition provided by the C language. A **while** repetition has this form:

```
while ( ctl_exp )
    statement
```

In the prototype of **while, ctl_exp** must be a numeric or pointer value, the same as **value** or **pointval,** as these types of operands were explained in Chapter 13. (For definitions, refer to Figure 13.6.) The **statement** component must be one of the following:

- a null statement, consisting of nothing but a semicolon

- a **ref_exp** expression, explained in Chapter 13, including at least one assignment operator, incrementing or decrementing operator, or function reference, followed by a semicolon

- a keyword statement, namely, **break, continue, return,** or **goto,** followed by a semicolon

- a statement of one of the preceding types, attached to any sequence of control clauses, namely, **if, if . . . else, while, for, switch,** and **do . . . while**

- a block of statements, enclosed in braces, including at least one statement of the preceding types or one other block of statements

When a statement controlled by **while** is encountered, the value of **ctl_exp** is evaluated. If TRUE (that is, nonzero), then **statement** is executed. Otherwise, program control continues with whatever follows **statement.** After **statement** has been executed, **ctl_exp** is again evaluated, with the same consequences. Iterations will continue until **ctl_exp** is FALSE (that is, zero) or the repetition is terminated by **break, return,** or **goto.**

The **for** repetition adds to the **while** repetition other expressions, not required for loop control, that are evaluated before a repetition begins and after each iteration. These expressions are useful in counting and other sequencing processes. A **for** repetition has this form:

```
for ( ref_exp ; ctl_exp ; ref_exp )
    statement
```

In the prototype of **for,** the components **ref_exp, ctl_exp,** and **statement** have the same meanings as in the **while** repetition.

The first expression of a **for** clause is evaluated before the repetition begins and whether or not any iteration takes place. It is purely a convenience and can be omitted. Anything it does can be performed by other statements preceding the appearance of **for.** If it is omitted, the semicolon that follows it must be supplied.

The second expression of a **for** clause is the control expression. It is evaluated before each iteration, including the first one. If it is TRUE (that is, nonzero), **statement** is executed. Otherwise, program control continues with whatever follows **statement.** After **statement** has been executed, **ctl_exp** is again evaluated, with the same consequences. Iterations will continue until **ctl_exp** is FALSE (that is, zero) or the repetition is terminated by **break, return,** or **goto.** The control expression of a **for** clause can be omitted. If it is, the semicolon that follows it must be supplied, and the expression has a default value of one.

The third expression of a **for** clause is evaluated after each interation of **statement** and before the control expression is next evaluated. It is also a convenience and can be omitted. Unless the repetition includes a **continue** statement, anything done by the third expression can be performed by other statements at the end of a **statement** block. If a **for** repetition is interrupted by **break,** its third expression will not be evaluated before leaving the repetition.

The **do . . . while** repetition inverts the syntax of **while,** placing a control expression after the statement controlled. This form of repetition guarantees that the statement controlled will always be executed at least once. A **do . . . while** repetition has this form:

```
do
    statement
while ( ctl_exp ) ;
```

In the prototype of **do . . . while,** the components **ctl_exp** and **statement** have the same meanings as in the **while** repetition. A semicolon is required after the **while (ctl_exp)** component of the **do . . . while** repetition. If the **statement** component is not a block, it will also end in a semicolon.

When **do** is encountered, **statement** is always performed. Then the value of **ctl_exp** is evaluated. If it is TRUE (that is, nonzero), **statement** is executed again. Otherwise, program control continues with whatever follows (**ctl_exp**). After **statement** has been executed, **ctl_exp** is again evaluated, with the same consequences. Iterations will continue until **ctl_exp** is FALSE (that is, zero) or the repetition is terminated by **break, return,** or **goto.**

The syntax of **do . . . while** is complex. The **while** clause stands alone, like a separate statement. However, a statement that is controlled by **do** must always be followed by a freestanding **while** clause. Unlike the **else** component of **if . . . else,** the **while** clause has a meaning of its own, namely, a null statement, controlled by **while.** If a **do** repetition is terminated by **break,** control passes not to the **while** clause but to whatever follows it.

Programmers tend to avoid **do** . . . **while** because of its complex syntax. Anything done with this repetition can also be performed with **for**, using a clause of this form:

for (x = 1 ; x ; x = (**ctl_exp**))

In this form, x is a variable of appropriate type that is initially set nonzero, causing a first iteration, and then set to a control value at the end of each iteration. This form or repetition has the advantage of using a compact syntax and of making the behavior of the repetition visible before it begins.

□ INTERRUPTIONS: **break** AND **continue**

The **break** statement, introduced in Chapter 2, stops a repetition of any type. It is also used with the **switch** conditional, as explained in the next section. The statement that will be executed after **break** is whatever immediately follows a repetition in which it appears. If the end of a function immediately follows the end of the repetition, **break** is equivalent to **return**.

When **break** is located within more than one repetition, it will interrupt only the innermost repetition of which it is a part. When **break** appears within a **for** repetition, the third expression of the **for** clause is not interpreted after the interruption. When **break** appears within a **do** . . . **while** repetition, the next statement executed is whatever follows the freestanding **while** clause. It is invalid to use **break** outside a repetition or a **switch**.

The C language provides another interruption statement, **continue**. Unlike **break, continue** interrupts a particular iteration but does not stop a repetition. After a **continue**, the control expression for a repetition will be evaluated again, to determine whether another iteration should be performed. A repetition interrupted by **continue** behaves as though the last statement of an iteration had just been completed. When **continue** is executed within a **for** repetition, the third expression of the **for** clause will be evaluated, as it normally is after an iteration has been completed. It is invalid to use **continue** outside a repetition.

The **return** statement, appearing anywhere in a function, interrupts the processing of any repetition or conditional, as well as all other processing of a function. The forms and actions of **return** statements were thoroughly discussed in Chapter 12.

As an example using interruption statements, the function listed in Figure 15.1 will convert a positive decimal number, expressed as a character string, to an **int** value. Characters that are not numerals are to be ignored. In this example, **break** interrupts an inner **for** repetition when a numeral has been identified; **continue** interrupts an outer **while** repetition when a character other than a numeral is to be ignored.

```
int icon( string )
char *string ;                  /* decimal number string*/
{
    static char numeral[ ] =     /* numeral characters    */
       "0123456789" ;
    char c, d, *p ;              /* utility characters    */
    int k, n ;                   /* numerical values      */

    n = 0 ;                      /* start result at zero */
    while ( c = *string++ )      /* go to end of string   */
    {
        for ( p = numeral ; d = *p ; ++p )
            if ( d == c )
                break ;          /* identify numeral      */
        if ( !d )                /* otherwise, ignore     */
            continue ;
        k = p - numeral ;        /* obtain digit value    */
        n = 10 * n + k ;         /* add to result         */
    }
    return n ;                   /* return integer value */
}
```

Figure 15.1: *A function using the interruption statements.*

A few software theologians categorically object to the use of interruption statements. Such an attitude has little relevance to practical software development. Judicious use of **break, continue,** and **return** often enhances the clarity and effectiveness of structured controls. The availability of these statements represents an intelligent alternative to both the lubricious embrace of nonstructured program control and the strictured structures of the "pure."

☐ CONDITIONALS: **if . . . else** AND **switch**

Conditionals cause parts of programs to be executed or not, depending on specified conditions. The **if** conditional, introduced in Chapter 2, has this form:

if (ctl_exp)
    statement

Here, components **ctl_exp** and **statement** have the same meanings that were explained under the **while** repetition.

When **if** is encountered, the value of **ctl_exp** is evaluated. If it is TRUE (that is, nonzero), **statement** is executed. Otherwise, whatever follows **statement** is executed. If there are no more statements in a function, control returns to the invoking function. If **statement** occurs at the end of a block, any control action specified for the block occurs.

A statement or block of statements controlled by **if** can be followed by another statement or block of statements, controlled by **else**:

if (ctl_exp)
    statement
else
    statement

When the value of **ctl_exp** is TRUE (that is, nonzero), the first **statement** will be executed and the second will not. When it is FALSE (that is, zero), the second **statement** will be executed and the first will not.

A **statement** following either **if** or **else** can be controlled by another **if**, in these forms:

if (ctl_exp)
  if (ctl_exp)
    statement

if (ctl_exp)
    statement
else
  if (ctl_exp)
    statement

In the first form, the second **if** clause will not be evaluated unless the first **if** clause is TRUE; **statement** will not be executed unless both are TRUE. In the second, the second **if** clause will not be evaluated unless the first **if** clause is FALSE; the second **statement** will not be executed unless the second **if** clause is TRUE when evaluated.

You may compound **if** clauses in this way to any depth. It is also possible to create an **if** . . . **else** pair of statements controlled by a preceding **if** or **else**, as in the following forms:

```
if ( ctl_exp )
    if ( ctl_exp )
        statement
    else
        statement


if ( ctl_exp )
    statement
else
    if ( ctl_exp )
        statement
    else
        statement
```

In the first form, neither **statement** can be executed unless the first **if** clause is TRUE. In the second form, neither the second nor the third **statement** can be executed unless the first **if** clause is FALSE. The second form occurs frequently in C programs. It is sometimes known as a *conditional cascade*.

A conditional cascade is a sequence of **if** . . . **else** conditionals, each attached to the preceding **else**. The control expressions of successive **if** clauses are not evaluated unless all the preceding control expressions are FALSE. In a conditional cascade, only one **statement** is executed. When no control expression is TRUE, this is the **statement** after the last **else**. As shown in Chapter 2, a conditional cascade is usually written in C by apposing **else** to **if** on one line and using only two indentation levels:

```
if ( ctl_exp )
    statement
else if ( ctl_exp )
    statement

    . . .

else if ( ctl_exp )
    statement
else
    statement
```

Whenever a statement controlled by **else** appears, the **else** control relates to the last preceding **if** to which an **else** has not already been attached. When you do not intend to create a conditional cascade, you may need to enclose some part of an **if** . . . **else** complex as a block. Look at the form shown in the following example:

```
if ( ctl_exp )
{
   if ( ctl_exp )
      statement
}
else
   statement
```

Without the braces, the **statement** controlled by **else** would relate to the second **if**, not the first. A statement controlled by **else** is invalid unless, within the same block, there is a preceding statement controlled by **if** to which a statement controlled by **else** has not already been attached.

The C language provides another conditional, **switch**, that operates somewhat like a cascade. It is used in the following form:

```
switch ( intvalue )
   statement
```

The **intvalue** component must be a numeric value of type **int**. (Refer to Figure 13.6 for a definition of a value.) The **statement** component has the same meaning as explained under the **while** repetition; it will usually be a block of statements.

The single statement following a **switch** clause or any of the individual statements within a block controlled by a **switch** clause may begin with the following prefix:

```
case intconst :
```

The component **intconst** must be an expression with an **int** value, involving only constants. No two **intconst** values in **case** prefixes for any one **switch** may specify the same value. There can be one statement beginning with the following:

```
default :
```

Like **switch**, **case** and **default** are keywords. A statement controlled by **switch** may have multiple prefixes.

When a **switch** is encountered, its control expression is evaluated. The result is compared with the values in **case** prefixes of statements that it controls. If one of them specifies a value equal to the **switch** control expression, execution begins with the statement to which it is a prefix. If no matching value is found and there is a statement with a **default** prefix, execution begins with that statement. Otherwise, no statement that is controlled by the **switch** is executed. Once execution of a statement controlled by **switch** begins, a program continues without regard for **case** or **default** prefixes, unless interrupted by **break, continue, return**, or **goto**.

Within a block of statements controlled by **switch**, a **break** statement terminates processing. The next statement after the block controlled by **switch** is then executed. If the end of a function follows immediately, **break** is equivalent to **return**. The behavior of **break** within a **switch** is similar to its behavior in a repetition. However, there is no parallel use of **continue** with a **switch**. If a **continue** statement does appear within a **switch**, it causes interruption of a repetition within which the **switch** is located.

In many applications, **switch** substitutes for a conditional cascade:

```
switch ( intvalue )
{
   case intconst :
      statement
      break ;
   case intconst :
      statement
      break ;

   . . .

   default :
      statement
}
```

This form is equivalent to a cascade, where ival is **int**:

```
ival = ( intvalue ) ;
if ( ival == intconst )
   statement
else if ( ival == intconst )
   statement

. . .

else
   statement
```

The **switch** conditional can be used as either a structured or a non-structured control. To use **switch** as a structured form of control, observe these restrictions:

- The **statement** component of **switch** must be a block of statements with no initializations.

- The **case** and **default** prefixes may not be located within any inner block of statements.

- The **case** and **default** prefixes may not be part of a **statement** component controlled by **if, else, while, for,** or **do**.

- The **case** and **default** prefixes may not be prefixed to **else** or to a freestanding **while** clause that is part of a **do** repetition.

- The first statement within the block controlled by **switch** must have a prefix.

- Immediately preceding every other statement with a prefix must be a **break**.

It is possible to write a **switch** within which there is no statement with a **case** or **default** prefix. A **statement** component can also consist of only a semicolon. In these cases, the only action performed is evaluation of the control expression. You may write a **switch** of the form

```
switch ( intvalue )
    default :
        statement
```

This will cause **intvalue** to be evaluated and then **statement** to be executed. If a statement has a **default** prefix, adding a **case** prefix does nothing. These are degenerate forms of **switch**; there is no good reason to use them. It is invalid to use **case** or **default** outside a prefix or outside a **switch**.

As a structured example using **switch**, the function listed in Figure 15.2 will edit a text string, placing one blank between words and two blanks after a period, question mark, or exclamation point.

As a nonstructured example using **switch**, the statements listed in Figure 15.3 will print square asterisks, whenever the value of square is a perfect square less than 10.

```
int enspace( textin, textout, versant )
char *textin ;                    /* unedited text        */
char *textout ;                   /* edited text          */
int versant ;                     /* nonblank status      */
{
    int c ;                       /* character value      */

    while ( c = *textin++ )       /* scan unedited text   */
    {
        switch ( c )              /* test character value */
        {
            case ' ' :            /* single blank         */
                if ( versant )
                    *textout++ = c ;
                versant = 0 ;
                break ;
            case '.' :            /* two blanks after     */
            case '?' :            /* period, question,    */
            case '!' :            /* or exclamation       */
                *textout++ = c ;
                *textout++ = ' ' ;
                *textout++ = ' ' ;
                versant = 0 ;

                break :
            default :             /* otherwise, copy      */
                *textout++ = c ;
                versant = 1 ;     /* set nonblank status  */
        }
    }
    return versant ;              /* return status        */
}
```

Figure 15.2: *A structured function using* **switch**.

☐ STATEMENT LABELS AND goto

As a nonstructured form of program control, the C language provides a **goto** statement, which can transfer control to any other statement within the same function. It also provides a form of prefix that can be attached to any statement, called a *label*. The sole use of a label is to identify a statement as the object of a **goto**.

A **goto** statement is written in the following form:

goto label ;

```
#include "stdio.h"
int square ;

switch ( square )
{
    case 9 :
        fprintf( stdout, "*****" ) ;
    case 4 :
        fprintf( stdout, "***" ) ;
    case 1 :
        fprintf( stdout, "*" ) ;
}
```

Figure 15.3: *A nonstructured statement using* **switch**.

The **label** component is an identifier that must appear in a prefix to some other statement within the same function:

label : statement

The **statement** component above has the same meaning as explained under the **while** repetition.

An identifier used for a label has the same format as any other identifier, explained in Chapter 10. Briefly, it consists of contiguous letters and numerals, the first of which must be a letter. The underscore character (_) is treated as a letter. In a statement label, the label identifier is followed by a colon (:) and then either another statement prefix or a statement. In a **goto** statement, the label identifier is followed by the semicolon that marks the end of the **goto** statement.

A label can be attached to a block of statements; in this form the colon is followed by an opening brace. A label can be attached to a null statement; the colon is followed by a semicolon. A statement label cannot be attached to a declaration or any part of a declaration. There are no arrays of labels, pointers to labels, or structures including labels. No operator accepts a label identifier as an operand. A label identifier cannot be a function argument.

The generally accepted conventions of the C language place label names in the same class of identifiers as variable names. C compilers that follow these conventions will not accept a label when a declaration using the same identifier has a scope that includes the label. Some of the more recent C compilers, however, treat labels as belonging to a separate class and will not confuse them with a variable or function of the same name.

A label identifier is both declared and defined by its appearance in a statement prefix. There is no other way to declare a label identifier. A label has local span; it is only available inside the function within which it appears. Unlike other identifiers with local span, however, a label identifier has a reach of an entire function, even though the label may appear within a block of statements. A label always behaves as though its identifier had been declared at the beginning of a function. No two statement labels in a function may use the same identifier.

According to a generally accepted convention of C, a label name can be superseded by a declaration occurring within a block of statements. Compilers following these conventions will not accept a **goto** if the label identifier it uses has been superseded within the part of a function where the **goto** appears. Compilers that place label identifiers in a separate class do not supersede label declarations and will always accept a **goto**, provided the identifier it specifies corresponds to a label that appears in the function.

Declarations inside blocks can cause problems with the **goto** statement and the nonstructured uses of **switch**. When control is transferred by means of either **goto** or **switch** to a statement with a prefix, any automatic allocation of storage required by declarations that occur within blocks will be performed. However, initializations of automatically allocated data that may be specified by such declarations will not be performed.[1] Since an executable statement cannot occur before a declaration, and since a label cannot be attached to a declaration, there is no general way to overcome this limitation.

Statement prefixes cannot be attached to the following parts of statements with compound syntax:

- before an **else**
- before the freestanding **while** clause of a **do . . . while** repetition

Statement prefixes cannot be placed before or within the control expressions of **if, while, for,** or **switch**. If a **goto** or **switch** located outside a conditional or repetition activates a statement located within the statements that are controlled by the conditional or repetition, no part of any control expression will be evaluated before the statement is activated. If a **goto** controlled by an **if** activates a statment controlled by the corresponding **else**, or vice-versa, the control expression

[1] Brian W. Kernighan and Dennis M. Ritchie, *The C Programming Language,* (Englewood Cliffs, N.J.: Prentice-Hall, 1978), p. 201.

of the **if** is not evaluated before the statement is activated.

The **goto** statement and the nonstructured applications of **switch** tend to complicate programs, make them difficult to read, and reduce their reliability. They frequently require additional overhead, reducing the efficiency of a program.[2] When used at all, they should be confined to small portions of a function, where they can be easily understood. These forms of control should generally be avoided in order to write robust, testable, and maintainable software.

□ USING CONTROLS IN PROGRAM STATEMENTS

As illustrated by most examples in this book that show whole functions, C programming tends to combine forms of control. Repetitions include conditionals, and conditionals determine whether repetitions are performed. Several examples have used loops inside loops and conditions within conditions. The structured controls can be combined in regular constructions that resemble expressions and declarations.

The fully structured controls of the C language have two general types of control formations:

- simple formations:

if (ctl_exp)
    statement

while (ctl_exp)
    statement

for (ref_exp ; ctl_exp ; ref_exp)
    statement

- compound formations:

if (ctl_exp)
    statement

---

[2] Practical examples of nonstructured control can be found in Donald E. Knuth, "Structured programming with goto statements," *ACM Computing Surveys* 6, no. 4 (1974): 261-301. Some examples in this paper are fairly easy to structure with the aid of **break**, **continue**, and arrays of function pointers; the most useful replace recursion with **goto**.

else
    statement

do
    statement
while (ctl_exp) ;

Each formation has one control expression. The compound formations have two parts that each resemble independent statements but are bound together in meaning. Compound **if** . . . **else** is the only formation that controls two statements or blocks of statements; the second part of **do** . . . **while** has a control expression but no statement.

The general rule for combining controls is that any of these control formations can be substituted as a **statement** component of another control formation. A block needs to be marked off with braces in the following circumstances:

- when more than one statement or control formation is being controlled as a **statement** component of a formation

- when an **else** that follows from a compound **if** would otherwise be related to the wrong **if**

The control flow of a function is expressed most clearly by careful use of indentation. The indentation rules observed in this book and recommended to the reader are these:

- Place each statement, statement prefix, and segment of a control formation on a separate line of the program text.

- Indent after **if, else, for, do, while** (without **do**), and **switch**, when followed by a single statement.

- Place each brace on a separate line; increase indentation after an opening brace, and decrease indentation before a closing brace.

- Where statement prefixes are being used, indent all statements.

- Use a consistent indentation increment of four to eight character widths; wider increments usually give clearer emphasis.

- When it is necessary to continue (or "wrap around") a line, stop before or after an operator and keep the same indentation, plus a character width or two.

This approach makes the scope of program control stand out from the appearance of the program text and makes it easy to match the braces around blocks of statements. Keep in mind that indentation is an aid to the reader of software but has no meaning to a C compiler:

```
if ( ctl_exp )
    if ( ctl_exp )
        statement
else
    statement
```

In this example, the **else** relates to the second **if**; the format of the program text cannot change this interpretation and should match the meaning of the program:

```
if ( ctl_exp )
    if ( ctl_exp )
        statement
    else
        statement
```

The **for** control is a great convenience, but its generality seems to encourage obscure usage. If the statements in a **for** loop don't involve any decisions or other loops, they can all be placed in one of the three expression components. For example, the following statements reverse the order of characters in a string:

```
char string[ ], c, *p, *q ;

for ( q = string ; *q ; ++q ) ;
for ( p = string ; p > --q ; c = *q, *q = *p, *p++ = c )
    ;
```

Much worse examples can be found. Not only is this crabbed style of programming difficult to read and understand, it is also difficult to test and maintain. The last statement has collected and conjoined too many actions. A more spacious alternative is much easier to follow:

```
for ( p = string, --q ; p > q ; ++p, --q )
{
    c = *q ;
    *q = *p ;
    *p = c ;
} ;
```

Now it is obvious that the two pointers move in opposite directions until they meet or cross. The "work" of the repetition has been located in its **statement** component.

Occasionally, you may encounter a **for** that seems to be involved in more than one type of control:

for (p = str, i = 0 ; i < MAX ; ++i)

Here, **p** is a pointer to **char**, **str** is an array of **char**, and **i** is an **int** intended to keep track of the index within the string. In this loop, the index manipulation is controlled by **for**, and the pointer manipulation is controlled by the body of the loop. The danger is that they will get out of step.

A better approach is to use a single control mechanism and generate dependent values when needed. For example, the following uses indexing for control and has an expression to generate a pointer value:

```
for ( i = 0 ; i < MAX ; ++i )
{
    p = str + i ;
```

The other approach is to use a pointer for control and generate an index when needed. On most computers, this is somewhat less efficient:

```
for ( p = str ; p < str + MAX ; ++p )
{
    i = p - str ;
```

In general, the expressions of **for** and **while** clauses are best used for operations directly related to loop control. For any one loop, decide on a single control mechanism, place that in the loop's control clause, and locate all other loop actions among the statements being controlled. This approach tends to make your programs more reliable and easier to understand and test.

□ EXERCISES

15.1: In many situations, it is necessary to partition a set of values into ranges, in such a way that an equal number of occurrences is found within each range.

(a) Write a program that will read a file of **int** values into an array, sort the array, and determine the median value (the value at the midpoint).

(b) Assume that the values to be partitioned are integers with a small enough range that it is possible to make an array with a member for each value. Write a program that will read a file of values, accumulate occurrences of each value, and print the values at the boundaries of quartiles (four divisions), deciles (10 divisions), and percentiles (100 divisions).

15.2: Many practical problems require fitting available items together to satisfy a requirement. Each of the following exercises presents such a challenge.

(a) Given an array with the available lengths of wire on spools, write a function that will determine the excess length in the most efficient combination of spools that can be combined to make a given length.

(b) Given counts of coins available at values of 1, 5, 10, 25, and 50 cents, write a function that will determine whether a given amount of change can be made from them and print out the denominations for the smallest number of coins that will add to this amount.

(c) Given an array with dimensions of available bolts of cloth, write a function that will determine the most efficient usage of each bolt to cover a rectangular area, in such a way that all seams run in the same direction.

15.3: Text analysis programs are useful for many applications. The following exercises focus on the analysis of words by a program that makes efficient use of dynamic storage.

(a) Write an efficient storage allocator module for word strings. It should obtain large blocks of storage, using the malloc function in the C library, then carve them up, on request, into short strings.

(b) Write an efficient structure allocator module for word strings and their counts. It should obtain large blocks of storage, using the malloc function, and carve them up into structures with this organization:

```
struct WRD
{
    struct WRD *wrd_left ;
    struct WRD *wrd_right ;
```

```
    int wrd_usage ;
    char *wrd_string ;
  } ;
```

In this structure, the first two pointers are to be used for building a binary tree, the **int** is to maintain a usage count, and the **char** pointer gives the location of a character string for a word.

(c) Write a searching and incrementing function, which should search the word tree for a given string. If it is found, the usage count should be incremented. If not, the word should be added to the tree by allocating a **WRD** structure, allocating a **char** string for the word, and setting the usage count to one. Keep the tree arranged in alphabetical order.

(d) Write a function to read text files. This should read a file, separate it into words, join words at the ends of lines that are hyphenated, remove any discretionary hyphens or other control information you may have in a file, and submit each word to the searching and incrementing function.

(e) Write a listing function. This should print a list of all the words in the tree, in alphabetical order, together with their usage counts.

(f) Write a **main** function to control this program and run it on text files of your own.

15.4: Write a program that reads a text file for a C program and reformats it, using the indentation rules suggested in this chapter.

(a) Make the program recognize comments first, place any comment on a separate line, and format only the text outside comments.

(b) Apply the first three indenting rules, using only spaces to create indentation. Define your indentation increment as a symbolic constant.

(c) Apply the continuation rule, stopping after a comma, equal sign, colon, or semicolon and before other operators.

(d) Leave one space around binary operators and no space between unary operators and their operands, except **sizeof**. This will require recognizing the different operators.

(e) Apply the rule regarding statement prefixes. This will require scanning each block to determine whether it contains statement prefixes.

(f) Format all comments on the right side of a listing, unless they begin in the first column. This will require splitting some comments. Split comments between words.

15.5: Perhaps you are familiar with such word processing assistance as *Sexist,* a program designed to identify gendered words and phrases. This exercise will construct a program that might be called "Lavage," to purge other words of vile and suspect origin.

(a) Begin by writing a program that can read a text file, divide it into words, and write an output file, word by word.

(b) Make this program submit each word to an **inquest** function, which will examine the word for proper sanitation. Unsanitary words should be quarantined from the remainder of the output text, with citations naming their diseases.

(c) There is deep prejudice against lefthandedness, revealed by the contrast between such words as "righteous" and "sinister" (the latter derived from the Latin word for "left"). Purge these and kindred:

portside	Gospel side	conservative
starboard	Epistle side	reactionary
left wing	verso	radical
right wing	recto	liberal
dextrous	larboard	dexter
southpaw	sinistral	nigh side
northpaw	dextral	off side

(d) Although less strident in the modern vernacular, suspicion attaches to curses of all varieties. Eliminate these and other oaths:

gosh	asterisk	rot
malaga	bloody	rubbish
feague	taffy	uzzard

(e) Society exhibits a consistent and poorly concealed bias against louts, oafs, and those through no fault of their own born slow or simple. Eject these and similar mean-spirited words:

clod	wretch	cabbagehead
creep	dolt	addlebrain
chuff	bungler	rube
moron	sop	chucklehead
fool	ass	lollard

(f) The mentally disturbed are savaged by language as well as by those who speak it. Expunge these and analogous deprecations:

crazy	lunatic	psycho
mad	insane	hyper
mental	freak	raving
sick	daft	loony

PART 4

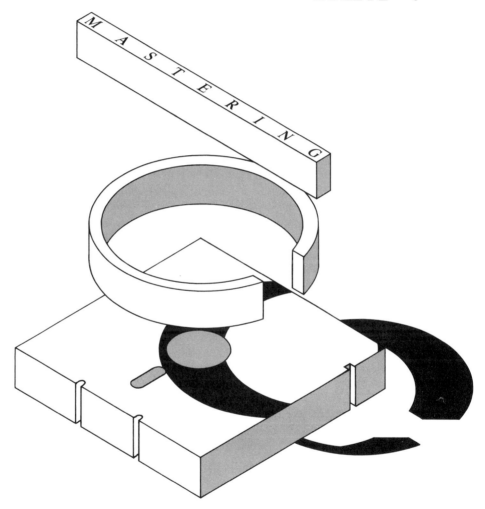

MASTERING

PROGRAMMING
ENVIRONMENTS

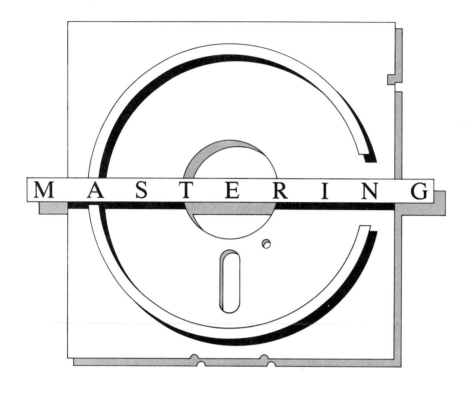

CHAPTER 16

IMPLEMENTATION
FEATURES

Implementations of C offer a small number of special features: several that depend on machine capabilities, a few resulting from evolution of the language, and others associated with a function library or an operating system. This chapter is concerned with special features of the language that are not related to function libraries or operating systems. In it, you will read about:

- the data types **float** and **double**
- conversions for **float** and **double**
- sizes and ranges of data elements
- specifying constant values
- unions and bit fields
- enumerated data types
- the data type specifier **void**
- structure and union assignments
- function parameters and values
- identifier class conventions

□ THE DATA TYPES **float** AND **double**

Chapter 10 introduced the data types **float** and **double**. Chapters 12, 13, and 14 explained some of the uses of these data types with functions, operators, and expressions. Details of these data types have been deferred until now, however, because of their restricted availability and their limited usefulness in C programming.

The **float** and **double** data types are a computer equivalent of scientific notation. In scientific notation, a number is expressed as a decimal value multiplied by a power of ten. For example, during the solar year, the maximum distance between the centers of the earth and the sun is about 1.4957×10^8 km. Written without scientific notation, this would be 149,570,000 km. In scientific notation, the precision is expressed by the number of digits, while the magnitude is mainly given by the power of ten. This practice makes it easy to designate quantities that span a wide range of magnitudes.

The *floating* data types provide an equivalent to scientific notation, using binary numbers. A floating value has two parts: a *mantissa,* a signed binary fraction, with a limiting value of one or two, and an *exponent,* a signed binary value that designates a multiplier as a power of two (not ten). Unfortunately, computers differ in details of format for a mantissa and an exponent. Often, the bitwise representation of a floating number that is generated by one type of computer cannot be used on another. A standard originated by the Institute of Electrical and Electronic Engineers (IEEE 754) is gradually gaining acceptance, but a majority of computers use incompatible formats.

The attributes of floating numbers that are of greatest concern to a programmer are the precision and the range of values that they can represent. Numbers cannot be expressed exactly in floating formats unless they are either integers or fractions whose denominator is a power of two. Even then, there are only a finite number of bits to represent a value. Estimating the error in a floating value is analogous to trying to represent a fraction as a decimal value with a maximum number of digits. For example, when a maximum of four digits is allowed, 3.333 is as close as possible to 10/3, but it is not exactly equal to 10/3.

Programs are most sensitive to precision when they use a wide range of values and when they subtract values that are nearly equal. For example, if the precision of floating values is limited to about six decimal digits, adding 2 to a value of 40 million will (probably) not produce any change at all, because the amount of change is too small to be represented.

Many computers provide two choices of floating formats. One usually provides about twice the number of bits of precision as the other; it may also provide a greater range of values. The C language accommodates these variations by the data types **float** and **double**. Where two different floating formats are available, the **double** data type designates the one with more precision. Where only a single floating format is available, the **float** and **double** data types are equivalent. As noted in Chapter 14, all operations using floating operands are performed in **double**, when this type is distinct from **float**, because of the automatic data type conversions that are a convention of the C language. A **long float** declaration is interpreted as **double**; there is no **long double**.

The **float** data type generally provides a precision equivalent to at least five decimal digits and a range of values spanning at least 10^{20} to 10^{-20}. Where a distinct **double** type is available, it generally provides at least twice the precision of **float**. Some implementations provide substantially greater precisions, ranges of values, or both.

Some implementations of C, particularly those designed for microcomputers, control computers, and signal processors, do not support floating data types at all. Where the floating types are available, they may be provided by software simulation rather than machine instructions, and their usage may be hedged with restrictions. In some implementations that use machine instructions, the linker, the operating system, or both must be informed that floating operations will be performed. In systems applications, interrupt routines may be restricted against floating operations.

There is wide variation in the speed of floating operations, as compared with the speed of integer operations. If machine instructions are available, adding **double** values can be as fast as adding **int** values, but it may also be 20 times slower. Most implementations that provide software simulation automatically invoke a function for each operation; the functions must be linked to a program before it can run. Software simulation of **double** operations is typically between 50 and 200 times slower than the speed of similar operations using **int**.

Floating operations can incur a number of exception conditions. A floating operation can result in overflow or underflow of the range of available values. Division by zero is invalid. These problems all have counterparts in integer arithmetic. A problem unique to floating operations is loss of significance, when two nearly equal values are subtracted or two widely different values are added. The instructions on many machines allow a choice about whether the results of computation are rounded up, down, or to the nearest value. The C language has no conventions for handling these conditions. Any action taken to notify a program of an exception, respond to an exception, or control the rounding of a result is implementation dependent.

□ CONVERSIONS FOR **float** AND **double**

As explained in Chapter 13, floating data elements and values can be used as operands with only some of the C operators. (Refer to Figure 13.2.) These are:

Function	argument or return value
Selection	structure or array member
Location	* &
Arithmetic	* / + − ++ −−
Comparison	< > <= >= == !=
Conditional	? :

Logical	&& || !
Assignment	= += -= * = /=
Sequence	,

For arithmetic, comparison, conditional (the last two operands), and (compound) assignment operations, if either operand is **float** or **double**, then before execution of the operation, the values of both operands will be converted to **double**. For the other operations, a **float** value is automatically converted to **double**. Floating values are not accepted where integer values are required; there is no automatic conversion from either floating type to any integer type. For example, an expression of type **float** or **double** cannot be used as an array index or in pointer arithmetic. An assignment or a cast can force conversion from **double** to **float** and from either **double** or **float** to **long int**, **unsigned int**, **int**, or **char**. Casts are implied by declarations of function parameters and return values.

In general, comparison of floating values will yield equal results only when the values are exactly the same. In many instances, practical comparisons involve a range of tolerance. If the values of tom and dick are to be considered equal when they do not differ by more than harry, then use the following sort of comparison:

```
float tom, dick ;
double harry, delta ;
delta = tom - dick ;
if ( delta < 0.0 )
    delta = - delta ;
if ( delta <= harry )
. . .
```

The use of floating operands for logical operations (and for the first conditional operand) can be hazardous. Some implementions allow zero values that do not have all zero bits or do not have a standard floating representation for zero. Whether such values can be generated and whether they will be considered logically FALSE are implementation dependent. A safer approach to such issues is to assign a floating value to an integer variable before testing it. However, even this risks implementation dependencies if the range of an integer data type does not accommodate a particular floating value.

When an integer value is converted to a floating data type, the floating value will be as close to the integer value as possible. If the precision of the floating type limits the conversion, low-order bits of the integer value will be lost. When a floating value is converted to an integer value and the floating value is integral, the integer value will be the same. Otherwise, the integer value will be within one of the floating value. Conventions of the C language do not otherwise describe how conversions of floating data types will be performed. If the range of values available in a target data type does not include a value to be converted, the result is implementation dependent. Conversion between **double** and **float** can produce errors if the ranges of values representable by these types differ.

The limited availability of floating data in C and the language's cavalier approach to conventions, exceptions, and conversions limit the usefulness of these data types. For most problems that involve numerical analysis, C is not the best choice of computer language. Floating data types in C can be useful for application programs that perform mostly logical analysis and require only a small number of routine calculations, where the ranges and precisions of data values do not present unusual problems.

□ SIZES AND RANGES OF DATA ELEMENTS

As noted in Chapter 5, the C language does not specify the sizes and ranges of data types. In all common implementations of the language, however, there are minimum sizes and ranges. The language has three standard signed integer data types: **int**, **long int**, and **short int**. Data types **int** and **short int** are normally at least 16 bits. The range of positive values available with this length is from 0 to 32,767. All but a few implementations of C provide a **long int** of at least 32 bits. The range of positive values available with this length is from 0 to 2,147,483,647.

The data type **int** is ordinarily the same size as either **long int** or **short int**. However, the data type **int** is chosen for efficiency rather than capacity. It is the standard word size for a particular computer.[1] For microcomputers with limited architectures, **int** is usually the same size as **short int**, frequently 16 bits. On large computers, and on some of the most powerful microcomputers, **int** is usually the same size as **long int**, often 32 bits. On a few computers, particularly those of older design, all three signed integer types have the same representation.

The **int** data type is intended for logical, control, and simple counting uses, where the range of values is limited and efficiency matters.

---

[1] Brian W. Kernighan and Dennis M. Ritchie, *The C Programming Language,* (Englewood Cliffs, N. J.: Prentice-Hall, 1978), p. 34.

When you must have a large range of values, you should use **long int**. On small computers, there will usually be a price in efficiency. When you have many values of restricted range to hold and you want to minimize the storage they consume, use **short int**. On large computers, there will sometimes be a price in efficiency.

The standard **unsigned int** data type has the same size as **int** but twice the range of positive values. The bit used for the sign of an **int** is interpreted as part of the value of an **unsigned int**. Most of the uses for this data type are implementation dependent. The sole portable use of **unsigned int** is to ensure that a right shift operation will shift in zero bits. Some recent implementations of C allow you to apply the **unsigned** modifier not only to **int** but also to **long int**, **short int**, and **char**. These implementations are not consistent about their automatic data type conversions. For example, some will automatically convert **unsigned short** to signed **int**, but others will preserve the **unsigned** attribute of data in any integer operation.

As explained in Chapters 13 and 14, unsigned operations follow modular arithmetic. Conversion of signed to unsigned values does likewise. Most modern computers use a twos complement representation for signed integers, for which no change to data bits is required. Changes will be required on a computer that uses a ones complement or sign-magnitude representation. Implementations that allow **unsigned** to be applied to all sizes of integers generally convert from one size to another by extending with high-order zero bits or by truncating high-order bits, as required.

As explained in Chapter 5, the **char** data type may be either signed or unsigned, as a feature of an implementation. All characters that are necessary to write C programs have positive values. There will always be at least 128 distinct character values; most modern computers provide eight-bit characters, with 256 available values.

□ SPECIFYING CONSTANT VALUES

Because data sizes in C are implementation dependent, so are the values of constants. Chapter 5 explained the forms of integer constants, which can use decimal, octal, or hexadecimal representation. Any of these forms can be followed by the letter L, in upper- or lowercase, to specify a **long int** data type for the constant. The **long int** form of integer constant is shown in the following examples:

```
0L   33l   −77L   012L   −0xadl
```

There is no way to specify a constant with the data type **short int** or with an **unsigned** data type of any kind.

The C language has an automatic type interpretation rule for integer constants. If a decimal constant exceeds the range of **int**, it is automatically interpreted as having data type **long int**. If an octal or hexadecimal constant without a minus sign exceeds the range of **unsigned int**, it is automatically interpreted as **long int**.[2] Unfortunately, because of the uncertainty as to whether **int** has the representation of **long int** or **short int**, this interpretation subjects the values of constants to a significant implementation dependency.

Automatic interpretation of an integer constant's data type has its most dramatic effect when a constant appears as a function argument. If the corresponding function parameter is declared **int**, this interpretation can work in some implementations but fail in others, for which the constant has a large enough value to be interpreted as **long int**. In general, it is unwise to include in expressions constant values outside the dependable range of the **int** data type.

A floating constant must be written in decimal and must include either a decimal point or an *exponent*. An exponent can be added to the end of the number. It consists of the letter E, in upper- or lowercase, followed by an integer, expressed in decimal. When a floating constant has an exponent, its value is whatever is specified by the part up to the exponent, times a power of ten given by the exponent. Both the main part of a floating constant and an exponent may have a minus sign. An exponent can be written with a plus sign. Valid floating constants are shown in the following examples:

$$0. \quad 12.3 \quad -7E3 \quad 243. \quad 37.7e-4 \quad -.0001 \quad -20E+20$$

All floating constants are of type **double**; there is no way to specify a constant of type **float**.

Character constants were explained in Chapter 5. The C language does not specify how character constants will be stored. As explained in Chapter 14, when character constants are used in expressions, they are automatically converted to **int**. Many C compilers store them in this form. Some C compilers allow a **char** constant to have more than one character. The number of characters allowed and the format in which they occur are both implementation dependent.

Character string constants were explained in Chapter 7. These automatically include a character with the integer value zero at the end.

---

[2] Ibid., p. 180.

Multiple appearances of the same string constant in a single function will cause multiple strings to be created.[3] A program should not attempt to change a string constant, because it may be placed in protected storage. A string constant can be continued across lines of program text by placing a backslash (\) at the end of a line and continuing the string at the beginning of the next line. A backslash used to continue a string does not become part of the string. Some compilers have maximum lengths of string constants that they will accept.

Chapters 5 and 7 showed how to specify integer values of characters, using backslash (\) followed by one to three octal digits. Some implementations also allow hexadecimal, using backslash followed by x or X and one or two hexadecimal digits, in either upper- or lowercase. Such a character value can be used with either a **char** or a quoted string constant. When used with a string constant, you must supply two hexadecimal digits, including a leading zero if necessary, if the next character in the string could be interpreted as a hexadecimal digit. Examples of valid integer character values specified in hexadecimal follow:

'\x3a'   '\XF'   "TAB \x078 times"

□ UNIONS AND BIT FIELDS

A *union* is a declaration of data that share the same storage space. Unions have the same formats of declaration and usage as structures, except that they use the keyword **union** instead of **struct**. A union of type CYST is declared in the following example:

```
union CYST ;
{
    double try ;
    int glion ;
    char grene ;
} gan ;
```

Separate storage is reserved for each member of a structure, but each member of a union shares the same storage. In the example, while gan.try is in use, the members gan.glion and gan.grene should not be active.

---

[3] Ibid., p. 181.

Chapter 9 explained data structures, and Chapter 14 described the use of structure-member–selection operators in expressions. Almost all the characteristics of structures also apply to unions. In particular, there are union tags, pointers to unions, members of unions, direct and indirect member selections, and arrays of unions. Structures and arrays may occur within unions, and unions may occur as structure members. A union may have any number of members. Implementations of C that provide structure assignment and the use of structures as function parameters, arguments, and return values generally permit unions to be used in the same contexts. The naming of union members has the characteristics described in Chapter 9 for the naming of structure members.

Both structures and unions can include a special form of declaration known as a *bit field*. A bit field is declared as type **int** or **unsigned int**. After an identifier is placed a colon, followed by an integer constant specifying the number of bits. The following example declares a structure of type **ADR** with two **unsigned** bit fields:

```
struct ADR
{
    unsigned segment : 16 ;
    unsigned offset : 16 ;
} address ;
```

In program statements, **address.segment** and **address.offset** will each behave as an **unsigned int** with a size of 16 bits.

Within structures, bit fields are packed into machine words, one after the other, in the order in which they are declared. Each bit field behaves like a small integer. An **unsigned** field with n bits can have values from zero through $2^n - 1$. A bit field may not overlap a machine word boundary. A compiler will move any field that would overlap a word boundary to the start of the next machine word. Fields without names may be included in declarations to specify unused bits. A field length of zero causes alignment to the start of the next machine word. The maximum size of a field is the number of bits in a machine word.

Bit fields are not provided by all compilers; where provided, they are heavily implementation dependent in two respects: the size of machine words and the choice of right-to-left or left-to-right packing of fields. Some compilers provide only **unsigned** bit fields, whether fields are so declared or not. Bit fields are not locatable in C; you cannot construct pointers to them. They cannot be parameters or return values of functions. If used in expressions, they will be converted to normal integer values of type **int** or **unsigned int**.

There is no feature of the C language to determine which member of a union was most recently used for storage. Therefore, any program that declares a union must carefully document and observe conventions for its use. This requirement tends to disrupt software modularity and structure, because effects of program actions cannot be traced through identifiers. A union also complicates testing and reduces robustness.

Most practical uses of unions and bit fields are for manipulating machine dependent data. Such applications require detailed knowledge of both machine characteristics and the manner in which these characteristics are used by a C compiler. Such applications of unions and bit fields are good for "hacks"—quick fixes by experts. Otherwise, they are obscure, generally unsatisfactory substitutes for assembler language, the clearly documented way to generate machine dependent code. Few, if any, circumstances warrant the use of a union or a bit field as a permanent part of software, either in an efficient but machine dependent program or in a soundly designed portable program.

□ ENUMERATED DATA TYPES

Many programs need control variables that can assume only a limited set of valid values. Often, these values are associated with specific data contents, control actions, or other meanings. Some of the more recent C compilers provide a special data definition feature that can assist in such circumstances, called *enumerated data types*.

An enumerated data type is a program defined integer data type. It can be declared using a keyword, **enum**, and a tag similar to a structure or union tag. The declaration of an enumerated type is followed by a list of identifiers, enclosed in braces, naming the *enumerators* for the type. Integer values associated with enumerators begin at zero and increase by one for each succeeding identifier in a declaration list. Only enumerators should be assigned, by name, to a data element of the specified type. Enumerated data types can be used in **typedef** declarations.

Variables can be declared to have an enumerated type either in the same declaration or in a declaration using an enumeration tag or a **typedef** symbol. A variable of such a type is allowed to assume values from the declared set. The following example declares an enumerated type and two identifiers using that type:

```
enum DAY
{
    mon, tue, wed, thu, fri, sat, sun
} new_years ;

enum DAY full_moon[ 14 ] ;
```

This example declares that a variable of type DAY has seven allowed values, whose enumerators are three-letter abbreviations for days of the week. The new_years data element and the full_moon array share this data type. The array has 14 members, each of which can have one of seven allowed values.

Compilers vary in the operations they allow with operands of enumerated data types. Simple assignments and comparisons for equality or inequality, where both operands have the same enumerated data type, are always allowed. The following examples are typical of the generally allowed uses for enumerated data:

```
full_moon[ 13 ] = sat ;

if ( new_years != wed )

if ( full_moon[ 0 ] == new_years )
```

Beyond these uses of enumerated data types, approaches of compilers vary from the rigid, allowing only these operations, to the lax, allowing values of enumerated data types to be used in all operations that accept integer operands and to be mixed freely with other integer data.

Compilers that permit additional uses of enumerated data also usually provide a form of declaration in which the integer values associated with enumerators can be specified. Any enumerator in a declaration list can be followed by an equal sign and an integer constant, specifying its integer value. Successive enumerators are associated with integer values that increase in steps of one, unless they, too, have specified values. The following example declares an enumerated data type using specified integer values:

```
enum PFX
{
    uni = 1, bi, tri, quadri, deci = 10, hecto = 100
} ;
```

The enumerators for the PFX data type, left to right, are associated with integer values of 1, 2, 3, 4, 10, and 100.

Unlike enumerated data in Pascal and other languages, enumerated values in the C language have an explicit internal form, the data type int and they have definite values in that data type. These values can be written into files and read from files as integers. They are portable across compilers, provided the compilers support an enumerated data type and the uses that a program makes of it. However, only simple assignments and comparisons for equality or inequality are generally supported uses.

□ THE DATA TYPE SPECIFIER **void**

Not all functions return values. Some of the more recent compilers provide a type specifier, the keyword **void**, to designate a function that does not return a value. If the definition of a function specifies **void**, then **return** statements may not include values. When the declaration of a function specifies **void**, the function may not be invoked in a context where its return value would be used. The **void** specifier cannot be attached to identifiers other than function names. The value of **sizeof(void)** is zero.

The sole purpose of **void** is to provide compiler checks as to whether values are returned and as to whether return values are used. Compilers that implement **void** generally allow it to be used in a cast, to indicate that a value may be obtained but is to be discarded. Some compilers will issue a warning if a function returning a value is invoked but the return value is not used, unless the name of the function is preceded by a **void** cast. These compilers may also issue a warning if a function that is supposed to return a value does not. The following example shows typical uses of the **void** specifier:

```
void release_space( records )
struct REC *records ;
{
    extern int free( ) ;

    ( void ) free( records ) ;
}
```

□ STRUCTURE AND UNION ASSIGNMENTS

As discussed in Chapter 13, some recent compilers will copy the contents of entire structures, by means of simple assignment operations. These compilers will also copy contents of unions, using the same operator formation. The internal data organization of a structure or union is implementation dependent. It can include unassigned and non-locatable areas required to satisfy machine characteristics. Contents of any such portions of a structure or a union are indeterminate and may or may not be copied by a structure or union assignment.

Most compilers that support structure and union assignments also permit structures and unions to be used as parameters, arguments, and return values of functions. When a structure or union, rather than a pointer to one, is used as a function argument, the corresponding function parameter will contain a copy of its contents. The function will be unable to change the contents of the structure or union that was used as an argument, just as a function cannot change the value of a variable used as an argument. When a structure or union is used as a return value, the invoking statement must make immediate use of the value, either by means of structure or union assignment or by means of direct member selection. Otherwise, the data returned is discarded.

The contents of an array cannot be copied by an assignment, because the meaning of an array name is not the contents of the array but a pointer constant, whose value is the location of the array. But if structure assignment is available, array contents can be copied by locating arrays within structures or unions and using structure or union assignment. The following example shows such a use of structure assignment:

```
typedef struct
{
    int sun[ 366 ] ;
    int fog[ 366 ] ;
} YEAR ;

YEAR current, next ;

next = current ;
```

A structure or union that is declared within an array or within another structure or union can also be copied by assignment and can be used as a function argument, provided it is assigned to another structure, union, or function parameter that has the same organization. C compilers do not usually provide other operations that involve entire structures or unions. In particular, neither comparison of structures or unions for equality or inequality nor compound assignments, such as += and *=, are available. The value of a structure assignment operation is the contents of a structure or union of the type assigned; this can be used as an operand of another assigment or as a function argument.

□ FUNCTION PARAMETERS AND VALUES

As just discussed, some of the more recent C compilers extend the language to accept structures and unions as function parameters and return values. As discussed in Chapters 7 and 12, the value of an array or function name is a pointer constant, providing the location of the array or function. Whole arrays cannot be transmitted as function arguments, and functions cannot be used as data at all. When a function parameter or return value is declared to be an array, it is understood that a pointer to the array will be transmitted. Some compilers also offer a similar interpretation for function names.

A C compiler that accepts a declaration of a function name for a function parameter or return value interprets the declaration as meaning that a pointer will be transmitted. With a permissive compiler, a function can use a parameter or a return value so declared without an indirection operator. Such a compiler will automatically apply an indirection operator, based on its adjustment of the declaration.

Figure 16.1 shows a **sort** function that declares one parameter to be a **value** array and another parameter to be a **decision** function. When it uses one of these parameters to manipulate the array or invoke the function, it does not apply an indirection operator. Instead, it depends on a permissive interpretation by the compiler.

Any parameter or return value used in such a way with a permissive compiler must be clearly understood to be transmitted as a pointer. A function that uses an array declared as a parameter is operating not on a copy of the array supplied as an argument but on the actual array, whose location was transmitted by a pointer value.

Returning a pointer to an array, however declared, has special hazards. The array must not be allocated automatically by the function that returns a pointer to it or by any other function which that

```
void sort( value, count, decision )
float value[ ] ;
int count ;
int decision( ) ;
{
    double vi, vj ;
    int i, j ;

    for ( i = 0 ; i < count - 1 ; ++i )
    {
        vi = value[ i ] ;
        for ( j = i + 1 ; j < count ; ++j )
        {
            vj = value[ j ] ;
            if ( decision( vi, vj ) )
                . . .
        }
    }
}
```

Figure 16.1: *A function that declares another function name as a parameter.*

function invokes, directly or indirectly. Once a function has returned, its automatic allocations are canceled. The space so allocated is eligible for other uses without notice. Any subsequent attempt to use the space risks conflict with other parts of a program.

□ IDENTIFIER CLASS CONVENTIONS

Classes of identifiers were introduced in Chapter 10. As noted there, C compilers differ in their assignments of identifiers to classes. The generally accepted conventions for C provide at least two classes:[4]

- all names of elements, pointers, structures, unions, arrays, functions, **typedef** organizations, statement labels, and enumerators
- all names of structure, union, and enumerator tags and of structure and union members

More recent C compilers provide additional classes. As noted in Chapter 10, most compilers produced since the early 1980s provide separate identifier classes for member names of each structure and union organization. Among the most common additional identifier classes are the following:

- names of **#define** constants and macro definitions, as discussed in Chapter 17.
- statement label names
- structure, union, and enumeration tags
- **typedef** symbols

Naming conventions for enumeration tags generally follow the same pattern as those for structure and union tags. Compilers may provide an identifier class for all tags or separate classes for the different types of tags. Unlike names of structure and union members, enumerator names cannot always be distinguished by use. They must belong to the same class of identifiers as names of variables and functions. See Chapter 10 for a discussion of overloading and supersession of identifiers.

---

[4] Ibid., p. 206.

□ EXERCISES

16.1: Programs can sometimes be made more portable by automatic determination of the characteristics of different data types. The objective of this exercise is to create functions that do this.

(a) Create a function that finds the largest and the smallest value of each integer type.

(b) Create a function that determines whether **int** is the same as **short int** or **long int**.

(c) Create a function that determines the number of bits in a machine word.

(d) Create a function that determines the precision of **float** and **double**. Start with a value of 1.0, then try adding values that are smaller by successive factors of two.

(e) Create a function that determines the maximum and minimum positive values of **float** and **double**.

(f) Create a function that determines quickly whether a **double** value can be assigned correctly to a variable of a specified type.

16.2: Some graphics functions become easier to write when floating data types can be used. This exercise presumes that you have them available to make a module of functions for scaling and windowing. This module obtains coordinates in **double** for two-dimensional display windows and transforms them to **long int** values that address "physical" display space.

(a) Write a function that accepts boundaries for the physical space.

(b) Write functions that keep track of multiple windows, each transforming a range of window coordinates to a range of physical coordinates. Windows may be overlaid onto physical space. Associated with each window should be a status, determining whether it is actively displayed and its priority with respect to other windows that may be overlaid.

(c) Write functions to keep track of a list of vectors in each window by start and end points in its display space.

(d) Write a function to map all vectors onto physical space, determining for each whether its window is active and, if so, the physical start and end points of each visible vector segment.

16.3: This exercise requires knowledge of the data format used by a particular machine for floating values. You should obtain a description of the format for the machine you will use.

(a) Exercise 13.2 discusses a way of making pseudorandom integers, by successive multiplication of an odd number by a prime number. If the bits so generated are used to populate the fraction bits of a floating point number, they will make random floating values between 0 and either 1 or 2, depending on the format of the number. Use this method, multiplying into a **long int** to generate bits. Then use unions, bit fields, or both to place bits resulting from multiplications into the fraction of a **double** variable, with an exponent such that the resulting **double** value will be greater than or equal to zero and less than one. Make a function that generates a random **double** by adding 0.0 to a variable so populated.

(b) It can be shown that random numbers with a normal distribution, having mean zero and variance one, are obtained by generating random numbers between zero and one until a pair (x, y) is found for which the sum of squares is not more than one, then by generating a third such number, z, and calculating the function

$$(-\log_e z)^{1/2} \, (x^2 - y^2) \, / \, (x^2 + y^2)$$

Using this approach, make a random generator for numbers from a normal distribution with specified mean and standard deviation.

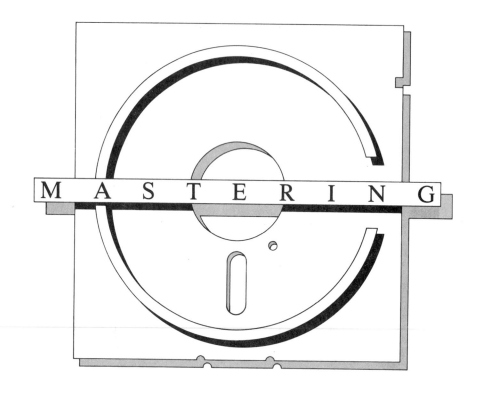

CHAPTER 17

PREPROCESSOR FACILITIES

Most implementations of C provide special facilities of the compiler, called preprocessor facilities, that can make changes to selected portions of a program by text substitutions. For example, preprocessor facilities include the #define constants, which have been used in numerous examples. In this chapter, you will read about:

- preprocessor operation

- symbol substitution

- conditional compilation

- file inclusion and line numbering

- organizing software development

□ PREPROCESSOR OPERATION

The symbol substitution, file inclusion, and conditional compilation capabilities of the C language are known collectively as *preprocessor facilities*. In the earliest versions of C, the preprocessor was a separate program. In more recent implementations, it is usually a service performed by the compiler on the source text of a program, before any other interpretation of the text but without special action on the part of a programmer.

Preprocessor operations are controlled by preprocessor statements, interspersed with the text of a program. Preprocessor statements are distinguished by a number sign (#), which precedes the name of a command and must be the first character in a line. Lines that begin in this way are acted upon by the preprocessor and are removed from the text of a program before it is otherwise interpreted.

Because the number sign has no other use in the C language, some compilers relax restrictions on preprocessor statements and allow spacing before and after a number sign. Use of this flexibility in formatting preprocessor statements is not recommended, because it makes a program nonportable. Comments may be placed in preprocessor statements. If a comment continues onto another line, the preprocessor statement continues with it.

Following the command in a preprocessor statement are instructions. A preprocessor statement may be continued, when necessary, by placing a backslash (\) at the end of a line and continuing the statement at the start of the next line. A backslash used to continue a statement does not become part of the statement. If a statement line ends with a backslash, the next line is always interpreted as part of that statement, even if it begins with a number sign. Most compilers have maximum lengths of preprocessor statements that they will accept, including continuation lines.

Preprocessor statements have their own syntax, which resembles that of C but is not identical. Preprocessor symbol definitions cause only text substitutions. They do not necessarily follow the syntax of C and may not respond to elements of source text according to their meanings as parts of a C program. When the preprocessor interprets the text of a C program, it will recognize the following features:

- comments

- identifiers

- string constants

- character constants

- other constants

The preprocessor **#define** facilities are capable of replacing identifiers with other text and of more complex actions, called *macro substitutions*. Macro substitution is activated by identifiers in the source text that are immediately followed by an opening parenthesis, as explained in the next section. The text substitutions performed by the preprocessor do not inspect for valid C syntax, and so they can result in invalid program statements.

□ SYMBOL SUBSTITUTION

Chapter 4 introduced the use of **#define** for symbolic constants. While this is the most common use of symbol substitution, the preprocessor will substitute text of any kind for an identifier. The format used to define symbol substitution is **#define**, followed by an identifier and then the text to be substituted for the identifier. Such a preprocessor statement is known as a *symbol definition*. The following example shows symbol definitions:

```
#define PHASE 3
#define LIMIT ( PHASE + 5 )
```

Notice that **#define** statements, like all other preprocessor statements, do not end with a semicolon. Unless continued by a backslash or a comment that spans a line, they are entirely contained within the line on which they occur.

The preprocessor will perform multiple symbol substitutions. Each line of source text is scanned for identifiers that have been defined as symbols, known as *symbol references*. When a symbol reference is found, the symbol is replaced by its substitution text. Then the line in which it occurred is rescanned, to see if there are any more symbol references. When no more symbol references can be found, the preprocessor continues with the next line.

Using symbols defined in the previous example, the following example shows the steps in text substitution performed on a sample line of source text:

```
if ( level > LIMIT )
if ( level > ( PHASE + 5 ) )
if ( level > ( 3 + 5 ) )
```

Notice that the definition of **PHASE** was not merged with the definition of **LIMIT**. Instead, substitutions are performed one at a time, and whatever definition is in effect when a symbol reference is found in source text is the one that will control a substitution. Substitution stops when there are no more symbol references. A process such as combining (3 + 5) into 8 is left for a later stage of a compiler.

Some compilers require spacing between a **#define** command and the identifier for the symbol being defined. Spacing is always required between an identifier and its substitution text if the first character of the substitution text is an opening parenthesis or could be used in an identifier. Spacing on both sides of a symbol identifier is recommended for clarity and portability.

Macro substitutions are more complex. They are specified by **#define** statements in which a symbol identifier is followed by an opening parenthesis, a list of other identifiers separated by commas, a closing parenthesis, and then the substitution text. The other identifiers are known as parameters of the macro definition. The substitution text may contain any number of references to the parameters named in the definition. Such a preprocessor command is known as a *macro definition*. Following is an example of macro definitions:

```
#define MEAN( a, b )   ( a + b ) / 2
#define STEP( a, b )   b * ( a / b )
```

In a macro definition, there can be no spacing between the identifier for a symbol and the opening parenthesis that follows it. Otherwise, an opening parenthesis will be interpreted as part of the substitution text for an ordinary symbol definition.

Macro substitution is performed when an identifier that has been defined as a macro symbol is encountered in the source text, followed immediately by an opening parenthesis. This is known as a *macro reference*. Macro substitution is performed as follows:

1. The source text is scanned for a matching closing parenthesis.

2. Between these parentheses, arguments separated by commas are extracted.

3. A copy of the substitution text is created.

4. Wherever a macro parameter appears in the substitution text, it is replaced by the corresponding argument from the source text.

5. In the source text, the **#define** symbol and its argument list are replaced by the processed copy of the substitution text.

Using macro symbols defined in the previous example, the following example shows the steps in text substitution performed on a sample line of source text:

```
hue = MEAN( gray, STEP( shade, color ) ) ;
hue = ( gray + STEP( shade, color ) ) / 2 ;
hue = ( gray + color * ( shade / color ) ) / 2 ;
```

Notice that these substitutions could have been performed in either order, but the result will be the same.

The number of arguments in a macro reference must match the number of parameters in the corresponding macro definition. A macro definition can be written with no parameters, and some compilers limit the maximum number of parameters. The identifiers of macro parameters are not symbols themselves. They are meaningful only inside the macro definition in which they appear. They may be identical to other identifiers in a program without causing conflict.

When a macro reference is scanned for arguments, commas inside character constants, string constants, and comments will be recognized as part of an argument; they will not act as argument separators. If an argument contains parentheses outside character or string constants, they must be balanced. Any text, including commas, brackets, braces, and sequences of characters that need not form valid C statements, will be included in a macro argument when it appears inside a pair of parentheses.

When the substitution text of a macro definition is scanned for occurrences of its parameters, most compilers recognize parameter identifiers in the same ways that identifiers are recognized in C program statements. They will not recognize identifiers inside character constants, string constants, or comments. Any character or string constant that appears in substitution text must have correct format.

In conventional implementations of C, a macro reference in source text will not be recognized by the preprocessor unless the macro symbol is immediately followed by an opening parenthesis.[1] A macro definition that is used to alter a function reference will not necessarily work unless a programmer leaves no space between the function name and an opening parenthesis. Since C libraries frequently use macro definitions for this purpose, a portable program must observe this practice for all uses of C library functions.

Macro substitutions can sometimes produce incorrect results, when operators in the resulting text do not have the intended priorities. Both of the following examples show a macro definition, reference, and substitution:

```
#define SUM( a, b )   a + b
amount = rate * SUM( principal, interest ) ;
amount = rate * principal + interest ;

#define PRODUCT( a, b )   a * b
length = last + PRODUCT( scale, top - bottom ) ;
length = last + scale * top - bottom ;
```

The first of these does not work as intended, because an operator outside the substitution text has higher priority than one generated by the substitution text. The second does not work either, because an operator in the substitution text has higher priority than an operator in an argument.

The way to solve such difficulties is to write "fully parenthesized" macro definitions. When you do this, all substitution text is enclosed by an outer pair of parentheses, and each appearance of a macro parameter in the substitution text is enclosed in parentheses. The preceding examples would be fully parenthesized as follows:

```
#define SUM( a, b )   ( ( a ) + ( b ) )
amount = rate * SUM( principal, interest ) ;
amount = rate * ( ( principal ) + ( interest ) ) ;
```

<hr>

[1] Brian W. Kernighan and Dennis M. Ritchie, *The C Programming Language,* (Englewood Cliffs, N. J.: Prentice-Hall, 1978), p. 87.

```
#define PRODUCT( a, b )   ( ( a ) * ( b ) )
length = last + PRODUCT( scale, top − bottom ) ;
length = last + ( ( scale ) * ( top − bottom ) ) ;
```

In many instances, the substituted text will contain unnecessary parentheses, but their appearance is harmless.

Use of incrementing, decrementing, or assignment operators in either macro definitions or references can be hazardous, as the following example shows:

```
#define SQUARE( a )   ( ( a ) * ( a ) )
modulus += SQUARE( span[ i++ ] ) ;
modulus += ( ( span[ i++ ] ) * ( span[ i++ ] ) ) ;
```

Evaluation of this statement yields an uncertain result, and the double incrementing of i is probably not wanted. Similar hazards occur if macro substitution can cause a function to be invoked more than once.

Symbol or macro definitions that affect program control or that contain operators without all the operands are also easy to misuse, as the following example shows:

```
#define LARGER( a )   > a
if ( tone − LARGER( semitone ) )
if ( tone −>semitone )
```

Another common source of error is to put a semicolon in a symbol definition:

```
#define HALF( a )   ( ( a ) >> 1 ) ;
t = r + HALF( s ) * zip ++ ;
t = r + ( ( s ) >> 1 ) ;
*zip ++ ;
```

An occasional source of error is an attempt to cancel a definition with a preprocessor statement such as

```
#define VANISH
```

This does not cancel the definition; it simply causes the symbol so defined to be replaced by spacing. Unless you avoid intentional uses of symbol substitution in these ways, it may be difficult to spot errors in your programs.

When more than one symbol reference appears in a line of source text, there is no convention for the order in which substitutions will be performed. For that reason, do not use symbol definitions or references that depend on an order of substitution. When a line of source text is rescanned after symbol substitution, it is scanned only for additional symbols. If, for example, you attempt to define and substitute a symbol that creates another preprocessor statement, substitution will occur, but the statement will not be acted on by the preprocessor.

Do not create symbol definitions that can lead to unlimited recursion, either directly or indirectly. Most compilers cannot detect indefinite preprocessor recursion, and they will continue to reprocess a line of text until stopped by excessive use of time, storage, or some other resource. The following example shows indefinitely recursive definitions and usage:

```
#define CASES( X )   X % 4 + MULTI( X )
#define MULTI( X )   3 * X - CASES( X )

iterations = MULTI( CASES( anything ) ) ;
```

Compilers vary in their interpretation of comments that may occur in symbol definitions and references. Many treat comments as spacing when scanning source or substitution text and include them in the substitution text. Others replace comments by single spaces before scanning any text. Still others treat the comments as spacing when scanning and delete them before substitution. For portability, do not place comments inside macro references. Place any comment in a **#define** statement after the substitution text, separated from it by at least one spacing character.

Generally accepted conventions of the C preprocessor do not allow the construction of identifiers by concatenating substituted text, because comments and the end of a definition line are treated as spacing in the substituted text. However, some deviant compilers may allow this. The following, egregious example shows three macro definitions and a pair of macro references for which an interpretation depends on the order of macro substitution:

```
#define NOSH()    EAR
#define TOSH    THWORM
#define EARTOSH    APPLE

NOSH()TOSH              /* ?? */

EARTOSH                 /* ?? */
APPLE                   /* ?? */

NOSH()THWORM            /* ?? */
EARTHWORM               /* ?? */
```

None of the practices illustrated is recommended. They depend on implementation dependent interpretations and will render a program nonportable.

Some compilers will perform substitutions for macro parameters that appear in character or string constants within substitution text, and they may also accept incomplete constants in substitution text. Any conventions for recognizing parameter identifiers inside constants will be implementation dependent. Some compilers will recognize a macro reference in source text when there is spacing between a macro symbol and an opening parenthesis. No such uses of macro definitions and references are portable.

A symbol has module span. An **#undef** preprocessor statement can cancel a symbol definition, and a symbol can be redefined. Otherwise, a symbol will be recognized in source text, except within comments, string constants, character constants, and preprocessor statement, from the line following its definition through the end of a source module.

The **#undef** statement simply names an identifier whose definition is to be cancelled. Some compilers keep track of multiple **#define** statements for the same identifier and cancel only the most recent of these for an **#undef** statement, reinstating the next most recent definition. A portable program cannot depend on this feature.

C compilers differ in their treatment of a **#define** statement that redefines a previously defined symbol. There are three common responses:

- No redefinition is permitted.

- A redefinition is permitted, and any previous definition is lost.

- A redefinition is permitted, and all previous definitions are remembered.

The last approach leads to the interpretation in which an **#undef** statement reinstates the last previous definition. Some compilers that follow either of the last two practices require that a redefinition match the original in defining either an ordinary or a macro symbol and in the number of macro parameters.

The only portable approach to these inconsistencies is to ensure that there is never an attempt at redefinition. In cases of doubt, the conditional compilation statements that are explained in the next section can be used to remove any previous definition before acting on another, as shown in the following example:

```
            /* old definition */
#define SYMBOL . . .
```

```
#ifdef SYMBOL
#undef SYMBOL
#endif
                              /* new definition */
#define SYMBOL . . .
```

□ CONDITIONAL COMPILATION

The preprocessor provides statements that control whether portions of a source text are compiled. These make decisions based on whether a symbol has been defined or on the value of an expression involving only constants. The control statements have the following forms:

```
#ifdef symbol
#ifndef symbol
#if intvalue
```

Each of these statements controls the compilation of source text beginning with the next line and continuing up to a matching statement of the form:

```
#endif
```

When an identifier appearing as **symbol** in an #ifdef statement has been previously defined by a #define statement (and the definition has not been canceled by an #undef statement), the source text between the #ifdef statement and its matching #endif statement will be included in the compilation. The #ifndef statement tests the reverse condition, that an identifier has not been defined as a symbol.

The source text between #if and its matching #endif is included in the compilation when **intvalue** is not zero. Appearing as **intvalue** can be any expression that uses integer constants, including those that have been previously defined as symbols, using #define commands, and any C operators that accept integers as operands, as in these examples:

```
#if SCALES < 5 && OCTAVES == 2
```

```
#if ( SELECT >> OFFSET ) & PEL
```

Between a preprocessor compilation control statement and its matching #endif can be a command of the form

```
#else
```

When the preprocessor control condition is satisfied, the source text from the control command up to the #else command will be included in the compilation. The source text following the #else command, up to the #endif command, will be excluded. When the preprocessor control condition is not satisfied, the source text from the control command up to the #else command will be excluded. The source text following the #else command, up to the #endif command, will be included in the compilation.

Preprocessor control statements can be nested to any depth. Once a control statement has excluded some portion of source text from further compilation, no statements in the excluded text, including preprocessor statements, will be acted upon, except for checking control statements to locate a matching #else or #endif statement. This convention can be applied to prevent symbol definition or to prevent file inclusion, which uses preprocessor statements that are explained in the next section.

Some C compilers provide another preprocessor control statement, #elseif or #elif, to test an additional constant expression and create a conditional cascade. In general, the expressions tested by these commands and by #if commands may not involve any knowledge about the program being compiled. For example, you cannot include **sizeof** (**gen_exp**) in an expression, where **gen_exp** involves some identifiers other than symbols, because the preprocessor will not have access to information about identifiers other than those previously defined as symbols.

Some compilers do provide access to certain forms of program dependent information, and some compilers allow control expressions that involve character and floating constants, in addition to integers. A few compilers provide a special preprocessor operator, **defined**, that has a value of 1 if a symbol has been defined and of 0 if it has not. This operator is of use in compound expressions, such as

```
#if defined( HILLS ) && defined( VALLEYS )
```

These features can be convenient, but their use will make a program nonportable.

□ FILE INCLUSION AND LINE NUMBERING

Preprocessor facilities provide a means of merging additional source text into a module being compiled. This is accomplished by an #include statement, which is written in one of these two forms:

```
#include "file_name"
```

#include <**file_name**>

These statements cause an entire file of source text to be merged with the module being compiled, immediately following the #include statement. The merged text may contain any valid C program statements, including preprocessor statements. It will be interpreted as though it had occurred in place of an #include statement.

The difference between the two forms of #include statement is significant for operating systems that group files under *directories* and that provide a *default* directory, which is searched when a file name has no directory information. For such a system, the first form of #include indicates the normal default directory, while the second form indicates an implementation dependent directory, generally used to hold C library functions. Some compilers do not support the second form of the #include statement.

Source files merged by an #include statement may themselves contain #include statement. Some compilers limit the depth of nesting for #include statements, to restrict the number of files that may require simultaneous access. The forms allowed as **file_name** information are subject to an operating system's restrictions. Most operating systems produced since the late 1960s allow file names that are divided into two portions by a period, as in

NAME.EXT

In such a naming system, it is common for the second part of a file name to indicate the type of data it contains. Of particular importance to C programmers: an extension .C is very common for C source text. Other common extensions are .H for C header files and .DAT for data files.

Some systems distinguish between upper- and lowercase letters in file names; many do not. Systems vary in the number of characters permitted. Among the most restrictive are systems that allow only one to six characters in the first part of a file name and only one to three characters in the second part. Some systems allow only letters and digits in file names, requiring that the first character of each part of a name be a letter. Other systems allow certain special characters, but conventions for allowed characters vary among these.

The preprocessor provides a statement to label lines of source text, as an aid in locating the causes of diagnostic messages from a compiler. It has the following form:

#line **intconst symbol**

An identifier appearing as **symbol** is optional. If present, it designates an identifier to be associated with compiler diagnostics until another #line command which has such an identifier appears. The parameter **intconst** must be an integer constant. That number will be associated with the next source line, for purposes of compiler diagnostics, and successively higher numbers will be associated with the following lines, until another #line command appears. Either of the #line parameters can use previously defined symbols.

□ ORGANIZING SOFTWARE DEVELOPMENT

The preprocessor facilities of C are convenient but troublesome features of the language. Disciplined uses of these facilities can help make programs more consistent and reliable, but careless or flamboyant uses can lead to programs that are extremely difficult to read, test, or change. The principal hazards of preprocessor facilities are these:

- Preprocessor statements use a syntax that differs from the rest of the C language.

- Preprocessor statements are disconnected from most other interpretation of source text by a C compiler.

- Preprocessor statements can change any element of source text, including keywords, operators, and the boundaries of functions, expressions, statements, and blocks.

- The ability to include nested files can create cross-threaded dependencies entirely outside dependencies of an executing program.

- Preprocessor statements can be (and often are) physically remote from the text elements on which they operate, making program source text difficult to understand.

- Preprocessor statements tend to couple a program to an operating system, in such matters as file name formats, directories, and command line options, making a program nonportable.

- Preprocessor conventions are poorly defined; critical details vary widely among compilers.

Productive uses of preprocessor facilities, however, support good organization. The major assistance that can be provided by preprocessor facilities to robust software design is help in ensuring coding consistency. The principal tools are:

- symbolic constants, created by preprocessor #define statements
- header files, merged into source text by preprocessor #include statements

Because of their importance in planned software development, these uses of preprocessor statements were introduced in Chapter 4. Projects aimed at developing robust, maintainable software will usually be strengthened by limiting their use of preprocessor facilities to these essentials.

All programs complex enough to be divided into functions and modules have at least three types of dependencies among these elements:

- *control dependencies,* evident in the flow of control from one function and module to another
- *sequence dependencies,* related to shared assumptions about the order in which events will occur and actions will be carried out
- *data dependencies,* consisting of formats for shared data and policies of use

These are primary dependencies, without which programmed processes usually could not be carried out.

First, consider control dependencies. A sound principle of C program development is that when one module makes use of functions that are defined in another module, the using module should include a header file that exports conventions of the providing module. This leads to a pattern of header file dependencies that parallels the program flow dependencies, as shown in Figure 17.1.

Software design should always aim to contain sequence dependencies within modules. Indeed, the need for having modules as the next stage of organization beyond functions is closely related to the need for constructing and managing sequence dependencies. Sequence dependencies must be carefully documented, and it is critical to software maintenance that both their documentation and their coding be centralized, so that it will always be encountered as an entity and cannot fissure into potentially conflicting pieces. Robust design minimizes and whenever possible eliminates sequence dependencies between modules. Sequence dependencies that cannot be eliminated are checked by each function in a module that is designed to be used from outside the module.

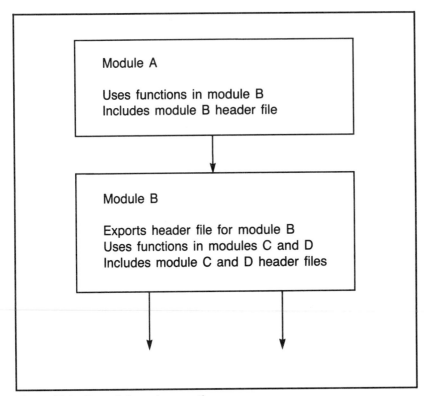

Figure 17.1: *Control dependency paths.*

In the C language, data dependencies within modules are generally tolerable, so long as the size and scope of a module is held to a reasonable limit. Planning, coding, and documentation can be kept together fairly easily for a single module. Data dependencies among different modules are created by defining data with global span that is accessed through **extern** declarations. A network of data dependencies can be substantially more difficult to manage.

Chapters 4 and 6 described a software organization in which modules that perform the most critical operations on data act as producers, exporting their data declarations to other, consumer modules that must use the data. Preprocessor facilities are helpful for ensuring consistent behavior. Usually, a module that performs the most critical operations on shared data carries the definitions of global data. The header file that exports conventions for the functions of such a module may also export declarations and symbols related to such global data, or the export of data conventions may be provided by a separate header file.

Producer-consumer relationships require careful documentation. As Chapter 6 pointed out, they can be difficult to test. They create a network of header file dependencies, mirroring the data dependencies, that is overlaid on the dependencies of control flow. Whenever any data definition or policy for data use changes, each of the consumer modules must be examined for compatibility, and its dependencies should be retested. A pattern of data dependencies overlaying control dependencies is shown in Figure 17.2.

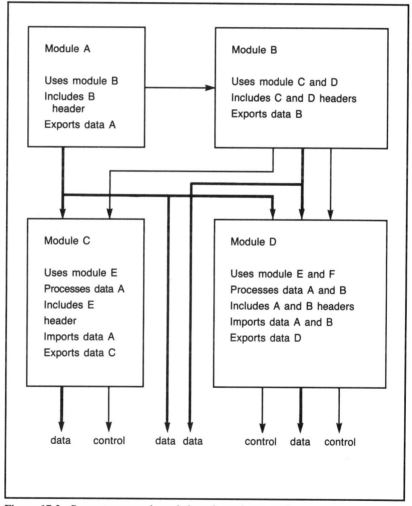

Figure 17.2: *Separate control- and data-dependency paths.*

Data dependencies form a separate network, which may or may not parallel control dependencies. Chaotic designs often exhibit data dependencies that flow "upstream" or across the streams of their control dependencies. Without careful planning, it is easy to generate such complex cross-threads of control and data dependencies that a program cannot be disassembled for testing. This type of software is a sad but characteristic product of talented people who lack experience with planned software development.

Chapter 12 introduced a more conservative organization called *data abstraction,* in which critical data collections are maintained by dedicated modules. In many applications, this approach improves on the "producer-consumer" organization by interposing program functions for all transactions involving data of a particular type. Data abstraction modules can often enforce policies for data use. Testing is substantially easier, because transactions of a given type flow through a common point of control.

Besides enhancing control and testability, data abstraction restructures a pattern of dependencies. Data dependencies become control dependencies. Software documentation and maintenance are usually expedited by such a single path dependency structure. The major cost of data abstraction is additional processing. When transactions do not constitute a critical component of software performance, this cost is easily borne. Often only a few—and sometimes none—of the transactions in a program need to be conveyed through data dependencies, in the interest of performance.

Many programs exhibit one or more of these additional types of dependencies:

- machine dependencies, embedded in the data communication, storage, or processing characteristics of equipment

- administrative dependencies, created by common mechanisms for access to data, user communication, or response to exceptions

- operational dependencies, generated by the capabilities and conventions of an operating environment

- coding dependencies, stemming from assumptions about coding details, forms of executable statements, and meanings of symbols.

These are secondary dependencies, which may be convenient to the programmer but are not strictly necessary for carrying out a programmed process.

A web of secondary dependencies is both a lure and a snare for software developers. Like a family relationship, it can provide and protect, yet when troubled it bids comparison to the Circles of Hell. Simply stated, the aim of robust software design is to reduce these dependencies to a serviceable minimum, so that a program more nearly resembles a democracy than either a dictatorship or a madhouse. It is naive to pretend, in the fashion of software theologians, that one can make sophisticated programs without these dependencies; but it is essential to keep them within manageable bounds.

The reason for including what may at first seem to be a philosophical statement in this section of the book is that header files are messages of dependencies in the C language. They communicate conventions of a program to those modules and functions that need to share them. As you build dependencies into a C program, you should, when possible, create header files that express them. Keep in mind that inclusion of any header file is evidence of a dependency. It entwines your software in a fabric of conditions and expectations. In addition, all dependencies contribute overhead costs to software development, testing, and maintenance. When you incur such a cost, make sure that your program receives a proportionate benefit.

Following are short lists of what is helpful and what can be harmful in C language header files:

HELPFUL:

- **extern** declarations of a module's external functions, specifying their return values

- declarations of data organizations for the parameters of external functions, when they are not fundamental data types

- symbols for values that have special meaning as arguments, array indexes, or return values

- names for functions, data, data organizations, structure members, and symbols that all begin with the same two or three characters, which are the same as the name of a module source file and its header file

HARMFUL:

- declarations of functions, data, data organizations, and symbols that are used only within an exporting module

- symbols that define or redefine any C language keywords, operators, or punctuation

- macro definitions that change the names or the arguments of any function references

- **typedef** declarations that redefine fundamental C language data types, unless such redefinition is necessary to manage machine dependencies

- macro definitions for data manipulations, unless these must be exported for consistency with policies governing use of shared data

- names of functions, data, data organizations, structure members, and symbols that lack a naming convention, closely related to the exporting module, that is designed to prevent conflict and confusion

Conditional compilation is sometimes used as an aid for adapting to machine or operational dependencies and to make "test" versions of modules. Both practices are generally undesirable and ineffective. The most practical and portable solution to machine and system dependencies is to recognize them as part of a software design process and to encapsulate them in implementation dependent modules. Any other approach will litter your code with poorly coordinated notes and exceptions, probably rendering it both unreliable and unreadable. The obvious problem with "test" sections of a module is that you are changing what you set out to test.

The major job of software is the management of external complexity. That is challenge enough. If you feel compelled to add an internal feature or convention to a program, look at it as an addition to a dependency network that must be mastered in order for a program to perform external tasks. Eliminating an unnecessary dependency is usually a step toward a more useful and reliable program.

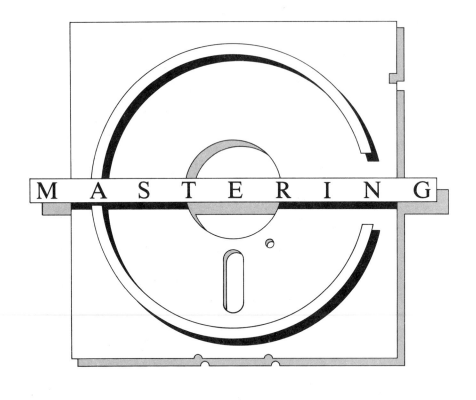

CHAPTER 18

THE C FUNCTION LIBRARY

Most implementations of C include a library of commonly needed data manipulation and input/output functions, called the C function library. Although not formally a part of the C language, these functions are so widely employed that only in specialized environments are you likely to find programs written without them. The next chapter discusses the input and output functions. In this chapter, you will read about:

- conventions and types of functions
- string manipulation functions
- storage allocation functions
- data conversion functions
- classification functions
- mathematical functions
- summary of library functions

□ CONVENTIONS AND TYPES OF FUNCTIONS

In addition to input and output, described in the next chapter, the C function library provides services for character string manipulation, dynamic memory allocation, data conversions between character formats and numeric values, classification of character values, and mathematics. This chapter and the next present only the functions that are usually available, in the most commonly encountered forms. The last section of this chapter gives a reference summary of the functions that it describes.

Many implementations provide functions in addition to those described. A few do not include all those described. The emphasis in this book is on describing the functions that are relatively dependable. Each C library function is presented in a consistent format. First, the general type of function—string, storage, and so on—is described in the section heading that precedes it. Then, under each function name, the following items appear:

PURPOSE
PROTOTYPE
ARGUMENTS
RETURN VALUE

ACTIONS
EXCEPTIONS
VARIANTS

The PURPOSE listed for a function will describe, in a phrase, the major service it provides.

The PROTOTYPE for a function gives a declaration of the return value and includes a parameter list. The names of parameters in a function prototype have no special significance. They are supplied only for reference in the description of arguments. However, any symbol appearing in place of a data type keyword must be used exactly as it appears. It will be defined by a header file.

To use many of the functions, you must include in your source text an implementation dependent header file. When this is necessary, the prototype will be preceded by an #include command, giving the name of the file. An #include command will be shown in the form that encloses a file name between a less-than sign and a greater-than sign. If you are working with an implementation that does not support this form of #include, locate copies of these files in an appropriate place, and use the form that encloses a file name between double quotes.

The ARGUMENTS for a function are each presented as a declaration, using the parameter names that appear in the function prototype, followed by text that explains the content or meaning of an argument. The RETURN VALUE of a function is presented in the same way. Any symbol appearing in place of a data type keyword must be used, exactly as it appears, in the declaration of an actual argument. It will be defined by a header file.

Normal ACTIONS will be described when all arguments in a function reference are valid and no unusual conditions interfere with performing the service. EXCEPTIONS include any characteristic that makes a parameter invalid, any condition that prevents performance of the function, and the response of the function in such an event. For some functions, there are no exception conditions.

VARIANTS outline the most common differences between a function as it is described and as it may actually be implemented. The functions commonly included in the C function library originated in the development of the Unix operating system. While the names of these functions have become a de facto standard, many details of their actions and exceptions vary from one implementation to another. Although the C library is sometimes referred to as a "portable" function library, the variations undermine portability. Descriptions of actions for the few functions that appear to have no variants will begin with the notation STANDARD.

It is unwise to presume that these functions are literally "portable." Until standardization of the C language has become widespread and has matured over several years, it is likely that significant variations in the implementation of these functions will persist. Use of C library functions should generally be encapsulated in program modules that are known to contain implementation dependencies. It is advantageous to plan software so that there are as few such modules as possible and to provide for each a unit test that will assess its performance in a new environment. Functions that are easy to make, such as those for string handling, are often produced (using different function names) as part of a portable software project.

In some implementations, certain functions are implemented as macro symbols, using preprocessor **#define** statements that are included in header files. Implementations that use macro substitution should provide substitution text that will cause parameters to be evaluated exactly as many times as would a function. However, it is recommended that you read the header files for any implementation carefully, so that you fully understand their behavior. In many implementations, recognition of a macro reference requires that an identifier be followed immediately by an opening parenthesis, with no intervening spacing. This format is recommended for all uses of C library functions.

□ STRING MANIPULATION FUNCTIONS

The string manipulation functions operate on character strings terminated by a null character. They are provided in two versions, bounded and unbounded. Bounded functions include arguments specifying maximum string lengths. These should be used unless a software design guarantees that all input strings to a function have null terminators and that sufficient storage has been allocated for any output string.

strlen

PURPOSE	Evaluate string length.
PROTOTYPE	**int strlen(string)**
ARGUMENTS	**char *string ;**
	Pointer to null-terminated character string.

RETURN VALUE	The length of the string in characters, up to but not including a null terminator.
ACTIONS	STANDARD. Measures and returns the string length.
EXCEPTIONS	If **string** is a null pointer value or fails to point to valid data, the results are unspecified. Should a string length exceed the largest value of an **int,** results are unspecified. If no null character is found, tests may extend into an invalid region of storage. An error may or may not occur.

strncmp

PURPOSE	Bounded comparison.
PROTOTYPE	**int strncmp(string1, string2, maxlen)**
ARGUMENTS	**char *string1, *string2 ;** Pointers to strings to be compared. **int maxlen ;** Maximum lengths before null terminator.
RETURN VALUE	Zero if the strings are the same, otherwise the difference between character values for the first character that disagrees.
ACTIONS	Comparison continues up to a position at which characters differ, a null character occurs in both strings, or the number of characters specified by **maxlen** has been compared, whichever occurs first. When a difference is found, the value returned is the character in **string1** less the character in **string2.**
EXCEPTIONS	If **maxlen** is zero or negative, the strings are considered equal. If either **string1** or **string2** is a null pointer value or fails to point to valid data, the results are unspecified. An error may or may not occur.
VARIANTS	Some implementations return values of 0, +1, or −1.

strncpy

PURPOSE	Bounded copy.
PROTOTYPE	**char** *strncpy(string1, string2, length)
ARGUMENTS	**char** *string1 ; Destination string. **char** *string2 ; Source string. **int** length ; Length of strings to copy.
RETURN VALUE	Value of **string1** argument.
ACTIONS	Copies **length** characters from **string2** to **string1**. Once a null character has been copied, pads any remaining length of **string1** with additional null characters.
EXCEPTIONS	If **length** is zero or negative, no characters are copied. Actions are unpredictable if the **length** characters beginning at **string1** overlap the **length** characters beginning at **string2**. If either **string1** or **string2** is a null pointer value or fails to point to valid data, the results are unspecified. An error may or may not occur.
VARIANTS	Padding of null characters may not occur. A null terminator may be added to **string1** if one is not copied. A value may not be returned. An **int** value equal to the number of characters copied may be returned.

strncat

PURPOSE	Bounded concatenate.
PROTOTYPE	**char** *strncat(string1, string2, length)
ARGUMENTS	**char** *string1 ; Destination string. **char** *string2 ; Source string. **int** length ; Length of strings to copy.

RETURN VALUE   Value of **string1** argument.

ACTIONS   Locates the first null character in **string1**. Beginning at that location, copies **length** characters from **string2** to **string1**. Once a null character has been copied, pads any remaining length of **string1** with additional null characters.

EXCEPTIONS   If **length** is zero or negative, no characters are copied. Actions are unpredictable if the **length** characters beginning at **string1** overlap the **length** characters beginning at **string2**. If either **string1** or **string2** is a null pointer value or fails to point to valid data, the results are unspecified. If no null character occurs in **string1**, a search may extend into an invalid region of storage. An error may or may not occur.

VARIANTS   Padding of null characters may not occur. A null terminator may be added to **string1** if one is not copied. A value may not be returned. An **int** value equal to the number of characters copied may be returned.

strcmp

PURPOSE   Unbounded comparison.

PROTOTYPE   **int strcmp(string1, string2)**

ARGUMENTS   **char *string1, *string2 ;**
Pointers to strings to be compared.

RETURN VALUE   Zero if the strings are the same, otherwise the difference between character values for the first character that disagrees.

ACTIONS   Comparison continues up to a position at which characters differ or a null character occurs in both strings, whichever occurs first. When a difference is found, the value returned is the character in **string1** less the character in **string2**.

EXCEPTIONS	If either **string1** or **string2** is a null pointer value or fails to point to valid data, the results are unspecified. An error may or may not occur. If no null character is found, comparison may extend into an invalid region of storage. An error may or may not occur.
VARIANTS	Some implementations return values of 0, +1, or −1.

strcpy

PURPOSE	Unbounded copy.
PROTOTYPE	**char** *strcpy(string1, string2)
ARGUMENTS	**char** *string1 ; Destination string. **char** *string2 ; Source string.
RETURN VALUE	Value of **string1** argument.
ACTIONS	Copies characters from **string2** to **string1** until a null character has been copied.
EXCEPTIONS	Actions are unpredictable if the characters beginning at **string2** up to a null character overlap an equal number of characters beginning at **string1**. If either **string1** or **string2** is a null pointer value or fails to point to valid data, the results are unspecified. If no null character is found, copying may extend into an invalid region of storage. An error may or may not occur.
VARIANTS	A value may not be returned. An **int** value equal to the number of characters copied may be returned.

strcat

PURPOSE	Unbounded concatenate.
PROTOTYPE	**char** *strcat(string1, string2)

ARGUMENTS   **char** *string1 ;
Destination string.
char *string2 ;
Source string.

RETURN VALUE   Value of **string1** argument.

ACTIONS   Locates the first null character in **string1**. Beginning at that location, copies characters from **string2** to **string1** until a null character has been copied.

EXCEPTIONS   Actions are unpredictable if the characters beginning at **string2** up to a null character overlap an equal number of characters beginning at the first null character in **string1**. If either **string1** or **string2** is a null pointer value or fails to point to valid data, the results are unspecified. If no null character occurs in **string1**, a search may extend into an invalid region of storage. An error may or may not be detected. If no null character is found in **string2**, copying may extend into an invalid region of storage. An error may or may not occur.

VARIANTS   A value may not be returned. An **int** value equal to the number of characters copied may be returned.

□ STORAGE ALLOCATION FUNCTIONS

The C library provides a simple mechanism for allocating dynamic storage, sometimes called *heap* storage. The heap is an unstructured pool of available space, from which regions of specified sizes are allocated on demand. The allocation functions return a pointer to the start of the region allocated. The size of a region should be determined by multiplying the number of data items it is to hold by **sizeof**, applied to their data type or organization.

Pointers returned by dynamic memory allocation have a special property: they can be used for a data element or aggregate of any type. Although the allocation functions are commonly designated as returning a pointer to **char**, they can be cast as returning a pointer to any data type except a function. Regions of memory that have been allocated can be released. After release, they may be used by the function library for any purpose, including satisfaction of subsequent demands for dynamic storage.

Dynamic memory allocation may be implemented in a variety of ways. The implementations are sometimes inefficient. When a large number of small segments of memory must be continually allocated and released, portability and performance are improved by constructing modules that obtain "wholesale" storage from the C function library and furnish "retail" quantities to consumers.

malloc

PURPOSE	Allocate a region.
PROTOTYPE	**char** *malloc(size)
ARGUMENTS	**int** size ; Size of region required, using **sizeof**.
RETURN VALUE	Pointer to region allocated. Need not be considered a pointer to **char**.
ACTIONS	Finds a storage region of sufficient size. Records that it has been allocated. Returns a pointer to the start of the region. No initialization of the region is performed.
EXCEPTIONS	A null pointer value is returned if insufficient storage is available to the function. Action if **size** is zero or negative is not specified.
VARIANTS	The **size** argument may be an integer value of some other data type. Some implementations have a limit on size of a region, regardless of the data type of **size**.

calloc

PURPOSE	Allocate and clear a region.
PROTOTYPE	**char** *calloc(size)

ARGUMENTS
int size ;
Size of region required, using **sizeof**.

RETURN VALUE
Pointer to region allocated. Need not be considered a pointer to **char**.

ACTIONS
Finds a storage region of sufficient size. Records that it has been allocated. Returns a pointer to the start of the region. Initializes the entire region to integer zero.

EXCEPTIONS
A null pointer value is returned if insufficient storage is available to the function. Action if **size** is zero or negative is not specified.

VARIANTS
The **size** argument may be an integer value of some other data type. Some implementations have a limit on the size of a region, regardless of the data type of **size**.

free

PURPOSE
Release an allocated region.

PROTOTYPE
int free(region)

ARGUMENTS
char *region ;
Pointer to previously allocated storage region. Need not be typed a pointer to **char**.

RETURN VALUE
Zero if region is successfully freed, otherwise a nonzero value.

ACTIONS
Checks that the region was previously allocated. If so, records its release.

EXCEPTIONS
An error will be detected if the value of **region** is not the location of a previously allocated region of dynamic storage.

VARIANTS
Some implementations do not check validity. A value may not be returned. Some implementations require that a region allocated by **calloc** be released through a function called **cfree**, which otherwise has the same behavior as **free**.

□ DATA CONVERSION FUNCTIONS

Two simple data conversion routines are available in most implementations, two more in those that include the floating data types. These convert between numeric values and character strings with a decimal representation. The strings must be null-terminated. Some implementations provide additional routines that handle integers of different data types and allow different number bases in the string representation, particularly octal and hexadecimal.

itoa

PURPOSE	Convert integer to alphanumeric.
PROTOTYPE	**int** itoa(ivalue, avalue)
ARGUMENTS	**int** ivalue ; Integer value to be converted. **char** *avalue ; Location for alphanumeric equivalent.
RETURN VALUE	Length of string placed in **avalue**.
ACTIONS	Converts the integer value to an alphanumeric string in decimal. Includes a leading minus sign if the value is negative.
EXCEPTIONS	None.
VARIANTS	No value may be returned. A function named ltoa may be available for **long int** values. The size of string required to hold **avalue** is implementation dependent.

atoi

PURPOSE	Convert alphanumeric to integer.
PROTOTYPE	**int** atoi(avalue)
ARGUMENTS	**char** *avalue ; Alphanumeric string to be converted.
RETURN VALUE	Integer equivalent.

ACTIONS | Converts the alphanumeric string to an integer value. Accepts a leading plus or minus sign. Otherwise stops at the first character not a decimal digit.

EXCEPTIONS | Unpredictable results occur when there are no decimal digits or the number to be converted is too large to be represented.

VARIANTS | The function may return an integer value of a different data type. A function named **atol** may be available for **long int** values. Some implementations require a sign and decimal digits only. Others accept spacing characters.

ftoa

PURPOSE | Convert floating to alphanumeric.

PROTOTYPE | **int ftoa(fvalue, avalue)**

ARGUMENTS | **double fvalue ;**
Floating value to be converted.
char *avalue ;
Location for alphanumeric equivalent.

RETURN VALUE | Length of string placed in **avalue.**

ACTIONS | Converts the floating value to an alphanumeric string in decimal. Includes a leading minus sign if the value is negative. Includes a signed exponent if the number cannot be represented with a decimal point within its range of significant digits.

EXCEPTIONS | None.

VARIANTS | No value may be returned. There may be additional arguments to control the format of **avalue.** The size of string required to hold **avalue** is implementation dependent.

atof

PURPOSE | Convert alphanumeric to floating.

PROTOTYPE	**double** atof(avalue)
ARGUMENTS	**char** *avalue ; Alphanumeric string to be converted.
RETURN VALUE	Floating equivalent.
ACTIONS	Converts the alphanumeric string to a floating value. Accepts a leading plus or minus sign, a decimal point, and a signed exponent. Otherwise stops at the first character not a decimal digit.
EXCEPTIONS	Unpredictable results occur when there are no decimal digits or the number to be converted is too large or small to be represented.
VARIANTS	Some implementations require a sign, decimal digits, decimal point, and exponent only. Others accept spacing characters.

□ CLASSIFICATION FUNCTIONS

The C library includes a number of functions that will check and change the classification of character values. A large proportion of implementations provide these by defining macro substitutions. The function prototypes show a header file named **ctype.h**, but some implementations provide the macro definitions in **stdio.h**, otherwise used as a header file for input/output functions.

isupper

PURPOSE	Test if uppercase character.
PROTOTYPE	#include <ctype.h> **int** isupper(cvalue)
ARGUMENTS	**int** cvalue ; Character value to test.
RETURN VALUE	Nonzero if an uppercase letter, otherwise zero.
ACTIONS	STANDARD. Tests the character for one of the following: ABCDEFGHIJKLM NOPQRSTUVWXYZ

EXCEPTIONS   None.

islower

PURPOSE   Test if lowercase character.

PROTOTYPE   #include <ctype.h>
               int islower(cvalue)

ARGUMENTS   **int cvalue ;**
               Character value to test.

RETURN VALUE   Nonzero if a lowercase letter, otherwise zero.

ACTIONS   STANDARD. Tests the character for one of
               the following:

                        abcdefghijklm
                        nopqrstuvwxyz

EXCEPTIONS   None.

isalpha

PURPOSE   Tests if alphabetic character.

PROTOTYPE   #include <ctype.h>
               int isalpha(cvalue)

ARGUMENTS   **int cvalue ;**
               Character value to test.

RETURN VALUE   Nonzero if an uppercase or a lowercase let-
               ter, otherwise zero.

ACTIONS   STANDARD. Tests the character for one of
               the following:

                        ABCDEFGHIJKLM
                        NOPQRSTUVWXYZ
                        abcdefghijklm
                        nopqrstuvwxyz

EXCEPTIONS   None.

isdigit

PURPOSE   Test if digit character.

PROTOTYPE	#include <ctype.h> **int** isdigit(cvalue)
ARGUMENTS	**int** cvalue ; Character value to test.
RETURN VALUE	Nonzero if a decimal digit character, otherwise zero.
ACTIONS	STANDARD. Tests the character for one of the following: 0123456789
EXCEPTIONS	None.

isalnum

PURPOSE	Test if alphanumeric character.
PROTOTYPE	#include <ctype.h> **int** isalnum(cvalue)
ARGUMENTS	**int** cvalue ; Character value to test.
RETURN VALUE	Nonzero if an uppercase letter, a lowercase letter, or a decimal digit, otherwise zero.
ACTIONS	STANDARD. Tests the character for one of the following: ABCDEFGHIJKLM NOPQRSTUVWXYZ abcdefghijklm nopqrstuvwxyz 0123456789
EXCEPTIONS	None.

isprint

PURPOSE	Test if printable character.
PROTOTYPE	#include <ctype.h> **int** isprint(cvalue)
ARGUMENTS	**int** cvalue ; Character value to test.

RETURN VALUE	Nonzero if a printable character, otherwise zero.
ACTIONS	Tests whether the character can be printed. Printable characters include spaces but not control characters that cause spacing.
EXCEPTIONS	None.
VARIANTS	The printable character set varies with the implementation.

isspace

PURPOSE	Test if spacing character.
PROTOTYPE	#include <ctype.h> int isspace(cvalue)
ARGUMENTS	int cvalue ; Character value to test.
RETURN VALUE	Nonzero if a spacing character, otherwise zero.
ACTIONS	Tests whether the character controls spacing.
EXCEPTIONS	None.
VARIANTS	The spacing character set varies with the implementation.

tolower

PURPOSE	Change to lowercase character.
PROTOTYPE	#include <ctype.h> int tolower(cvalue)
ARGUMENTS	int cvalue ; Character value to change.
RETURN VALUE	Equivalent lowercase letter.
ACTIONS	Tests the character for one of the following: ABCDEFGHIJKLM NOPQRSTUVWXYZ

If found, returns the matching equivalent from:

abcdefghijklm
nopqrstuvwxyz

Otherwise, returns the character unchanged.

EXCEPTIONS   None.

VARIANTS   Some implementations convert without a test.

toupper

PURPOSE   Change to uppercase character.

PROTOTYPE   #include <ctype.h>
int toupper(cvalue)

ARGUMENTS   int cvalue ;
Character value to change.

RETURN VALUE   Equivalent uppercase letter.

ACTIONS   Tests the character for one of the following:

abcdefghijklm
nopqrstuvwxyz

If found, returns the matching equivalent from:

ABCDEFGHIJKLM
NOPQRSTUVWXYZ

Otherwise, returns the character unchanged.

EXCEPTIONS   None.

VARIANTS   Some implementations convert without a test.

□ MATHEMATICAL FUNCTIONS

Mathematical functions are available in most implementations that provide floating data types. They calculate absolute value, bounding integers, roots, powers, and transcendental functions. Logarithm and exponential functions use base e. Trigonometric functions use angles stated in radians. Other functions will split a floating value into a mantissa and exponent and recombine these. The exponent base depends on the radix used by a floating representation.

Many implementations require a header file called math.h, as shown in the prototypes. In some implementations, this file provides access to a variable named errno, which will be set to a nonzero but implementation dependent code number when one of the mathematical functions returns with an error. Some C compilers, contrary to the usual conventions of C, automatically recognize the types of return values of these library functions.

frexp

PURPOSE	Decompose floating number.
PROTOTYPE	#include <math.h> double frexp(value, xpon)
ARGUMENTS	double value ; Signed floating value. int *xpon ; Signed exponent from floating value.
RETURN VALUE	Signed mantissa from floating value.
ACTIONS	Separates the exponent of value and expresses it as int. Stores it in xpon. Returns the mantissa.
EXCEPTIONS	If an invalid pointer value is supplied for xpon, data may be stored in an invalid region of storage. An error may or may not be detected.
VARIANTS	The base of the exponent depends on the radix of the double representation. Most computers use radix 2, but some use 16 or another power of 2. The mantissa in a radix 2 representation usually has a value from 0.5 up to but not including 1. However, some representations use a different range or may produce unnormalized values.

ldexp

PURPOSE	Recompose floating number.

PROTOTYPE	#include <math.h> **double** ldexp(value, expon)
ARGUMENTS	**double** value ; Signed mantissa for floating value. **int** expon ; Signed exponent for floating value.
RETURN VALUE	Signed floating value.
ACTIONS	Combines the mantissa and the exponent. Returns the equivalent floating value.
EXCEPTIONS	If the resulting value exceeds the representable range, unpredictable actions occur.
VARIANTS	May or may not provide an **errno** code when arguments are not representable. Some implementations do not check for representability. Others return zero or a large value if the arguments are not representable. The base of the exponent depends on the radix of the **double** representation. Most computers use radix 2, but some use 16 or another power of 2. The mantissa in a radix 2 representation usually has a value from 0.5 up to but not including 1. However, some representations use a different range and may accept or produce unnormalized values.

abs

PURPOSE	Absolute value.
PROTOTYPE	#include <math.h> **double** abs(value)
ARGUMENTS	**double** value ; Signed floating value.
RETURN VALUE	Absolute value of the argument.
ACTIONS	If the argument is less than zero, returns the negative of the argument. Otherwise, returns the argument unchanged.

EXCEPTIONS   None.

VARIANTS   Some implementations name the function **fabs**.

ceil

PURPOSE   Next higher integer value.

PROTOTYPE   #include <math.h>
double ceil(value)

ARGUMENTS   **double** value ;
Signed floating value.

RETURN VALUE   Next more positive integer value.

ACTIONS   If the argument has an integer value, returns its value unchanged. Otherwise, returns the next more positive integer value.

EXCEPTIONS   Unpredictable action when the value exceeds the range at which the significance of a floating value makes it possible to determine whether it has an integer value.

VARIANTS   May or may not provide an **errno** code when significance is exceeded.

floor

PURPOSE   Next lower integer value.

PROTOTYPE   #include <math.h>
double floor(value)

ARGUMENTS   **double** value ;
Signed floating value.

RETURN VALUE   Next more negative integer value.

ACTIONS   If the argument has an integer value, returns its value unchanged. Otherwise returns the next more negative integer value.

EXCEPTIONS   Unpredictable action when the value exceeds the range at which the significance of a floating value makes it possible to determine whether it has an integer value.

VARIANTS
May or may not provide an **errno** code when significance is exceeded.

sqrt

PURPOSE
Square root.

PROTOTYPE
#include <math.h>
double sqrt(value)

ARGUMENTS
double value ;
Signed floating value.

RETURN VALUE
Square root of the argument.

ACTIONS
If the argument is zero or greater, computes and returns its square root.

EXCEPTIONS
If the argument is less than zero, the function is mathematically complex.

VARIANTS
May or may not provide an **errno** code when the argument is less than zero. Most implementations return zero, but some will return the square root of the absolute value. The precision is implementation dependent.

log

PURPOSE
Natural logarithm.

PROTOTYPE
#include <math.h>
double log(value)

ARGUMENTS
double value ;
Signed floating value.

RETURN VALUE
Natural logarithm of argument.

ACTIONS
Tests whether the argument is greater than zero. If so, computes and returns the logarithm to the base *e*.

EXCEPTIONS	If the argument is zero or negative, returns zero.
VARIANTS	May or may not provide an **errno** code when the argument is zero or negative or when it is too close to zero for its logarithm to be representable. The latter boundary is implementation dependent. The precision is implementation dependent.

exp

PURPOSE	Natural exponential.
PROTOTYPE	#include <math.h> **double** exp(value)
ARGUMENTS	**double** value ; Signed floating value.
RETURN VALUE	Natural exponential of argument.
ACTIONS	Tests whether the magnitude of the argument is within an allowed range. If so, computes and returns an exponential using the base *e*.
EXCEPTIONS	If a positive argument is less than an allowed value or a negative argument is less than a different allowed value, returns zero. If a positive argument is greater than an allowed value or a negative argument is greater than a different allowed value, returns a large positive value.
VARIANTS	May or may not provide an **errno** code when the argument is outside a range within which the exponential is representable. The range of representability and the large positive value that can be returned on an exception are implementation dependent. The precision is implementation dependent.

pow

PURPOSE	Power function.

PROTOTYPE	#include <math.h> **double** pow(value, exponent)
ARGUMENTS	**double** value ; Signed floating value. **double** exponent ; Signed floating exponent for floating value.
RETURN VALUE	Value raised to power of exponent.
ACTIONS	Takes the natural logarithm of **value**. Multiplies that by **exponent**. Takes the natural exponential of the product.
EXCEPTIONS	The function is mathematically undefined when both arguments are zero and when the first argument is zero and the second is less than zero. The function is mathematically complex when the first argument is negative and the second is not an integer value. The exceptions for the natural logarithm and exponential functions apply. If the logarithm of **value** can be obtained, there may be a representation or significance error in the multiplication step.
VARIANTS	May or may not provide an **errno** code when any of the exceptions occurs. Argument values that lead to representation exceptions are implementation dependent. The precision is implementation dependent.

sin

PURPOSE	Sine of an angle.
PROTOTYPE	#include <math.h> **double** sin(angle)
ARGUMENTS	**double** angle ; Angle in radians.
RETURN VALUE	Sine of the argument.
ACTIONS	Checks for an angle within a range for which the argument is significant. If so,

finds the value modulo 2π, then computes and returns the sine.

EXCEPTIONS   The sine cannot be determined if the value of the angle is outside a range for which **angle**, modulo 2π, lacks significance in the floating representation.

VARIANTS   May or may not provide an **errno** code when an exception occurs. The argument values that will lead to representation exceptions are implementation dependent. The precision is implementation dependent.

cos

PURPOSE   Cosine of an angle.

PROTOTYPE   #include <math.h>
double cos(angle)

ARGUMENTS   **double angle ;**
Angle in radians.

RETURN VALUE   Cosine of the argument.

ACTIONS   Checks for an angle within a range for which the argument is significant. If so, finds the value modulo 2π, then computes and returns the cosine.

EXCEPTIONS   The cosine cannot be determined if the value of the angle is outside a range for which **angle**, modulo 2π, lacks significance in the floating representation.

VARIANTS   May or may not provide an **errno** code when an exception occurs. The argument values that will lead to representation exceptions are implementation dependent. The precision is implementation dependent.

tan

PURPOSE   Tangent of an angle.

PROTOTYPE

#include <math.h>
double tan(angle)

ARGUMENTS

double angle ;
Angle in radians.

RETURN VALUE

Tangent of the argument.

ACTIONS

Checks for an angle within a range for which the argument is significant. If so, finds the value modulo π. Checks for a value sufficiently far from π/2 that the result will be significant. If so, computes and returns the tangent.

EXCEPTIONS

The tangent cannot be determined if the value of the angle is outside a range for which **angle**, modulo π, lacks significance in the floating representation. The tangent also cannot be determined if the angle, modulo π, is too close to π/2.

VARIANTS

May or may not provide an **errno** code when an exception occurs. The argument values that will lead to representation exceptions are implementation dependent. The precision is implementation dependent.

asin

PURPOSE

Angle given the sine.

PROTOTYPE

#include <math.h>
double asin(sine)

ARGUMENTS

double sine ;
Sine of an angle.

RETURN VALUE

Angle in radians whose sine is the argument.

ACTIONS

Checks for an argument in the range from −1 through 1. If so, computes the principal angle whose sine has the value of the argument. The range of the result is from −π/2 through π/2.

EXCEPTIONS   If an argument is outside the allowed range, a value of 0 is returned.

VARIANTS   May or may not provide an **errno** code when an exception occurs. The precision of the result is implementation dependent.

acos

PURPOSE   Angle given the cosine.

PROTOTYPE   #include <math.h>
double acos(cosine)

ARGUMENTS   **double** cosine ;
Cosine of an angle.

RETURN VALUE   Angle in radians whose cosine is the argument.

ACTIONS   Checks for an argument in the range from -1 through 1. If so, computes the principal angle whose cosine has the value of the argument. The range of the result is from 0 through π.

EXCEPTIONS   If an argument is outside the allowed range, a value of 0 is returned.

VARIANTS   May or may not provide an **errno** code when an exception occurs. The precision of the result is implementation dependent.

atan

PURPOSE   Angle given the tangent.

PROTOTYPE   #include <math.h>
double atan(tangent)

ARGUMENTS   **double** tangent ;
Tangent of an angle.

RETURN VALUE   Angle in radians whose tangent is the argument.

ACTIONS	Computes the principal angle whose tangent has the value of the argument. The range of the result is from $-\pi/2$ through $\pi/2$.
EXCEPTIONS	None.
VARIANTS	The precision is implementation dependent.

□ SUMMARY OF LIBRARY FUNCTIONS

The C library functions described in this chapter are summarized by the following list, in the order of description in the text. For each function, a function-reference prototype and a one-line description of the purpose are listed.

String-Manipulation Functions:

int strlen(string)

   Evaluate string length.

int strncmp(string1, string2, maxlen)

   Bounded comparison.

char *strncpy(string1, string2, length)

   Bounded copy.

char *strncat(string1, string2, length)

   Bounded concatenate.

int strcmp(string1, string2)

   Unbounded comparison.

char *strcpy(string1, string2)

   Unbounded copy.

char *strcat(string1, string2)

   Unbounded concatenate.

Storage Allocation Functions:

char *malloc(size)

   Allocate a region.

char *calloc(size)

   Allocate and clear a region.

int free(region)
   Release an allocated region.

Data Conversion Functions:

int itoa(ivalue, avalue)
   Convert integer to alphanumeric.

int atoi(avalue)
   Convert alphanumeric to integer.

int ftoa(fvalue, avalue)
   Convert aloating to alphanumeric.

double atof(avalue)
   Convert alphanumeric to floating.

Classification Functions:

#include <ctype.h>

int isupper(cvalue)
   Test if uppercase character.

int islower(cvalue)
   Test if lowercase character.

int isalpha(cvalue)
   Test if alphabetic character.

int isdigit(cvalue)
   Test if digit character.

int isalnum(cvalue)
   Test if alphanumeric character.

int isprint(cvalue)
   Test if printable character.

int isspace(cvalue)
   Test if spacing character.

int tolower(cvalue)
   Change to lowercase character.

int toupper(cvalue)

Change to uppercase character.

Mathematical Functions:

#include <math.h>

double frexp(value, xpon)

Decompose floating number.

double ldexp(value, expon)

Recompose floating number.

double abs(value)

Absolute value.

double ceil(value)

Next higher integer value.

double floor(value)

Next lower integer value.

double sqrt(value)

Square root.

double log(value)

Natural logarithm.

double exp(value)

Natural exponential.

double pow(value, exponent)

Power function.

double sin(angle)

Sine of an angle.

double cos(angle)

Cosine of an angle.

double tan(angle)

Tangent of an angle.

double asin(sine)

Angle given the sine.

double acos(cosine)

Angle given the cosine.

double atan(tangent)

Angle given the tangent.

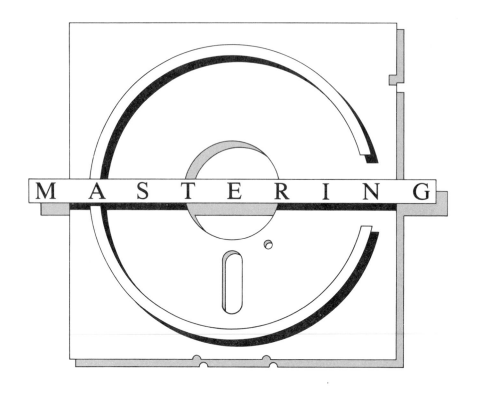

MASTERING

CHAPTER 19

INPUT AND OUTPUT
FUNCTIONS

Most C function libraries include commonly used input and output functions. The previous chapter described general conventions for the C function library and the characteristics of its other contents. This chapter discusses only the functions related to input and output. In it, you will read about:

- organization and conventions

- data access functions

- unformatted input and output functions

- formatted input and output functions

- input formats

- output formats

- nonbuffered input and output functions

- summary of input/output functions

□ ORGANIZATION AND CONVENTIONS

The C library functions for input and output were designed primarily to provide transmission of character data. Each input and output action is associated with some particular data source or destination. These are sometimes known as *input/output streams, I/O streams,* or just *streams.*

A stream is an unstructured sequence of character data. Data may reside in a physical file; they may also be transferred to and from terminals or other communications devices. In addition, they may flow to or from *virtual* files, used to communicate between simultaneously or sequentially active programs. (These are known as *pipes* in Unix systems.) The C library functions help to make a program device-independent, so that it can work in the same way regardless of the source or destination of a stream.

The input/output functions are often used to structure a stream into *text.* When interpreted as text, a stream is divided into *lines,* each of which ends with a *line marker.* The Unix systems generally use a newline character (\n) as a line marker in the actual data of a stream. Other systems may use a different line marker. For example, many microcomputers use carriage return followed by line feed. When a stream is interpreted as text, the input/output functions automatically recognize and generate line markers. Functions that transmit characters directly, with or without structuring as text, are called *unformatted* input/output functions.

The input/output functions also translate between data represented by characters and by other, internal data types. They are capable of reading and writing all of the data types provided by the C language. Several of these functions use a character string, called a *format,* that describes in detail translations to be performed. Functions that perform transformation between internal data and character strings, under format control, are known as *formatted* input/output functions.

Whether accessed as formatted text, unformatted text, or unstructured characters, streams are subjected by the C library functions to data manipulations designed to increase the efficiency of processing. The most important of these involves collecting data into sizable blocks, or *buffers,* when transferring data from a source or to a destination. Most implementations also provide lower-level, *nonbuffered* functions, which offer the programmer more direct control of input and output.

The actual origins and destinations of streams are addressed through *path names.* Like the other functions in the C library, the input/output functions originated during development of the Unix operating system. The term *path name* is an inheritance from the Unix system. It means a character string that describes a source or destination of data. In many systems, path names are called *file names.* All path names are implementation dependent. As described in the next section, most implementations provide two or more streams that are automatically available when a program uses any of the input/output functions.

In order to use any of the I/O functions, a module must include a header file, named **stdio.h**, that contains implementation dependent definitions. This file will define at least the following symbols:

FILE a **typedef** symbol or #define symbol for a data organization that records information about an active stream

EOF an **int** value returned whenever a stream encounters an end of data condition or an input/output error

stdin a pointer to FILE for an automatically activated source of input, often an interactive terminal

stdout a pointer to FILE for an automatically activated destination of output, often the same interactive terminal as stdin

The input/output functions are not consistent in the order of arguments. When a function requires a pointer to **FILE** as an argument, this will be the first argument for a data access function or a formatted I/O function. However, for an unformatted I/O function, it will be the last argument.

□ DATA ACCESS FUNCTIONS

To obtain access to a stream, a program must use the data access functions. Gaining access to a stream generally involves at least these steps:

LOOKUP   Determine the validity of a path name. If it designates a physical or a virtual file, determine whether it currently exists.

ATTACH   Determine whether access is available for the desired operations. If it is, set status to indicate allocation.

ACTIVATE   Initialize data structures, as needed, to begin data access.

In order to provide a relatively simple means of data access, there is a function, named **fopen,** that performs all the foregoing steps, given a path name and an indication of the type of operations to be performed. Another function, named **fclose,** reverses the actions of **fopen,** terminating data access. These functions must be used for all streams except those provided automatically by the C library.

The **fopen** function returns a pointer to **FILE,** otherwise known as a *stream pointer,* which must be supplied as an argument to the other functions that utilize streams. Whenever C library functions are in use, at least two streams are automatically activated before a program begins. The header file **stdio.h** provides implementation dependent definitions of pointer constants for these files, using the symbols **stdin** and **stdout.** Both are often directed to an interactive terminal.

In some implementations, certain C library functions, particularly those for input/output, can produce status messages when an error occurs. Those implementations frequently provide another automatically activated stream, named **stderr,** that receives the messages. This stream is also often directed to an interactive terminal, generally the same as the normal destination for **stdout.**

When a stream is activated, a program must declare the type of operations to be performed. All systems provide at least the options of input and output. Some systems also provide options to append (add to the end of existing data) and to update (change parts of existing data). Most systems provide text interpretation by default. Many have an option (sometimes called "binary") that suppresses text interpretations. However, some systems do not provide a "binary" option. Usually, **stdin** is a text input stream, **stdout** and **stderr** are text output streams.

Associated with each stream is a status that describes the current *position* in the stream. This commonly counts the number of characters read or written. However, counting of line markers is implementation dependent. A function called **ftell** will provide the current position, and another function named **fseek** will reset the position. The latter will not work on a communications stream and may or may not work on a stream associated with a virtual file.

Many path names are the names of physical files. As explained in Chapter 17, most systems provide a two-part file name format. In systems with a directory structure, a path name can also include directory information. The format of this information is implementation dependent. Most such systems include concepts of the *root directory* or *main directory* and the *current directory.* Unix systems use the following format for directory information:

/dir_1/dir_2. . ./dir_n/file_name

The successive directories in a chain are designated **dir_i**. If the first virgule (slash) is omitted, the search begins at the current directory; otherwise, it begins at the root directory. Some microcomputers use a similar syntax with a backslash instead of a virgule.

A format for directory information encountered on large computers and some of the larger minicomputers is this:

[dir_1.dir_2. . . dir_n]file_name

In this format, periods separate the directory names in a chain, which always begins at the main directory.

Some path names include device designations or symbols that an operating system will associate with devices or files. These path names are implementation dependent, and their forms vary widely. Some systems also make a variety of assumptions about the second part of a two-part file name if it is omitted.

The C library functions provide a relatively simple means of communicating information about exception conditions. Most functions return a status value. When an end of data condition or an error condition is encountered, the value returned is **EOF**, as defined in the header file. By calling a function named **ferror**, a program can determine whether this value indicates an error. If it does not, it indicates an end of data condition. Some systems distinguish between different types of errors with coded values, but meanings of these values are implementation dependent.

fopen

PURPOSE	Open a stream.
PROTOTYPE	`#include <stdio.h>` `FILE *fopen( pathname, option )`

ARGUMENTS	`char *pathname ;`
	Null-terminated path name string.
	`char *option ;`
	Null-terminated option string.

RETURN VALUE	Stream pointer for an active stream.
ACTIONS	Opens the path with requested options. The option string may specify:

"r"	read operations only
"w"	write operations only
"a"	write operations appended to stream
"r+"	read and update existing data
"w+"	write and update existing data
"a+"	append and update existing data
"rb"	read, without text interpretation
"wb"	write, without text interpretation
"ab"	append, without text interpretation
"rb+"	read and update, without text interpretation
"wb+"	write and update, without text interpretation
"ab+"	append and update, without text interpretation

A file must already exist to be opened for reading. If a file is opened for writing, an existing file is deleted and a new file is begun. These considerations do not apply to communications streams.

EXCEPTIONS   If the function cannot be performed, a null pointer value is returned.

VARIANTS   Some implementations do not provide operations without text interpretation or specify it in a different way. Some implementations specify update as an **rw** option. Some implementations will not delete an existing file; others will create a new "version" of an existing file. Some implementations accept upperor lowercase in the option string; others allow only lowercase. The sequences of operations allowed with update are implementation dependent. If an error occurs, some implementations store a value in an **int** defined as **errno.**

fclose

PURPOSE   Close a stream.

PROTOTYPE   #include <stdio.h>
int fclose(stream)

ARGUMENTS   **FILE *stream ;**
Active stream pointer.

RETURN VALUE   Zero if successful, otherwise **EOF.**

ACTIONS   STANDARD. Closes the stream. Records status for any file that has been created.

EXCEPTIONS   An error will be reported if **stream** does not have the location of a **FILE** structure for an active stream. Other errors can occur while recording status information for files.

ftell

PURPOSE   Obtain stream position.

PROTOTYPE	#include <stdio.h> **int** ftell(stream)
ARGUMENTS	FILE *stream ; Active stream pointer.
RETURN VALUE	Positive value if successful, otherwise **EOF.**
ACTIONS	Returns the current stream position.
EXCEPTIONS	An error will be reported if **stream** does not have the location of a **FILE** structure for an active stream. Other errors can occur while inspecting status information for files.
VARIANTS	Some implementations use a different data type for the return value. Some implementations do not return an error indication.

fseek

PURPOSE	Set stream position.
PROTOTYPE	#include <stdio.h> **int** fseek(stream, position, reference)
ARGUMENTS	FILE *stream ; Active stream pointer. **int** position ; New stream position. **int** reference ; Coded value for position reference.
RETURN VALUE	Zero if successful, otherwise nonzero.
ACTIONS	If **reference** is zero, sets the stream position according to the value of **position**. If **reference** is 1, changes the current position according to the value of **position**. If **reference** is 2, sets the position to the end of data, plus the value of **position**. These actions treat **position** as a signed value. When **position** and **reference** are both zero, the position is the start of data.
EXCEPTIONS	An error will be reported if **stream** does not have the location of a **FILE** structure for an

active stream. Other errors can occur while inspecting status information for files. An error can also occur if the stream cannot be repositioned or if the requested position is invalid. Communications files cannot be repositioned.

VARIANTS

Some implementations use different data types for the integer arguments. Some implementations do not return an error indication. The actions when **reference** is 2 or 3 are implementation dependent. An error can be always avoided by assuring that a stream can be repositioned and by using a value for **reference** of zero and a value for **position** obtained from **ftell**.

ferror

PURPOSE

Obtain stream error status.

PROTOTYPE

```
#include <stdio.h>
int ferror( stream )
```

ARGUMENTS

FILE *stream ;
Active stream pointer.

RETURN VALUE

Zero if no error has occurred, otherwise a nonzero value.

ACTIONS

Returns the error status for the stream. Once an error has been reported, an error will continue to be reported until the stream is closed.

EXCEPTIONS

An error will be reported if **stream** does not have the location of a **FILE** structure for an active stream.

VARIANTS

The meanings of nonzero return values are implementation dependent. Some implementations provide a procedure named **clearerr** to reset error status.

□ UNFORMATTED INPUT AND OUTPUT

Unformatted input and output functions provide transmission of character data without interpretation, except for structuring a character stream into text. Most of these functions require a stream pointer as an argument. A few of the functions assume either the **stdin** or the **stdout** stream. In many implementations, such functions are provided by macro substitutions defined in the **stdio.h** header file. You can interleave unformatted input and output with formatted input and output, which is described in the next section.

fgetc

PURPOSE	Read a character.
PROTOTYPE	#include <stdio.h> **int** fgetc(stream)
ARGUMENTS	FILE *stream ; Active stream pointer.
RETURN VALUE	Character value or **EOF**.
ACTIONS	Obtains and returns the next character. With text interpretation, a line marker is returned as a newline character. Otherwise, characters are transmitted as read.
EXCEPTIONS	If an error or end of data condition is encountered, **EOF** is returned. An error will occur if **stream** does not supply the location of a **FILE** structure for a stream that is open for input.
VARIANTS	Some implementations support only input with text interpretation. Some implementations provide an equivalent function named **getc**.

getchar

PURPOSE	Read a character from **stdin**.
PROTOTYPE	#include <stdio.h> **int** getchar( )

ARGUMENTS	None.
RETURN VALUE	Character value or EOF.
ACTIONS	Obtains and returns the next character. With text interpretation, a line marker is returned as a newline character. Otherwise, characters are transmitted as read.
EXCEPTIONS	If an error or end of data condition is encountered, EOF is returned.
VARIANTS	Some implementations support only input with text interpretation. Some implementations recognize end of data from stdin when a certain control character is read. Many implementations provide this function by macro substitution.

fputc

PURPOSE	Write a character.
PROTOTYPE	#include <stdio.h> int fputc(character, stream)
ARGUMENTS	char character ; Character value to be written. FILE *stream ; Active stream pointer.
RETURN VALUE	Character value or EOF.
ACTIONS	Writes and returns the character value. With text interpretation, a newline character is written as a line marker. Otherwise, characters are transmitted unchanged.
EXCEPTIONS	If an error condition is encountered, EOF is returned. An error will occur if stream does not supply the location of a FILE structure for a stream that is open for output.
VARIANTS	Some implementations support only output with text interpretation. Some implementations provide an equivalent function named putc.

putchar

PURPOSE   Write a character to **stdout**.

PROTOTYPE
```
#include <stdio.h>
int putchar( character )
```

ARGUMENTS
char character ;
Character value to be written.

RETURN VALUE   Character value or **EOF.**

ACTIONS   Writes and returns the character value. With text interpretation, a newline character is written as a line marker. Otherwise, characters are transmitted unchanged.

EXCEPTIONS   If an error condition is encountered, **EOF** is returned.

VARIANTS   Some implementations support only output with text interpretation. Many implementations provide this function by macro substitution.

fgets

PURPOSE   Read a string.

PROTOTYPE
```
#include <stdio.h>
char *fgets( string, maxlen, stream )
```

ARGUMENTS
char *string ;
Location for data read.
int maxlen ;
Maximum characters to read.
FILE *stream ;
Active stream pointer.

RETURN VALUE   Value of **string** argument or null pointer.

ACTIONS   Reads from input into **string** until a line marker has been read or end of data is encountered or (**maxlen** − **1**) characters have been read. Adds a terminating null character to the string. With text interpretation, a line marker is entered into the string as a newline character. Otherwise, characters are transmitted as read. At least **maxlen** characters of storage must be allocated, beginning at **string**.

EXCEPTIONS   If an error or end of data condition occurs before normal actions are completed, a null pointer value is returned. In such a case, **string** may be unchanged or may contain a partial string. An error will occur if **stream** does not supply the location of a **FILE** structure for a stream that is open for input.

VARIANTS   Some implementations support only input with text interpretation. When **stdin** is used for **stream,** some implementations do not place newline characters into **string**. Some implementations limit the length of an input string to a maximum number of characters, regardless of the value of **maxlen**.

fputs

PURPOSE   Write a string.

PROTOTYPE   #include <stdio.h>
char *fputs(string, stream)

ARGUMENTS   **char** *string ;
Location of data written.
FILE *stream ;
Active stream pointer.

RETURN VALUE   Character value or **EOF.**

ACTIONS   Writes from **string** to output until a null character is found. The null character is not transmitted. With text interpretation, a newline character is written as a line marker. Otherwise, characters are transmitted unchanged.

EXCEPTIONS   If an error condition occurs before normal actions are completed, **EOF** is returned. In such a case, the output may be nothing, a partial string, or a complete string. An error will occur if **stream** does not supply the location of a **FILE** structure for a stream that is open for output.

VARIANTS

Some implementations support only output with text interpretation. When **stdout** is used for **stream**, some implementations write an additional line marker at the end of the string. Provided an error does not occur, some implementations return the value of the last character written; others return zero. Some implementations limit the length of an output string to a maximum number of characters, regardless of the length of **string**.

fread

PURPOSE

Read a block.

PROTOTYPE

\#include <stdio.h>
int fread(data, size, count, stream)

ARGUMENTS

char *data ;
Location for data read.
int size ;
Size of a data item.
int count ;
Number of data items.
FILE *stream ;
Active stream pointer.

RETURN VALUE

Number of items read or zero.

ACTIONS

Reads items from input into **data**. Returns the number of items read. The **data** argument may be of any type; **sizeof** applied to this type should be used to obtain the value of **size**. Fewer than **count** items may be read; this should not be considered to be an error. If the value of either **size** or **count** is less than 1, nothing is read and a value of 0 is returned.

EXCEPTIONS

If an error or end of data condition occurs during transfer of an item, a value of 0 is returned. In such a case, **data** may be unchanged or it may contain some input. An error will occur if **stream** does not supply the location of a **FILE** structure for a stream that is open for input.

VARIANTS

With text interpretation, some implementations terminate input when a line marker is read. They may enter the line marker into **data** as a newline character. Some implementations limit the length of input to a maximum number of characters, regardless of the values of **size** and **count**.

fwrite

PURPOSE

Write a block.

PROTOTYPE

```
#include <stdio.h>
int fwrite( data, size, count, stream )
```

ARGUMENTS

char *data ;
Location of data written.
int size ;
Size of a data item.
int count ;
Number of data items.
FILE *stream ;
Active stream pointer.

RETURN VALUE

Number of items written or zero.

ACTIONS

Writes items from **data** to output. Returns the number of items written. The **data** argument may be of any type; **sizeof** applied to this type should be used to obtain the value of **size**. Fewer than **count** items may be written; this should not be considered to be an error. If the value of either **size** or **count** is less than 1, nothing is written and a value of 0 is returned.

EXCEPTIONS

If an error condition occurs during transfer of an item, a value of 0 is returned. In such a case, the output may be nothing, some of **data**, or all of **data**. An error will occur if **stream** does not supply the location of a **FILE** structure for a stream that is open for output.

VARIANTS

With text interpretation, some implementations may write a newline character from **data** as a line marker. Some implementations limit the length of output to a maximum number of characters, regardless of the values of **size** and **count**.

□ FORMATTED INPUT AND OUTPUT

A formatted input or output operation is controlled by a character string, called a *format,* describing the organization of data in character form and its translation between the character form and the internal data representations supported by C. A format string contains a sequence of items, coded as characters, each describing an element of a fundamental data type.

Unlike any ordinary C functions, formatted I/O functions have a variable number of arguments. One of these arguments is always a format string. Another argument, with most of the functions, specifies a stream or string to be used as the source or destination of character data. Following these arguments come data arguments. For each data argument, there must be a specification in the format.

When writing formats, it is important to keep in mind how they are used. When one of the formatted I/O functions is called, after determining the data stream or string, it begins to interpret the format as instructions. As each *item,* or data specification, in the format is interpreted, the routine looks for a corresponding data argument. The function learns how many data arguments there are and the types of data they represent by interpreting the format.

There are formatted I/O functions for transmission of data encoded as characters both to and from a stream and to and from an internal character string. When converting data for interactive uses, particularly data from keyboard input, it is usually advisable to perform formatted I/O on data in a string and to use another function to transfer data as characters between the string and the external environment.

There are significant differences between formats for input and for output. The remainder of this section will describe the formatted input and output functions. Descriptions of how to construct formats for these functions are in the following two sections. You can interleave formatted input and output with unformatted input and output, which is described in the previous section.

fscanf

PURPOSE	Read from a stream.
PROTOTYPE	#include <stdio.h> **int** fscanf(stream, format, ptr, ptr, . . .)
ARGUMENTS	**FILE** *stream ; Active stream pointer. **char** *format ; Format string. . . ., ptr, . . . Pointers to data elements.
RETURN VALUE	Number of data arguments processed or **EOF**.
ACTIONS	Interprets the format. For each item in the format, obtains characters from the stream and translates them into the value of a data element, as specified. Assigns the value to a data element at the location specified by the corresponding data argument. Returns the number of data arguments for which values have been assigned.
EXCEPTIONS	If there is an error reading characters from the stream, or if there is a conflict between a format item and the characters read from the stream, or if an end of data condition occurs while reading characters for an item other than a character string, then **fscanf** ends the operation and returns **EOF**.
VARIANTS	Some implementations return a count of data characters rather than a count of arguments. Some implementations return zero on an error rather than **EOF**. Some implementations do not support all of the format fields described or do not support them in exactly the ways described.

scanf

PURPOSE
Read from **stdin**.

PROTOTYPE
#include <stdio.h>
int scanf(format, ptr, ptr, . . .)

ARGUMENTS
char *format ;
Format string.
. . ., **ptr**, . . .
Pointers to data elements.

RETURN VALUE
Number of data arguments processed or **EOF**.

ACTIONS
Interprets the format. For each item in the format, obtains characters from **stdin** and translates them into the value of a data element, as specified. Assigns the value to a data element at the location specified by the corresponding data argument. Returns the number of data arguments for which values have been assigned.

EXCEPTIONS
If there is an error reading characters from **stdin**, or if there is a conflict between a format item and the characters read from the stream, or if an end of data condition occurs while reading characters for an item other than a character string, then **scanf** ends the operation and returns **EOF**.

VARIANTS
Some implementations return a count of data characters rather than a count of arguments. Some implementations return zero on an error rather than **EOF**. Some implementations do not support all of the format fields described or do not support them in exactly the ways described. Some implementations recognize end of data from **stdin** when a certain control character is read. Many implementations provide this function by macro substitution.

sscanf

PURPOSE	Read from a string.
PROTOTYPE	#include <stdio.h> **int** sscanf(string, format, ptr, ptr, . . .)
ARGUMENTS	**char** *string ; Null-terminated input character string. **char** *format ; Format string. . . ., ptr, . . . Pointers to data elements.
RETURN VALUE	Number of data arguments processed or **EOF**.
ACTIONS	Interprets the format. For each item in the format, obtains characters from the input string and translates them into the value of a data element, as specified. Assigns the value to a data element at the location specified by the corresponding data argument. Returns the number of data arguments for which values have been assigned.
EXCEPTIONS	If there is a conflict between a format item and the characters read from the stream, or if the null terminator of **string** is encountered while reading characters for an item other than a character string, then **sscanf** ends the operation and returns **EOF**.
VARIANTS	Some implementations return a count of data characters rather than a count of arguments. Some implementations do not support all of the format fields described or do not support them in exactly the ways described.

fprintf

PURPOSE	Write to a stream.

PROTOTYPE   #include <stdio.h>
            int fprintf(stream, format, val, val, . . .)

ARGUMENTS   FILE *stream ;
            Active stream pointer.
            char *format ;
            Format string.
            . . ., val, . . .
            Data values.

RETURN VALUE Number of characters written or **EOF**.

ACTIONS   Interprets the format. For each item in the
            format, obtains a value from a data argu-
            ment. Translates it into characters and writes
            it to the stream. Returns the number of
            characters written.

EXCEPTIONS If there is an error writing to the stream,
            fprintf ends the operation, and returns **EOF**.

VARIANTS   Some implementations do not return a value.
            Some return zero on an error rather than
            EOF. Some implementations do not support
            all of the format fields described or do not
            support them in exactly the ways described.

printf

PURPOSE   Write to **stdout**.

PROTOTYPE   #include <stdio.h>
            int printf(format, val, val, . . .)

ARGUMENTS   **char** *format ;
            Format string.
            . . ., val, . . .
            Data values.

RETURN VALUE Number of characters written or **EOF**.

ACTIONS   Interprets the format. For each item in the
            format, obtains a value from a data argu-
            ment. Translates it into characters and writes
            it to **stdout**. Returns the number of charac-
            ters written.

EXCEPTIONS   If there is an error writing to **stdout, printf** ends the operation and returns **EOF**.

VARIANTS   Some implementations do not return a value. Some return zero on an error rather than **EOF**. Some implementations do not support all of the format fields described or do not support them in exactly the ways described. Many implementations provide this function by macro substitution.

sprintf

PURPOSE   Write to an array.

PROTOTYPE   #include <stdio.h>
             int sprintf(string, format, val, val, . . .)

ARGUMENTS   **char** string[ ] ;
             Output character array.
             char *format ;
             Format string.
             . . ., val, . . .
             Data values.

RETURN VALUE   Number of characters written or **EOF**.

ACTIONS   Interprets the format. For each item in the format, obtains a value from a data argument. Translates it into characters and writes it to the output character array. Returns the number of characters written.

EXCEPTIONS   If there is an error writing to the array, **sprintf** ends the operation and returns **EOF**. Unless controlled by a match between the format and output array length, output characters may be stored in an invalid region of storage. An error may or may not be detected.

VARIANTS   Some implementations do not return a value. Some return zero on an error rather than **EOF**. Some implementations do not support all of the format fields described or do not support them in exactly the ways described.

☐ INPUT FORMATS

Input formats provide a picture of expected input. The characters in a format are interpreted as fields. After a field has been decoded from a format, input data are scanned to match the field. The scan position in the input is remembered from one field and from one operation to the next. There are three types of fields in format strings:

- *Spacing.* This includes blanks, tabs, and newline characters. Spacing in a format is ignored. The input is not scanned.

- *Items.* The specification for a data item begins with a percent sign (%). Items cause characters to be extracted from the input, and most items cause a value to be assigned to one data argument.

- *Text characters.* Any character other than spacing or part of an item causes spacing in the input to be skipped, and then it must match the next input character. The case of alphabetic characters is significant. A mismatch will cause an input function to terminate with an error. A mismatched character will remain in the input data.

Except for single character items, data for a format item are extracted from input by scanning over spacing until a character other than spacing is found; this is the *start* position. Then the input is scanned up to the next spacing character; this is the *end* position. An item may specify a maximum width; if spacing has not been found, this will terminate a scan.

Spacing in the input data includes blanks, tabs, and newline characters. In a stream with text interpretation, it includes line markers. An end of data condition in a stream or a null terminator in a string is considered an error if it occurs before a start position has been found. Otherwise, it provides an end position for a field.

Fields for data items in a format contain up to five elements, in the following order:

1. An *item flag,* the percent sign (%). This element is required.

2. A *suppression flag,* the asterisk (*). This element is optional. If present, the item is processed up to the point of assignment to a data argument, but assignment is suppressed and no data argument used.

3. A *width,* an unsigned decimal integer greater than zero. This element is optional. If present, it specifies a maximum number of characters to be accepted from input.

4. A *size,* the lowercase letter l (for long). This element is optional. If present, it specifies the size of a data element. This option can be used with fields of type d, e, f, o, or x.

5. A *type,* one of the following:
    lowercase c, d, e, f, h, o, s, or x
    percent sign %
    This element is required. A width, size, or suppression flag cannot be used with the percent sign.

If an item does not have one of these forms, an error will be reported, and the input will not be scanned. Otherwise, data characters from the start position up to the end position are extracted from the input, and the scan position is advanced to the end position. The characters extracted are converted as specified by the item. An error can occur if the data characters extracted for an item do not form a valid sequence for an item of the specified type. After an error has been reported, the scan position in the input should be regarded as indefinite; if necessary, it can be determined by using the **ftell** function.

Data extraction and conversion are performed according to item types, as follows:

%   This has the same effect as would a text field consisting of a percent sign. It is included among the format items because a single percent sign marks the start of an item.

c   Scanning over leading spacing does not occur for an item of this type. A single character is extracted from the input. It is assigned without conversion to a **char** whose location is given by a data argument.

d   The input is expected to be a decimal integer with an optional leading sign. The value is assigned to an **int** whose location is given by a data argument. If the size of the item is long, the value is assigned to a **long int**.

e   The input is expected to be a floating constant with an optional leading sign, optional decimal point, and optional exponent with an optional leading sign. The value is assigned to a **float** whose location is given by a data argument. If the size of the item is long, the value is assigned to a **double**.

f   The processing is the same as for an item of type e.

h The input is expected to be a decimal integer with an optional leading sign. The value is assigned to a **short int** whose location is given by a data argument.

o The input is expected to be an unsigned octal integer, with or without a leading zero. The value is assigned to an **unsigned int** whose location is given by a data argument. If the size of the item is long, the value is assigned to a **long int**.

s The input is a character string. It is assigned without conversion to successive **char**, the first of whose locations is given by a data argument. A null terminator is added after the last character assigned.

x The input is expected to be an unsigned hexadecimal integer, with or without a leading 0x or 0X. Hexadecimal digits represented by letters can be in either upper- or lowercase. The value is assigned to an **unsigned int** whose location is given by a data argument. If the size of the item is long, the value is assigned to a **long int**.

Some implementations do not ignore spacing in a format. Instead, spacing in a format causes any spacing in the input to be skipped over. This has an effect only on a following format item of type c, because all other format fields automatically skip leading spacing. Some implementations allow additional input format item types of lowercase g and upper case E, G, and X for compatibility with output format types. Items of types E, G, and g will be processed in the same way as an item of type e. An item of type X will be processed in the same way as an item of type x.

Some implementations differ in their scanning mechanism for numeric fields. They inspect successive characters to see whether they could belong to a value of the specified type, and they stop extracting characters at the first one that would be invalid. If no characters have been extracted, the numeric value is interpreted as zero. Some implementations accept a floating exponent with no digits.

Some implementations do not accept leading plus signs. Some implementations allow a leading sign for items of types o and x. Some implementations provide a type u for an unsigned integer represented in decimal. Some implementations treat h as a size rather than a type; in these implementations, it may apply to types d, o, u, and x.

Some implementations ignore an invalid size, width, or suppression flag. Some implementations process a width for an item of type c by assigning the specified number of characters to successive **char**, the first of whose locations is given by a data argument, without adding a terminating null character. Some implementations allow uppercase L as a size element.

Some implementations provide an item type represented by a pair of brackets with one or more characters between them. This is treated as an item of type s, except that the characters between brackets control the scanning mechanism. Leading spacing is not skipped. Only the characters between brackets are accepted as part of the input string. An input string is terminated by either the first input character not in the specified set or an end of data. Some implementations offering this feature provide an extension in which a caret (^) following the opening bracket indicates that the succeeding characters are to be excluded from string acceptance, while all others are to be permitted. The syntax of this feature does not permit a closing bracket to be named as a specificially included or excluded character.

Input items of type s are hazardous unless limited by maximum widths, because a string assignment can extend into an invalid region of storage. An error may or may not be detected. Numeric input values that are too large to be represented by a data element of the specified type may or may not be detected. If such errors are not detected, the values that will be assigned are implementation dependent.

Following are some examples of formatted input. For each is shown an input format, the available input characters, and the assignments that will occur. Initial and final scan positions in the input are shown by carets (^) underneath the characters to be scanned next. The values that will be assigned are then shown, in the order to which data arguments should correspond. A value is preceded by a data type. Single characters are between apostrophes, and character strings are between double quotes. If an error will occur during scanning, the list of values ends with the notation ERROR. The features and rules of interpretation are those described for conventional implementations of C:

FORMAT   "%d %lo %s"

INPUT   − 58 204516 filigree
                ^   ^

VALUES   **int**   − 58
               long int   0204516
               char [9]   "filigree"

FORMAT	"%s%c%5x68"	
INPUT	CV 3abcd6 789	
VALUES	char [3]	"CV"
	char	' '
	unsigned int	0x3abcd
	ERROR	

FORMAT	"%*f %7lf%2h"	
INPUT	8.6 −537E−94abc	
VALUES	double	−0.537E−6
	ERROR	

FORMAT	"%f%1s&%lo %6r"	
INPUT	.96 V& 0504 #2	
VALUES	float	0.96E0
	char [2]	"V"
	long int	0504
	ERROR	

There are no input formats for data aggregates, other than strings of **char**. To use formatted input for arrays or structures you must perform input for each data element contained in an aggregate. There are no formats for input of pointer values. It may be possible to read pointer values as integers, but this will be implementation dependent. Input of pointer values is particularly hazardous, because most implementations do not guarantee that data locations will be the same each time a program runs.

□ OUTPUT FORMATS

Output formats specify the appearance of output. As with input formats, the characters in an output format are interpreted as fields. After a field has been decoded from a format, a value may be obtained from a data argument and converted to characters. Some fields designate literal characters to be used for output. There are three types of fields in format strings:

- *Spacing.* This includes blanks, tabs, and newlines. Spacing is written out as it appears in the format, except that when text interpretation is in effect for a stream, a newline character is written as a line marker.

- *Items.* The specification for a data item begins with a percent sign (%). Each item causes a field of characters to be written out. Most items use a value from a data argument.

- *Text characters.* Any character other than spacing or part of an item is written out without change.

Data items in a format specify the layout of an output field. A field can be of automatic or specified width. A field of automatic width is made just wide enough to accomodate the characters required to express a data value. In a field of specified width, data characters may be adjusted to begin at the left of the field or to end at the right of the field; unused positions in the field may be filled with blanks or zeros. A data item in a format may include up to six elements, in the following order:

1. An *item flag,* the percent sign (%). This element is required.

2. *Adjustment flags,* a minus sign, a zero, or a minus sign followed by a zero. This element is optional. A minus sign causes characters for a data item to be left-adjusted. Otherwise, they are right-adjusted. A zero causes unused positions to be filled with zeros; otherwise, they are filled with blanks.

3. A *width,* an unsigned decimal integer greater than zero. This element is optional. If present, it specifies a minimum number of characters to be written as output.

4. A *precision,* a period followed by a positive decimal integer or zero. This element is optional. If present, it specifies the number of digits written to the right of a decimal point for **float** or **double** or the maximum number of characters written from a string of **char**. If only a period is supplied, the precision is zero. A precision can be used with fields of type e, f, g, or s. If not specified, a default precision of 6 applies to types e, f, and g.

5. A *size,* the lower case letter I (for long). This element is optional. If present, it specifies the size of a data element. This option can be used with fields of type d, e, f, g, o, u, or x, but it has no effect on the interpretation of types e, f, and g.

6. A *type,* one of the following:
   lowercase c, d, e, f, g, o, s, u, or x.
   percent sign %
   This element is required. A width, precision, size, or adjustment flag cannot be used with the percent sign.

If an item does not have one of these forms, an error will be reported, and no output will be generated. Otherwise, for all types but the percent sign, a value corresponding to the specified type of item is obtained from a data argument, converted to characters, adjusted as required, and written as output. If the number of characters written is not returned by an output function, it can be determined by using the ftell function.

Data conversion and adjustment are performed according to item types, as follows:

%   This has the same effect as would a text field consisting of a percent sign. It is included among the format items because a single percent sign marks the start of an item.

c   The data value is expected to be a character value contained in an **int**. It is written without change.

d   The data value is expected to be **int**. If the size is long, it is expected to be **long int**. It is written as a decimal integer. If the value is negative, a leading minus sign is included.

e   The data value is expected to be **double**. It is written as a decimal number, with one digit before the decimal point, followed by an exponent which consists of uppercase E, a plus or minus sign, and a decimal integer of at least two digits.

f   The data value is expected to be **double**. It is written as a decimal number with at least one digit before the decimal point.

g   The data value is expected to be **double**. It is converted according to e or g, depending on which requires fewer characters. Trailing zeros after a decimal point are not printed.

o   The data value is expected to be **unsigned int**. If the size is long, it is expected to be **long int**. It is written as an unsigned octal integer, without a leading zero.

s   The data value is expected to be a pointer to **char**. The character string is written without change, up to but not including a terminating null character.

u   The data value is expected to be **unsigned int**. If the size is long, it is expected to be **long int**. It is written as an unsigned decimal integer.

x   The data value is expected to be **unsigned int**. If the size is long, it is expected to be **long int**. It is written as an unsigned hexadecimal integer, without a leading 0x or 0X.

The conventions for automatic conversion of data type will convert any data value appearing as a function argument to one of the types listed for the different format item types. In particular, **char** and **short int** will be converted to **int**. A **float** value will be automatically converted to **double**.

The choice between type e and type f conversion for an item of type g is implementation dependent. Many implementations use type e when the value of the exponent for type e is greater than the precision or less than −3. Some implementations suppress a decimal point for types e, f, and g if a precision of zero is specified. The convention for rounding types e, f, and g is implementation dependent.

Some implementations provide a variation for format types e and g, using uppercase E and G. In these implementations, the letter E in an exponent is written in lowercase for types in lowercase and in uppercase for types in uppercase. Some implementations provide a variation for format type x, using uppercase X. In these implementations, letters representing hexadecimal digits are written in lowercase for type x and in uppercase for type X. The choice of case for letters used as hexadecimal digits is otherwise implementation dependent; uppercase is the more common choice.

Some implementations provide an additional format type b. The data value is expected to be **unsigned int**. It is written as a binary integer, consisting of ones and zeros. Some implementations use uppercase B, D, O, U, and X as equivalent to size l followed by the same letters in lowercase, that is lb, ld, lo, lu, and lx. In the case of X, this practice conflicts with the X feature that causes uppercase to be used for letters that are hexadecimal digits.

Some implementations do not write output for type c if the value is a null character. Some implementations treat a precision of zero applied to type s as allowing an unlimited length of output. Some implementations ignore invalid specifications for adjustment flags, widths, precisions, and sizes. Some implementations accept a width for percent sign. Some implementations interpret a precision for types d, u, o, or x as requiring a minimum number of digits and will prepend leading zeros, if necessary; they may produce no output if a precision of zero is specified. Some implementations allow uppercase L as a size element. Some implementations interpret an invalid character immediately following an item flag as a text character.

Some implementations provide additional adjustment flags. A plus sign as a flag causes a plus sign to be prepended and a blank as a flag causes a blank to be prepended, to the output of a positive value with a numeric format type. In some implementations, a number sign (#) used as an adjustment flag causes 0 to be prepended to output for type o and 0x or 0X to be prepended to output for types x and X; it may also force output of a decimal point when a precision of zero is specified with format type e, E, f, g, or G; and it may force output of trailing zeros with format types g or G.

Some implementations allow data arguments of type **int** to specify widths and precisions instead of integer values that appear in a format. This is indicated in a format by an asterisk (*) in place of a width element, a precision element, or both. If one of these is present, an argument providing an **int** value must immediately precede the argument for the value to be written. If both are present, two such arguments must precede the value to be written, the value for width first.

Following are some examples of formatted output. For each is shown an output format, a list of output values, and the output that will occur. The positions of the first output character and of the next available output location are shown by carets (^) underneath these positions. A value is preceded by a data type. Single characters appear between apostrophes, character strings between double quotes. If an error will occur during output, under the output appears the notation ERROR. The features and rules of interpretation are those described for conventional implementations of C:

VALUES	int	−58
	long int	0204516
	char *	"filigree"

FORMAT	''%d %lo %s''	
OUTPUT	− 58 204516 filigree	
	^ ^	

VALUES	**char**	'r'
	char *	"Moonscape"
FORMAT	''Least Hea%ct%5.4s''	
OUTPUT	Least Heart Moon	
	^ ^	

VALUES	**int**	− 123
	float	0.000059
FORMAT	''PROTO%−5d %8g''	
OUTPUT	PROTO−123 5.9E-05	
	^ ^	

VALUES	**long int**	47838
	unsigned int	0372
	char *	"REWELLING"
	double	2.718
FORMAT	'' %lx%3x%.6s %7r''	
OUTPUT	BADE FAREWELL	
	^ ^	ERROR

There are no output formats for data aggregates other than strings of **char**. To use formatted output for arrays or structures, you must perform output for each data element contained in an aggregate. It is usually possible to write pointer values as integers, but the integer data type associated with a pointer is implementation dependent. When formatting text, remember that the formatted output routines do not create lines automatically. A line ends only when a newline character is explicitly written.

☐ NONBUFFERED INPUT AND OUTPUT FUNCTIONS

Some programs need input or output of data other than text or need additional control of character oriented input and output. Most implementations of C provide additional input/output functions to assist in these circumstances. These are known collectively as *nonbuffered* input and output functions. They may not provide mechanisms to insure the efficiency of data transmission. Operations of these functions are implementation dependent; they should be used only when a program requires services that are not provided by formatted or unformatted input/output functions. Their use will make a program nonportable.

Two nonbuffered functions, named **read** and **write**, provide direct transfer of blocks of data. Three functions, called **open, creat,** and **close,** control file access. Two functions, called **lseek** and **ltell,** are involved with file positioning. Two functions, called **rename** and **delete,** can remove and change the names of files without performing input or output. This collection of functions is designed to transfer "binary" data without interpretation. Some implementations provide a text translation option. The amount of data that can be transferred in one operation may be limited by physical storage mechanisms. Some implementations provide buffering for these functions at a lower level.

When using the **read** and **write** series of functions, sources and destinations of data are addressed as *files* (sometimes known as *units*), whether data actually reside in files or flow to and from terminals, communications lines, or other devices. Access is through a *file descriptor,* an **int** value that is returned by **open** or **creat.** Path names and other designations of I/O sources and destinations are implementation dependent. They usually follow the same conventions as the formatted and unformatted I/O functions, but additional options may be available. Control of implementation dependent file storage parameters may be available through the **creat** function.

Some implementations that include a directory structure for files provide functions to inspect directory contents. One of these may perform a "lookup," often with the same syntax that an operating system command uses to list directory contents. Some systems, including Unix, maintain directories in text files using standardized directory file names and a standardized file format; they supply header files defining data structures, to assist C programmers in reading directory files.

Special controls are sometimes useful for interactive terminals. Functions named **getch** and **putch** are often available. The **getch** function receives one character from the keyboard without interpretation and without an echo to the display. The **putch** function transfers one character to the display without interpretation. Many systems automatically collect input from a terminal in a "type-ahead" buffer. Some of these provide different functions to obtain input from the type-ahead buffer and directly from the terminal. Some provide a function to empty the type-ahead buffer. Some provide a function to determine whether there is a character in the type-ahead buffer.

Two screen manipulation functions are sometimes provided for video displays with addressable character positions. The **curpos** function obtains the position on the screen where the next displayable character will appear. The **curset** function changes this position. Functions performing these services do not always have these names. Some implementations provide a much more elaborate repertoire of screen manipulations, including menus, switchable and overlappable display windows, and graphics.

Because the nonbuffered I/O functions are so heavily implementation dependent, it is not possible to provide a satisfactory description of conventional forms. To use these functions, you must consult the documentation for your C function library.

□ SUMMARY OF INPUT/OUTPUT FUNCTIONS

The input/output functions of the C function library are summarized in the following list, in the order of the descriptions in the text. For each function, a function reference prototype and a one line description are listed.

Data Access Functions:

```
#include <stdio.h>
FILE *fopen( pathname, option )
```

Open a stream.

int fclose(stream)

Close a stream.

int ftell(stream)

Obtain stream position.

int fseek(stream, position, reference)

Set stream position.

int ferror(stream)

Obtain stream error status.

Unformatted Input and Output Functions:

```
#include <stdio.h>
int fgetc( stream )
```

Read a character.

int getchar( )

Read a character from **stdin**.

int fputc(character, stream)

Write a character.

int putchar(character)

Write a character to **stdout**.

char *fgets(string, maxlen, stream)

Read a string.

char *fputs(string, stream)

Write a string.

int fread(data, size, count, stream)

Read a block.

int fwrite(data, size, count, stream)

Write a block.

Formatted Input and Output Functions:

#include <stdio.h>
int fscanf(stream, format, ptr, ptr, . . .)

Read from a stream.

int scanf(format, ptr, ptr, . . .)

Read from **stdin**.

int sscanf(string, format, ptr, ptr, . . .)

Read from a string.

int fprintf(stream, format, val, val, . . .)

Write to a stream.

int printf(format, val, val, . . .)

Write to **stdout**.

int sprintf(string, format, val, val, . . .)

Write to an array.

CHAPTER 20

TESTING AND MAINTAINING
C PROGRAMS

Software testing and maintenance, unlike the weather, are things that hardly anybody talks about but almost everybody works on. As Chapter 4 mentioned, these activities commonly consume three-quarters or more of the effort spent on a given software project over its life cycle. This chapter discusses the testing and maintenance of software written in C, including the following topics:

- test and maintenance cycles
- testing environments
- defect prevention
- software documentation
- software libraries

□ TEST AND MAINTENANCE CYCLES

The term *software testing,* as used in this chapter, refers to deliberate procedures designed to reveal defects or performance limitations in programs. *Software maintenance* refers to changes, made after an initial version of a program, that remove defects or meet new requirements. These activities grow in scope as software becomes more complex, as it affects more people or property, as it is used over longer periods of time, and as the gap widens between users and developers.

Testing begins as soon as anything is written down. The simplest tests are simply to reread requirements, designs, and code, to see if they make sense. With the advent of interactive computers, this discipline, formerly called "desk checking," has been badly neglected. A large proportion of problems can be prevented in this way. The "code and go" approach to software reaches its practical limit at a few hundred lines. An attempt to create anything larger this way usually generates a larger mess.

There are at least three distinct kinds of testing for defects in program code:

1. *General testing,* designed to explore all the services that software is supposed to deliver or to exercise every part of the code

2. *Focused testing,* designed to reveal the presence of suspected defects, most often ones found in some combination of circumstances

3. *Debugging,* designed to show details of program execution near the point where a defect is suspected

Nearly all software developers perform some kind of general testing. They regard it as basic insurance against problems. General testing may be concerned with either the outside of software, testing every external service, or with the inside of software, causing execution of every line of code. Sometimes it is concerned with both. Whatever the focus, it is impossible to test every combination and sequence of operations. There is always a potential for latent defects, not detected by general testing. When latent defects are found, software developers turn to focused testing and debugging, to identify and correct the failures.

Maintenance begins as soon as code is written; it is rare to find a hundred lines of newly written code containing no defects. Since the late 1950s, specialists in computer algorithms and languages have tried to develop methods to insure against software defects. So far, the best that can be said of these approaches is that, like fluoridated toothpaste, they can be "of significant value when used in a conscientiously applied program of . . . hygiene and regular professional care."

Tests and maintenance tend to occur in cycles. As major portions of requirements and designs are completed, they are usually subject to formal review and revision procedures. While the backbone of a new program is being set up, there is an intense burst of effort to catch and correct mistakes that have somehow slipped in. As each new subsystem is grafted on, there is a less chaotic round of testing. In sizable development efforts, it is often necessary to keep logs and make changes in batches. Otherwise, people become confused about the current status of software, and the amount of testing can explode.

In contrast to the number of books on computer languages, algorithms, and applications, there are relatively few that deal with software testing and maintenance. In practice, successful strategies are found mainly in business environments. They help meet deadlines and control costs. Often, their real substance is not written down but is embedded in a local culture of technology. While these "cultures" all have peculiarities, the effective ones differ mainly in the forms that people fill out. Their methods ultimately resolve to T. J. Watson's motto:[1]

THINK

A key element in mature software cultures is to have people other than the developers of a program do some of the testing. It is notoriously difficult to spot the shortcomings in one's own work. However,

---

[1] THINK was long used as an internal motto by International Business Machines, Inc.

such an arrangement is expensive. If you cannot afford it, the next best thing is to let some time elapse between writing and checking.

□ TESTING ENVIRONMENTS

The work of testing is affected by a number of factors, including the type of application, the computer system, the programming language, and special facilities. These can have large effects on the productivity of people who perform testing. For testing programs written in C, the testing environment usually includes a computer or a terminal, a text editor, a compiler, and a linker. If this is all that is available, then you will have to perform most tests in one of two ways:

1. *Test harnesses.* Write code that activates services or calls functions to be tested and checks them.

2. *Test modifications.* Put code inside functions to be tested, usually to print checkpoints and data values.

Although these methods are laborious, sometimes they are the only ones possible. Method 1 is often used for general testing. Method 2 is used almost exclusively for focused testing and debugging.

Test harnesses can perform unit tests and most levels of integration tests. A harness usually includes a main function, which calls the code to be tested. It may also include *stub* functions, which substitute for functions that the code under test will call. Sophisticated stubs may be necessary for unit tests. These quickly reach a point of diminishing returns, as it becomes more likely that problems are caused by the test code than by the code to be tested.

One of the most common sources of error in C programs is to change a header file, altering some program convention, and then forget to recompile all the modules affected by the change. Test harnesses must follow the conventions of the code they are testing. They must have #include statements for any header files originated or used by the modules under test, and they must be recompiled whenever any of these header files is changed.

Test modifications are typically made when the search for a defect has narrowed to one module or one function. The most common modifications invoke printf, to indicate that control has reached a certain point or to display the contents of variables. These modifications may be inserted at many points in the code, so that more than one possible problem is checked with one test. It is useful to flag the lines inserted with /* */ or some other notation in the form of a C comment, so that they can be removed easily once a problem has been corrected.

C programmers usually notice that test modifications can be inserted automatically by preprocessor facilities. However, any modification inserted into code runs a risk of introducing new defects and concealing existing ones. As noted in Chapter 17, preprocessor statements are less portable and more subject to misinterpretation than ordinary C statements. Code modifications, whether made by the preprocessor or by some other means, are useful for debugging, but they are an unreliable approach to general testing.

Some environments provide special facilities that aid in testing code. Such facilities can substantially increase the productivity of testing personnel. They are of two major types:

- software that automates library maintenance procedures

- hardware or software to perform debugging without changing code

Software library automation can greatly reduce the risk that an obsolete version of code is being used or that a change to the software conventions has not been propagated to all the modules that depend on it. Good software library automation can also reduce the time needed to run tests, by performing only the compilations necessitated by changes.

Debugging systems allow the software tester to observe code under test, by stopping at selected points and displaying the values of variables. The best of these systems give access to the program using source code lines and data names. More primitive systems use machine locations and give access only to global variables. For time-critical problems, debugging systems may not suffice. The tester may need hardware monitors that record a sequence of machine states or may have to insert test modifications into code.

In the mid-1980s, interpreters and incremental compilers began to be introduced for C on microcomputers. These can speed testing for some applications. Typically, the user of such a system works in an environment that resembles an interactive editor, except that the program being edited can be run by typing a command. Unfortunately, these systems are relatively slow, produce inefficient code, handle only fairly small programs, mismanage header files, and do not always process C statements according to standard syntax.

□ DEFECT PREVENTION

Planning greatly affects the efforts spent in testing and maintenance. The cost of correcting a defect after a program is in service can be thousands of times greater than the cost of revising requirements or rewriting a design. Carefully planned software tends to have fewer defects. A software system planned around potential requirements is likely to be easier to adapt than a system that was grown like weeds or cast in cement. When tests and maintenance are planned, software developers tend to spend their time identifying potential needs and problems rather than fighting fires.

Consistent use of procedures is critical to reliable software. If a C function is invoked with arguments that differ from its parameters, it is likely to fail. When defining a C function, the type of value it will return should always be stated, for example:

int *testval(arg1, arg2) ;

It is useful to declare these return value data types in a header file, for example:

extern int *testval( ) ;

This illustration exhausts the support provided by the original versions of C for consistent procedure usage. ANSI standard C will provide a function "prototype," allowing C compilers to check for the proper number and data types of arguments.

Using shared data causes difficulty in many programs, because of opportunities for incorrect use. One approach to preventing such problems is called *data abstraction;* this means providing access to data through procedures. A design employing data abstraction will include a module to manage each type of data. Only these modules have direct access to the data; other modules inspect or modify information by using the data abstraction procedures.

All programs need to perform range and bounds checking on data for reliability. However, doing so tends to reduce performance. To provide both reliability and performance, a robust software design often divides a program into data validation environments. Data entering a particular environment will be checked at entry. Thereafter, they will be presumed to have passed a certain set of tests. Within the environment, those tests will not be repeated.

All programs use some resources in addition to routine processing capabilities and a fixed allocation of main memory for data storage. The most common is a facility to read input and write output. Most programs can encounter conditions in which such resources are not available or have become encumbered because of errors. A robust program checks for these conditions each time a resource is required and has one or more ways to respond to each possible error.

Programs that use dynamic memory face a problem of overcommitment, when no more storage is available. Sometimes, this condition will require termination of a program; work simply can't be completed. Under these circumstances, a robust program will stop gracefully. It will not, for example, leave data files in some indeterminate state, possibly corrupting them for future use. In other circumstances, it may be possible for a program to reduce its demands, to reuse previously allocated storage, or to adapt by taking a different approach to its work.

Design decisions can make testing easy or difficult. Factors that reduce the cost of testing and increase software reliability include:

- readable, unambiguous specifications

- regularity of dependencies

- low complexity within procedures

- avoidance of recursive procedures

Every cute trick tends to generate a countervailing cost in testing. Standard procedure interfaces are of much greater value than the condensation of an occasional argument.

The issue of complexity is often treated as though it were the same as length. A short procedure is not necessarily simple, nor is a long one necessarily complex. For example, if an operation requires nothing but invoking many functions in sequence, you can put all of this into one C function. If you split it up, you probably increase the complexity of data connections, and you make anyone reading the code look in several places instead of one.

The use of private data and private procedures can strongly affect testability. The advantage of private data is protection against errors caused by another module; a disadvantage is that private data will be inaccessible to test functions. Private procedures are less valuable than private data, because most programs have fewer procedures to confuse than data items. To maximize testability, no C function should be declared **static**.

A naming convention helps to document linkages and prevent confusion. One good approach is to reserve the first two or three characters of every procedure name and global data name for a module identifier, naming the module producing the data or containing the procedure.

The C preprocessor statements are open to promiscuous usage. For a program to be testable, they must be used with limitations. A good policy is to employ **#define** only to specify constants and provide access to data structures. If you use it to specify function names or other program elements, changes in a definition can produce disorderly side effects that are very difficult to trace.

Experienced software developers generally become skeptical about coding for efficiency in a high-level language. Surveys show that 90 percent of most software consumes less than 10 percent of run time. Rather than writing obscure or nonportable code, you are usually better off identifying functions that are consuming large amounts of processing time and recoding them in assembler language.

□ SOFTWARE DOCUMENTATION

The documentation for a software system consists of the following major components:

- specifications
- software designs
- program code
- test procedures
- user manuals

Timely completion of these documents is essential. Recording project details soon after they are developed is relatively inexpensive, but trying to reconstruct them later can be exasperating and costly.

The planning effort for a software system should produce specification and design documents. As a system is implemented, however, there are usually changes in both areas. The documents will be useful in maintenance only if they are kept current, so that they always describe a system as it has been implemented.

Software maintenance often fails to keep design documents in step with changes to code. This problem can be alleviated by placing design detail directly in the code. After a detailed design is originally written, sections of it are formatted as long C comments, and code is written between the comments. When the code is changed, design documentation is directly available to a programmer making changes, and it can easily be updated at the same time.

A typical module with an embedded design starts with information for the module. After this may be another section detailing data shared within the module and with other modules. Then come procedures of the module, each preceded by its design information. When a change is required, it is made first to the design text and then to program statements. Such a module looks like this:

```
/*
    (text of detailed design for module)
*/
/*
    (detailed design for shared data)
*/
    (data-definition statements)
/*
    (detailed design for procedure)
*/
    (C function statements)
/*
    (detailed design for procedure)
*/
    (C function statements)
```

The statements of a program are its ultimate documentation. Since they will remain the fundamental description of a program's methods, they should be written with readability in mind. Your program code gains readability from:

- clear format

- meaningful names

- intelligible comments

The outline format used for programs throughout this book shows the flow of control in a structured language such as C; it is strongly recommended. Among the most common errors in C programs are replacing semicolons with commas and double equal signs with single equal signs.

Since these errors often result in valid syntax, they may not be caught by a compiler. In general, because symbols are employed so extensively in C, it is helpful to emphasize them by leaving spaces on both sides. Examples in this book do so, with the following exceptions:

1. Braces are placed on lines by themselves, without extra indentation. This makes it easy to match pairs of braces that set off blocks of statements.

2. Symbols that couple data elements or operate on a single data element are written without spacing. These include an open parenthesis, when it designates a function, an open bracket for an array, the exclamation point, the comma, and the minus sign (when used to indicate a negative value).

Meaningful names help your program statements explain themselves. In C, you choose three major types of names:

- data names

- procedure names

- symbol names

Early C compilers accepted long names but required that names be distinguished within the first eight characters. Since the late 1970s, most C compilers will distinguish between long names, typically 15 to 31 characters. Make choices with care. Good names describe what is being named. They are easy to remember.

□ SOFTWARE LIBRARIES

Every project to make a substantial program builds a software library. The project library consists of source code files, header files, and documentation files. Because it is impractical to compile all the code for each addition or change, a software library is usually extended to include *object* programs, an intermediate, linkable form of code that has been reduced to machine instructions. Most projects also use code from other libraries, particularly the C library. Care in keeping library contents orderly can be critical to the success of a complex project and to long-term maintenance of any software system.

The two greatest problems in building and maintaining software libraries are:

- accounting for versions
- managing dependencies

Versions can apply to single procedures, modules, larger subsystems, header files, test code, and an entire system. Dependencies in C programs include function calls, global data, and program conventions.

Despite the large amount of effort expended to maintain software libraries, all done directly on computers, there is relatively little comprehensive software available to assist in it. Most of what exists was made for large, mainframe computers, and little of it was designed for the special features of C and the needs of complex programs. Until this situation improves, it is likely that significant parts of library maintenance in which you may be involved will be done with manually maintained records.

Management of versions is primarily a task of assigning numbers according to some consistent scheme, making them part of the file names or other file data, and remembering for each version at a particular level of assembly what versions of lower-level components it was made from. This task is simple for a program with three modules and twenty functions, but it becomes substantial for a program with dozens of modules and hundreds of functions. In the original development of software, it is generally unwise to discard old versions until a complete system has been assembled, tested, and accepted.

Unless software dependencies are determined by sound planning, their management in a software library can become an enormous headache. It is possible—indeed, all too easy—to generate software totally interlocked with dependencies, so that no single piece of it can be removed for testing or reused in other software. Most developers use data abstraction to eliminate or greatly reduce globally shared data. Program conventions should be shared only through header files. As recommended in Chapter 4, the simplest way to manage these dependencies is to keep their paths strictly parallel to the flow of control.

There is a myth that dividing software into modules makes it maintainable and that smaller modules make it more maintainable. This notion can be made to seem credible to anyone but the software librarian who has confronted several hundred faceless little modules. What makes a program maintainable is what makes it understandable. You can't work with something you don't understand.

1. An understandable program has clear objectives.

2. An understandable program has integrity of design.

3. An understandable program's objectives and organization are positively conveyed by its documentation.

And so we have come nearly full circle in the cycle of software development. Where we end is where we began. The future of software belongs to those who plan for it.

□ Index

Selections from The SYBEX Library

Introduction to Computers

OVERCOMING COMPUTER FEAR
by Jeff Berner
112 pp., illustr., Ref. 0-145
This easy-going introduction to computers helps you separate the facts from the myths.

INTRODUCTION TO WORD PROCESSING
by Hal Glatzer
205 pp., 140 illustr., Ref. 0-076
Explains in plain language what a word processor can do, how it improves productivity, how to use a word processor and how to buy one wisely.

PARENTS, KIDS, AND COMPUTERS
by Lynne Alper and Meg Holmberg
145 pp., illustr., Ref. 0-151
This book answers your questions about the educational possibilities of home computers.

PROTECTING YOUR COMPUTER
by Rodnay Zaks
214 pp., 100 illustr., Ref. 0-239
The correct way to handle and care for all elements of a computer system, including what to do when something doesn't work.

YOUR FIRST COMPUTER
by Rodnay Zaks
258 pp., 150 illustr., Ref. 0-142
The most popular introduction to small computers and their peripherals: what they do and how to buy one.

THE SYBEX PERSONAL COMPUTER DICTIONARY
120 pp., Ref. 0-199
All the definitions and acronyms of microcomputer jargon defined in a handy pocket-sized edition. Includes translations of the most popular terms into ten languages.

Computer Books for Kids

MONICA THE COMPUTER MOUSE
by Donna Bearden, illustrated by Brad W. Foster
64 pp., illustr., Hardcover, Ref. 0-214
Lavishly illustrated in color, this book tells the story of Monica the mouse, as she travels around to learn about several different kinds of computers and the jobs they can do. For ages 5–8.

POWER UP! KIDS' GUIDE TO THE APPLE IIe® /IIc™
by Marty DeJonghe and Caroline Earhart
200 pp., illustr., Ref. 0-212
Colorful illustrations and a friendly robot highlight this guide to the Apple IIe/IIc for kids 8–11.

BANK STREET WRITING WITH YOUR APPLE®
by Stanley Schatt, Ph.D. and Jane Abrams Schatt, M.A.
150 pp., illustr., Ref. 0-189
These engaging exercises show children aged 10–13 how to use Bank Street Writer for fun, profit, and school work.

POWER UP! KIDS' GUIDE TO THE COMMODORE 64™

by Marty DeJonghe and Caroline Earhart
192 pp., illustr., Ref. 0-188
Colorful illustrations and a friendly robot highlight this guide to the Commodore 64 for kids 8–11.

Humor

COMPUTER CRAZY

by Daniel Le Noury
100 pp., illustr., Ref. 0-173
No matter how you feel about computers, these cartoons will have you laughing about them.

MOTHER GOOSE YOUR COMPUTER: A GROWNUP'S GARDEN OF SILICON SATIRE

by Paul Panish and Anna Belle Panish, illustrated by Terry Small
96 pp., illustr., Ref. 0-198
This richly illustrated hardcover book uses parodies of familiar Mother Goose rhymes to satirize the world of high technology.

CONFESSIONS OF AN INFOMANIAC

by Elizabeth M. Ferrarini
215 pp., Ref. 0-186
This is one woman's tongue-in-cheek revelations of her pursuit of men, money, and machines. Learn about the many shopping services, information banks, and electronic dating bulletin boards available by computer.

Special Interest

THE COLLEGE STUDENT'S PERSONAL COMPUTER HANDBOOK

by Bryan Pfaffenberger
210 pp., illustr., Ref. 0-170
This friendly guide will aid students in selecting a computer system for college study, managing information in a college course, and writing research papers.

CELESTIAL BASIC

by Eric Burgess
300 pp., 65 illustr., Ref. 0-087
A collection of BASIC programs that rapidly complete the chores of typical astronomical computations. It's like having a planetarium in your own home! Displays apparent movement of stars, planets and meteor showers.

ESPIONAGE IN THE SILICON VALLEY

by John D. Halamka
200 pp., illustr., Ref. 0-225
Discover the behind-the-scenes stories of famous high-tech spy cases you've seen in the headlines.

ASTROLOGY ON YOUR PERSONAL COMPUTER

by Hank Friedman
225 pp., illustr., Ref. 0-226
An invaluable aid for astrologers who want to streamline their calculation and data management chores with the right combination of hardware and software.

Computer Specific

Apple II—Macintosh

THE MACINTOSH™ TOOLBOX

by Huxham, Burnard, and Takatsuka
300 pp., illustr., Ref. 0-249
This tutorial on the advanced features of the Macintosh toolbox is an ideal companion to The Macintosh BASIC Handbook.

THE PRO-DOS HANDBOOK

by Timothy Rice/Karen Rice
225 pp., illustr., Ref. 0-230
All Pro-DOS users, from beginning to advanced, will find this book packed with vital information. The book covers the basics, and then addresses itself to the

Apple II user who needs to interface with Pro-DOS when programming in BASIC. Learn how Pro-DOS uses memory, and how it handles text files, binary files, graphics, and sound. Includes a chapter on machine language programming.

THE MACINTOSH™ BASIC HANDBOOK

by Thomas Blackadar/Jonathan Kamin

800 pp., illustr., Ref. 0-257

This desk-side reference book for the Macintosh programmer covers the BASIC statements and toolbox commands, organized like a dictionary.

PROGRAMMING THE MACINTOSH™ IN ASSEMBLY LANGUAGE

by Steve Williams

400 pp., illustr., Ref. 0-263

Information, examples, and guidelines for programming the 68000 microprocessor are given, including details of its entire instruction set.

THE EASY GUIDE TO YOUR APPLE II®

by Joseph Kascmer

147 pp., illustr., Ref. 0-122

A friendly introduction to the Apple II, II plus, and the IIe.

BASIC EXERCISES FOR THE APPLE®

by J.P. Lamoitier

250 pp., 90 illustr., Ref. 0-084

Teaches Applesoft BASIC through actual practice, using graduated exercises drawn from everyday applications.

THE APPLE II® BASIC HANDBOOK

by Douglas Hergert

250 pp., illustr., Ref. 0-115

A complete listing with descriptions and instructive examples of each of the Apple II BASIC keywords and functions. A handy reference guide, organized like a dictionary.

APPLE II® BASIC PROGRAMS IN MINUTES

by Stanley R. Trost

150 pp., illustr., Ref. 0-121

A collection of ready-to-run programs for financial calculations, investment analysis, record keeping, and many more home and office applications. These programs can be entered on your Apple II plus or IIe in minutes!

YOUR FIRST APPLE II® PROGRAM

by Rodnay Zaks

182 pp., illustr., Ref. 0-136

This fully illustrated, easy-to-use introduction to Applesoft BASIC programming will have the reader programming in a matter of hours.

THE APPLE® CONNECTION

by James W. Coffron

264 pp., 120 illustr., Ref. 0-085

Teaches elementary interfacing and BASIC programming of the Apple for connection to external devices and household appliances.

THE APPLE IIc™: A PRACTICAL GUIDE

by Thomas Blackadar

175 pp., illustr., Ref. 0-241

Learn all you need to know about the Apple IIc! This jargon-free companion gives you a guided tour of Apple's new machine.

CP/M Systems

THE CP/M® HANDBOOK

by Rodnay Zaks

320 pp., 100 illustr., Ref 0-048

An indispensable reference and guide to CP/M—the most widely-used operating system for small computers.

MASTERING CP/M®

by Alan R. Miller

398 pp., illustr., Ref. 0-068

For advanced CP/M users or systems programmers who want maximum use of the CP/M operating system . . . takes up where our *CP/M Handbook* leaves off.

THE BEST OF CP/M® SOFTWARE
by John D. Halamka
250 pp., Ref. 0-100
This book reviews tried-and-tested, commercially available software for your CP/M system.

THE CP/M PLUS™ HANDBOOK
by Alan R. Miller
250 pp., illustr., Ref. 0-158
This guide is easy for beginners to understand, yet contains valuable information for advanced users of CP/M Plus (Version 3).

IBM PC and Compatibles

THE ABC'S OF THE IBM® PC
by Joan Lasselle and Carol Ramsay
143 pp., illustr., Ref. 0-102
This book will take you through the first crucial steps in learning to use the IBM PC.

THE BEST OF IBM® PC SOFTWARE
by Stanley R. Trost
351 pp., Ref. 0-104
Separates the wheat from the chaff in the world of IBM PC software. Tells you what to expect from the best available IBM PC programs.

THE IBM® PC-DOS HANDBOOK
by Richard Allen King
296 pp., Ref. 0-103
Explains the PC disk operating system. Get the most out of your PC by adapting its capabilities to your specific needs.

THE MS™-DOS HANDBOOK
by Richard Allen King
320 pp., illustr., Ref. 0-185
The differences between the various versions and manufacturer's implementations of MS-DOS are covered in a clear, straightforward manner. Tables, maps, and numerous examples make this the most complete book on MS-DOS available.

SELECTING THE RIGHT DATA BASE SOFTWARE FOR THE IBM® PC

SELECTING THE RIGHT WORD PROCESSING SOFTWARE FOR THE IBM® PC

SELECTING THE RIGHT SPREADSHEET SOFTWARE FOR THE IBM® PC
by Kathleen McHugh and Veronica Corchado
100 pp., illustr., Ref. 0-174, 0-177, 0-178
This series on selecting the right business software offers the busy professional concise, informative reviews of the best available software packages.

ESSENTIAL PC-DOS
by Myril and Susan Shaw
300 pp., illustr., Ref. 0-176
Whether you work with the IBM PC, XT, PCjr, or the portable PC, this book will be invaluable both for learning PC-DOS and for later reference.

Software Specific

Spreadsheets

VISICALC® FOR SCIENCE AND ENGINEERING
by Stanley R. Trost and Charles Pomernacki
203 pp., illustr., Ref. 0-096
More than 50 programs for solving technical problems in science and engineering. Applications range from math and statistics to electrical and electronic engineering.

DOING BUSINESS WITH MULTIPLAN™
by Richard Allen King and Stanley R. Trost
250 pp., illustr., Ref. 0-148
This book will show you how using Multiplan can be nearly as easy as learning to use a pocket calculator. It presents a collection of templates for business applications.

MASTERING VISICALC®
by Douglas Hergert
217 pp., 140 illustr., Ref. 0-090
Explains how to use the VisiCalc "electronic spreadsheet" functions and provides examples of each. Makes using this powerful program simple.

DOING BUSINESS WITH VISICALC®
by Stanley R. Trost
260 pp., illustr., Ref. 0-086
Presents accounting and management planning applications—from financial statements to master budgets; from pricing models to investment strategies.

DOING BUSINESS WITH SUPERCALC™
by Stanley R. Trost
248 pp., illustr., Ref. 0-095
Presents accounting and management planning applications—from financial statements to master budgets; from pricing models to investment strategies.

MULTIPLAN™ ON THE COMMODORE 64™
by Richard Allen King
260 pp., illustr., Ref. 0-231
This clear, straighforward guide will give you a firm grasp on Multiplan's functions, as well as provide a collection of useful template programs.

Word Processing

INTRODUCTION TO WORDSTAR®
by Arthur Naiman
202 pp., 30 illustr., Ref. 0-134
Makes it easy to learn WordStar, a powerful word processing program for personal computers.

PRACTICAL WORDSTAR® USES
by Julie Anne Arca
303 pp., illustr., Ref. 0-107
Pick your most time-consuming office tasks and this book will show you how to streamline them with WordStar.

THE COMPLETE GUIDE TO MULTIMATE™
by Carol Holcomb Dreger
250 pp., illustr., Ref. 0-229
A concise introduction to the many practical applications of this powerful word processing program.

THE THINKTANK™ BOOK
by Jonathan Kamin
200 pp., illustr., Ref. 0-224
Learn how the ThinkTank program can help you organize your thoughts, plans, and activities.

Data Base Management Systems

UNDERSTANDING dBASE III™
by Alan Simpson
250 pp., illustr., Ref. 0-267
For experienced dBASE II programmers, data base and program design are covered in detail; with many examples and illustrations.

UNDERSTANDING dBASE II™
by Alan Simpson
260 pp., illustr., Ref. 0-147
Learn programming techniques for mailing label systems, bookkeeping, and data management, as well as ways to interface dBASE II with other software systems.

Integrated Software

MASTERING SYMPHONY™
by Douglas Cobb
763 pp., illustr., Ref. 0-244
This bestselling book provides all the information you will need to put Symphony to work for you right away. Packed with practical models for the business user.

SYMPHONY™ ENCORE: PROGRAM NOTES
by Dick Andersen
325 pp., illustr., Ref. 0-247
Organized as a reference tool, this book gives shortcuts for using Symphony commands and functions, with troubleshooting advice.

JAZZ ON THE MACINTOSH™
by Joseph Caggiano and Michael McCarthy
400 pp., illustr., Ref. 0-265
The complete tutorial on the ins and outs of the season's hottest software, with tips on integrating its functions into efficient business projects.

MASTERING FRAMEWORK™
by Doug Hergert
450 pp., illustr., Ref. 0-248
This tutorial guides the beginning user through all the functions and features of this integrated software package, geared to the business environment.

ADVANCED TECHNIQUES IN FRAMEWORK™
by Alan Simpson
250 pp., illustr., Ref. 0-267
In order to begin customizing your own models with Framework, you'll need a thorough knowledge of Fred programming languages, and this book provides this information in a complete, well-organized form.

ADVANCED BUSINESS MODELS WITH 1-2-3™
by Stanley R. Trost
250 pp., illustr., Ref. 0-159
If you are a business professional using the 1-2-3 software package, you will find the spreadsheet and graphics models provided in this book easy to use "as is" in everyday business situations.

THE ABC'S OF 1-2-3™
by Chris Gilbert and Laurie Williams
225 pp., illustr., Ref. 0-168
For those new to the LOTUS 1-2-3 program, this book offers step-by-step

instructions in mastering its spreadsheet, data base, and graphing capabilities.

MASTERING APPLEWORKS™
by Elna Tymes
250 pp., illustr., Ref. 0-240
Here is a business-oriented introduction to AppleWorks, the new integrated software package from Apple. No experience with computers is assumed.

Languages

BASIC

YOUR FIRST BASIC PROGRAM
by Rodnay Zaks
182 pp., illustr. in color, Ref. 0-092
A "how-to-program" book for the first time computer user, aged 8 to 88.

FIFTY BASIC EXERCISES
by J. P. Lamoitier
232 pp., 90 illustr., Ref. 0-056
Teaches BASIC through actual practice, using graduated exercises drawn from everyday applications. Programs written in Microsoft BASIC.

EXECUTIVE PLANNING WITH BASIC
by X. T. Bui
196 pp., 19 illustr., Ref. 0-083
An important collection of business management decision models in BASIC, including inventory management (EOQ), critical path analysis and PERT, financial ratio analysis, portfolio management, and much more.

BASIC PROGRAMS FOR SCIENTISTS AND ENGINEERS
by Alan R. Miller
318 pp., 120 illustr., Ref. 0-073
This book from the "Programs for Scientists and Engineers" series provides a library of problem-solving programs while developing the reader's proficiency in BASIC.

Pascal

INTRODUCTION TO PASCAL
(Including UCSD Pascal™)
by Rodnay Zaks
420 pp., 130 illustr., Ref. 0-066
A step-by-step introduction for anyone who wants to learn the Pascal language. Describes UCSD and Standard Pascals. No technical background is assumed.

THE PASCAL HANDBOOK
by Jacques Tiberghien
486 pp., 270 illustr., Ref. 0-053
A dictionary of the Pascal language, defining every reserved word, operator, procedure, and function found in all major versions of Pascal.

APPLE® PASCAL GAMES
**by Douglas Hergert and
Joseph T. Kalash**
372 pp., 40 illustr., Ref. 0-074
A collection of the most popular computer games in Pascal, challenging the reader not only to play but to investigate how games are implemented on the computer.

PASCAL PROGRAMS FOR SCIENTISTS AND ENGINEERS
by Alan R. Miller
374 pp., 120 illustr., Ref. 0-058
A comprehensive collection of frequently used algorithms for scientific and technical applications, programmed in Pascal. Includes programs for curve-fitting, integrals, statistical techniques, and more.

DOING BUSINESS WITH PASCAL
**by Richard Hergert and
Douglas Hergert**
371 pp., illustr., Ref. 0-091
Practical tips for using Pascal programming in business. Covers design considerations, language extensions, and applications examples.

Other Languages

FORTRAN PROGRAMS FOR SCIENTISTS AND ENGINEERS
by Alan R. Miller
280 pp., 120 illustr., Ref. 0-082
This book from the "Programs for Scientists and Engineers" series provides a library of problem-solving programs while developing the reader's proficiency in FORTRAN.

A MICROPROGRAMMED APL IMPLEMENTATION
by Rodnay Zaks
350 pp., Ref. 0-005
An expert-level text presenting the complete conceptual analysis and design of an APL interpreter, and actual listing of the microcode.

UNDERSTANDING C
by Bruce H. Hunter
320 pp., Ref 0-123
Explains how to program in powerful C language for a variety of applications. Some programming experience assumed.

FIFTY PASCAL PROGRAMS
by Bruce H. Hunter
338 pp., illustr., Ref. 0-110
More than just a collection of useful programs! Structured programming techniques are emphasized and concepts such as data type creation and array manipulation are clearly illustrated.

Technical

Assembly Language

PROGRAMMING THE 6502
by Rodnay Zaks
386 pp., 160 illustr., Ref. 0-135
Assembly language programming for the 6502, from basic concepts to advanced data structures.

6502 APPLICATIONS
by Rodnay Zaks
278 pp., 200 illustr., Ref. 0-015
Real-life application techniques: the input/output book for the 6502.

ADVANCED 6502 PROGRAMMING
by Rodnay Zaks
292 pp., 140 illustr., Ref. 0-089
Third in the 6502 series. Teaches more advanced programming techniques, using games as a framework for learning.

PROGRAMMING THE Z80®
by Rodnay Zaks
624 pp., 200 illustr., Ref. 0-069
A complete course in programming the Z80 microprocessor and a thorough introduction to assembly language.

Z80® APPLICATIONS
by James W. Coffron
288 pp., illustr., Ref. 0-094
Covers techniques and applications for using peripheral devices with a Z80 based system.

PROGRAMMING THE 6809
by Rodnay Zaks and William Labiak
362 pp., 150 illustr., Ref. 0-078
This book explains how to program the 6809 microprocessor in assembly language. No prior programming knowledge required.

PROGRAMMING THE Z8000®
by Richard Mateosian
298 pp., 124 illustr., Ref. 0-032
How to program the Z8000 16-bit microprocessor. Includes a description of the architecture and function of the Z8000 and its family of support chips.

PROGRAMMING THE 8086™/8088™
by James W. Coffron
300 pp., illustr., Ref. 0-120
This book explains how to program the 8086 and 8088 microprocessors in

PROGRAMMING THE 68000™
by Steve Williams
250 pp., illustr., Ref. 0-133
This book introduces you to microprocessor operation, writing application programs, and the basics of I/O programming. Especially helpful for owners of the Apple Macintosh or Lisa.

Hardware

FROM CHIPS TO SYSTEMS: AN INTRODUCTION TO MICROPROCESSORS
by Rodnay Zaks
552 pp., 400 illustr., Ref. 0-063
A simple and comprehensive introduction to microprocessors from both a hardware and software standpoint: what they are, how they operate, how to assemble them into a complete system.

MICROPROCESSOR INTERFACING TECHNIQUES
by Rodnay Zaks and Austin Lesea
456 pp., 400 illustr., Ref. 0-029
Complete hardware and software interfacing techniques, including D to A conversion, peripherals, bus standards and troubleshooting.

THE RS-232 SOLUTION
by Joe Campbell
194 pp., illustr., Ref. 0-140
Finally, a book that will show you how to correctly interface your computer to any RS-232-C peripheral.

Operating Systems

REAL WORLD UNIX™
by John D. Halamka
209 pp., Ref. 0-093
This book is written for the beginning and intermediate UNIX user in a practical, straightforward manner, with specific instructions given for many business applications.